How Healthy Is Your Organization?

How Healthy Is Your Organization?

THE LEADER'S GUIDE TO CURING CORPORATE DISEASES AND PROMOTING JOYFUL CULTURES

Imre Lövey and Manohar S. Nadkarni
with Eszter Erdélyi

Creating Corporate Cultures
Fred Massarik, Series Editor

PRAEGER

Westport, Connecticut
London

Library of Congress Cataloging-in-Publication Data

Lövey, Imre.
   How healthy is your organization? : the leader's guide to curing corporate diseases and
promoting joyful cultures / Imre Lövey and Manohar S. Nadkarni with Eszter Erdélyi.
     p. cm. — (Creating corporate cultures, ISSN 1935–6560)
   Includes bibliographical references and index.
   ISBN-13: 978–0–275–99776–2 (alk. paper)
   1. Organizational behavior. 2. Corporate culture. 3. Psychology, Industrial. 4. Leadership.
I. Nadkarni, Manohar S. II. Erdélyi, Eszter. III. Title.
HD58.7.L684 2007
658.4′063—dc22   2007014263

British Library Cataloguing in Publication Data is available.

Library of Congress Catalog Card Number: 2007014263
ISBN-13: 978–0–275–99776–2
ISBN-10: 0–275–99776–6
ISSN: 1935–6560

First published in 2007

Praeger Publishers, 88 Post Road West, Westport, CT 06881
An imprint of Greenwood Publishing Group, Inc.
www.praeger.com

Printed in the United States of America

The paper used in this book complies with the
Permanent Paper Standard issued by the National
Information Standards Organization (Z39.48–1984).

10 9 8 7 6 5 4 3 2 1

Contents

Illustrations

Tables

Figures

Series Foreword

Culture is everywhere! Its study is not, for example, a narrow specialty confined to anthropology. Nor is it a specialty for those who seek to "change corporate culture," as proposed by many a consultant.

No one owns the word or concept *culture*. Indeed, it has numerous facets and complex ways of manifesting its impact on people and institutions. Nor is it defined exclusively by any one category of activity, such as language, ritual, housing, literature, or modes of dress, or by whatever is considered to be "good behavior," as in, "I met this really cultured person at a party last night..."

So what then is culture? In spite of the elaborate definitions and the extensive writings, there is no cut-and-dried single definition that serves all purposes. This series, Creating Corporate Cultures, takes a broad view of the subject. However one may seek the false security of one definition to fit all, it is our view that it is best to be eclectic and broad-gauge, exploring insights from many disciplinary viewpoints—including but not confined to anthropology, psychology, sociology, management, philosophy, and organizational development, among others—and as viewed from the vantage points of executives, consultants, academics, and hands-on people at work. Thus this series regards culture not as a "silo," but as a field of many interacting forces, as a stream of human activities involving ideas, behaviors, norms, and manifestations of many kinds in which everyone is enmeshed day by day. Complexity rules!

One view of culture proposes that "it's just the way we do things around here." And as such this may be a reasonable starting point for getting at corporate cultures in action. It does not tell us, however, what things should be looked at and what "around here" really means. We will find that many authors focus on different "things" and bound their areas of interest "around here" in varied ways. We leave the specifics to the authors contributing to the Series.

One aspect is clear: Cultures involve norms and values, and they usually have quite long durations in time. Sudden change is possible but rare. Mostly, cultures do not change overnight, and they manifest some measure of resistance to change. It does no good to simply yell at somebody, "Go change your culture!" This must be evident, if you consider the multiplicity of forces that act on people, especially when norms and values are taken into account. But as cultures *do* change, we know that this change can be purposefully facilitated by the people involved.

With this in mind, the series does not propose any quick-fix solutions. We hope, however, that each volume will constitute a substantial basis for thought and for action, helping along creative culture change—in management, consulting, teaching, and in improving the quality of the human condition at work.

ABOUT THIS BOOK

The first in this series is this book by Imre Lövey, Manohar S. Nadkarni, with Eszter Erdélyi: *How Healthy Is Your Organization? The Leader's Guide to Curing Corporate Diseases and Promoting Joyful Cultures*. In a readable style, Lövey and his colleagues suggest that an organization indeed can embrace joy and health, while overcoming the potentially conflicting experiences of work and joy. Work need not be a burden, and the attainment of positive pleasure and a sense of daily vitality constitute reachable goals. In this mode the book considers a balance among objectives and examines the numerous "diseases" of organizations. These include customer exploitation, aggressive approaches to the environment, alienation, shortsightedness, and workaholism. Symptoms include self-centered leadership, isolation, and insensitivity—all of which frustrate organizational health.

In the proposed approach for making things better, the authors' exposition avoids oversimplification, and it builds on a sound theoretic base for understanding human behavior. It draws on a wide range of disciplines and considers varied points of experience. We hope that in this sense, *How Healthy Is Your Organization?* provides readers with a helpful platform for learning, and for practical application in their fields of practice, to change cultures for the better in ways that matter.

Fred Massarik
Series Editor

Acknowledgments

I first met Manohar in 1979, when, somewhat miraculously, a large-scale UN project happened to land in Hungary, one involving the training of a dozen local people in organizational development consulting. Fortunately, I happened to be one of them. After a bit of initial resistance, I fell in love with the approach, a love that has lasted ever since. I developed what became a life-long friendship with one of the lead instructors, Manohar S. Nadkarni. We visited each other from time to time, and over the years we have enjoyed working with several new generations of consultants.

A few years ago we decided to make an attempt to capture the essence of what we had learned about organizations, by that time having worked with hundreds of them around the world. We had a memorable time putting our thoughts together, which activity resulted in a great flow of ideas we were sure would somehow naturally organize itself into a book. At this point fortune smiled on us, and we were able to bring our mutual friend Eszter Erdélyi into the process to turn the potential into reality by actually structuring and writing the book with us. Without her persistence, tolerance, and rigorous logic, this book may not have ever made it to our own shelves, let alone anyone else's. The first edition came out in South Asia, with the title *The Joyful Organization: Understanding Organizational Health, Diseases and Joy*. We then published a translation in Hungary, titled *Az örömteli szervezet: Szervezeti egészség, betegség, öröm—és a vezetés*.

Not long thereafter my American colleague and friend, Fred Massarik, provided us the opportunity to publish our book with Praeger/Greenwood as the first volume of their Creating Corporate Cultures series. The suggestions of Fred's colleague Nick Philipson represented very important improvements in the book.

While we were completing the work for this edition, Manohar became ill and passed away. We were blessed with his friendship, his scholarship, and his teachings to us personally. We hope that he would have been as proud of the completion of this edition as we are to have begun it with him.

We extend our heartfelt thanks to Manohar's son Manoj, who, following Manohar's passage, helped us extensively to translate ideas and style. In a sense, we began this book as a family, and we have completed it as such.

There are many people who have contributed directly or indirectly to this book. First, we must thank our clients in India, Hungary, the United States, and many other countries. We have learned a great deal from them and with them. We thank them for making it possible for us for so many years to make a living, and to make a difference, in such an enjoyable way.

We have also received a great deal of encouragement from our colleagues in the international organizational development community, who have assisted us in summarizing our concepts, filling the gaps, building a consistent framework, and assessing the evidence supporting our thesis. Without their support, interest, and encouragement this book would not have come to life at all.

There are others who more directly helped us with polishing our concepts, giving feedback or technical advice and support. I would like to thank all of my dear colleagues from Concordia, the organization and management development consulting firm with which I have served for many years. And I extend thanks from all of us to Kim Barnes, Karen Davis, Ferenc Erdélyi, Jay Fogelman, Brenda Johns, Agnes Laborci, Endre Lövey, Fred Massarik, Joan Pearce, Annette Simons, Peter Szirmai, Janos Vecsenyi, Laksana Watthanakul, Berne Weis, and Carey White.

Budapest, Hungary, November 2006
Imre Lövey

Introduction

Let us try an exercise of imagination. Have you ever stood in front of a group of people who looked at you with expressionless eyes, indifferent to what you had to say, clearly thinking that nothing would change their situation at work for the better and too burned out to pretend otherwise? Have you ever thought while commuting to work that you may just as well turn back because you cannot make enough of a difference there and that you are doing meaningless work for incompetent and petty if not downright mean bosses while your personal life scrambles?

A managing director called us to help him promote managers who would be able to speed up the adaptation of the organization to the changing economic environment. We went and interviewed everyone involved, people in their mid-forties and fifties. Instead of getting on with the task at hand, we made a disturbing discovery. Perhaps to a different degree, but they all appeared to be overwhelmed, cynical, and uninterested, not just in work, but in life itself! They thought of work as a burden and only a source of income, rather than an activity in which they were absorbed and took delight. Listening to their emotionless and hopeless comments about the sustained lack of any challenge or excitement in their work, it hit us how much an organization could contribute to people feeling like this. Perhaps an organization could make people feel the opposite, too.

Now let us continue our exercise of imagination. Have you ever sung a song on your way to work? Have you ever lost sleep over the excitement of what you and your team could accomplish, with new ideas popping up in your head, making it difficult to wait until the morning? Have you visited somewhere where you felt the liveliness and the attitude of serious achievement to be contagious?

The greater part of society admits to spending a significant portion of life uninterested and unengaged at work. However, every now and then one meets a group where instead of stress and dissatisfaction, the group members are characterized by a strong sense of purpose, efficiency, creativity, mastery, and pride. To our great pleasure, we observe an organization visibly thriving and people experiencing—of all things possible!—joy, while working. It is so contagious that we feel motivated and energized just by visiting. Inevitably, the questions arise: Why does this organization reach its objectives—providing unbeatable customer value, operating more efficiently, and having members who grow and live fuller, more satisfying lives—more often than other organizations? How was this organization created? How does it operate? Who has the biggest influence on it? What exactly leads to the observable people derive from performing tasks not intrinsically different from work in other organizations? Above all, how can we become members? We can tell a joyful organization when we see one, rare as it is, but can we contribute to developing one?

Joy, of course, is an elusive experience, but we can outline its characteristics with precision. When individuals feel connected to a larger purpose, apply their skills and discretion, and sustain focused concentration, they begin to experience the feeling of being one with what they do. Entirely absorbed and thus not conscious of the effort of doing the activity, they live through the experience as self-fulfillment. They find the most efficient ways to achieve their purpose and lose minimal energy in the process. Yet their vision and skills guide them toward creating the highest quality.

Early in life, as we begin to discover the world surrounding us, we experience joy naturally. Most of us lose this ability through the process of socialization, in which rather than learning, we are taught, and rather than being creative, we are instructed to be obedient. This is also how we are brought up. We separate curricular activity and extracurricular activity. Study is a burden and a compulsion, whereas play is for enjoyment. This process may be efficient for passing down accumulated knowledge, but it certainly does not encourage us to work in a joyful way. The premise of this book is that we can rekindle in ourselves the ability to experience joy from what we do, even if we have already grown up!

Until recently, the admitted bottom line on a company's purpose around the world was to make a profit. While satisfying this demand most efficiently is still required, successful organizations are increasingly characterized by a different set of measures as well: their ability to capture emotions and the mind-set of customers and employees and the credibility of their promises. To be able to present a compelling story consciously rather than instinctively, and consistently rather than temporarily, organizations need something other than a zesty sounding vision, cheerleading, and a productivity boosting. This book proposes to dispel the myth that we have limited influence over this process. Indeed our objective is to help organizations thrive and readers to come closer to finding joy in their work lives.

Much of the existing literature puts the burden of finding satisfaction in work on the employee, as well as assumes that it is mostly in the interest of the individual to do so. If there have appeared attempts to look at the role of a leader in creating a work environment conducive to individual fulfillment, they have focused on limited aspects of the issue. Our research examines explicitly the structural barriers leaders' personal beliefs create on the organizational culture and their impact on how successfully the organization can fulfill its vision.

In order to become joyful, an organization has to become healthy first. When an organization is not healthy, people are necessarily preoccupied with fighting the lack of functionality, taking energy and resources away from the effort to realize the vision. Reading through the symptoms of organizational diseases, readers will probably be tempted to assess the state of health of the organization they belong to. Recognizing the symptoms of real-life diseases leads to a better understanding of their causes and origins, which allows for informed decisions to improve organizational health—the magnitude of which depends on the reader's position in the organization. For this purpose, after each disease we have listed several possible actions to improve organizational health.

In the process, readers will question some generally held notions. Common understanding holds that management is about identifying priorities and producing results in a short time frame. This book challenges this view and proposes that the most frequently ignored criterion for organizational health is achieving and maintaining a balance among fundamental objectives such as the needs of the customer, the organization, and its members.

Also, we argue that people are not simply a resource for an organization, but also a crucial reason the organization exists in the first place. It is a basic requirement of organizational health that organizations satisfy the needs of members. A healthy organization is a context in which people invest themselves and blossom, a fact that makes a healthy organization not at all in conflict with being profitable; and, in fact, quite the contrary.

We also show that executives' awareness of how their personal beliefs impact on organizational health and their personal capacity for joy determines whether an organization is going to be healthy and joyful: Some belief systems lead to organizational health while others lead to diseases. Only executives who are consciously aware of their own belief system and its impact on the organization are able to change or counteract possible negative impact.

Once an organization is on its way to improve and maintain health, and executives counterbalance their beliefs influencing organizational health negatively, practical steps can be implemented to create a more joyful organizational culture.

Building a joyful organization, as worldwide experience shows, is a counterintuitive exercise. Joy also appears an unlikely driving force of organizational longevity. While joy is fleeting, people expect an organization to endure. An important implication of applying this organizational philosophy is that this elusive driving force can be tamed to serve the organization. The attributes of an organization, which reinforce the "self" of its members rather than weakening them in the service of somebody else's goals, can be consciously built.

We have over 70 years of combined experience in organizational development, gained on five continents. The most significant and influential common characteristic of our background is that throughout our careers we worked among conditions of social and economic transformation. While working with hundreds of organizations of all kinds undergoing massive changes, and training thousands of leaders and managers in the process, we had an uncommon exposure to a plethora of organizational problems and individual behavior patterns. Our extensive exposure to the teaching and consulting environment in countries such as the United States, India, Hungary, France, Russia, Indonesia, Nigeria, Thailand, or Macedonia has helped us crystallize our messages and deepen our understanding beyond cultures and borders. Although our experience originates in different cultures, it has led us to remarkably convergent views. Perhaps this unique exposure is the single most important qualifying factor in our attempt to develop this holistic framework to better understand organizational prosperity in today's world.

From this experience we selected examples, or "mini-cases," to illustrate the characteristics of a joyful organization, organizational health criteria, disease symptoms, and the pragmatic steps encouraging the development of a joyful organization. The cases represent real-life events from our consulting practices and are unchanged. However, unlike other management books, we have chosen to focus on the point to illustrate and reveal only one identity: our own. To be consistent in our logic, we also focus on building a coherent logic by arguments and take responsibility for all statements in the book. This does not mean, however, that we have not learned a great deal from other management theorists and "organizational philosophers," whose ideas we internalized. At the end, we include a reading list with authors whose concepts have had a deep impact on us and whose work could further contribute to our readers' understanding of organizations.

The book is divided into three parts. In Part I we define the experience of joy in the organizational context, organizational health, and examine how these definitions relate to success. In Part II we discuss criteria for organizational health and the diseases that arise when some functionality is consistently missing. We identify symptoms, analyze causes, and propose possible treatments for these. In Part III we investigate the distinguished role executives play in creating a healthy and joyful organization. We answer the question most often asked us: Does the executive's capacity for experiencing joy confine the organization's capacity to be joyful? The reader will also be introduced to how the very personal beliefs of leaders on issues such as how to run an organization, remain in business, deal with human beings, and organize human communities mirror organizational health characteristics that define the health and joy of our organization. Finally, we propose some specific measures that can be taken to encourage joy.

PART I

Joy and Health in Organizations

CHAPTER 1

The Joyful Organization

Why do we regard work and the consequent membership of an organization as a burden? Could work ever become so engaging that we could experience joy from its accomplishment? Is the phenomenon of joy incompatible with organizations? What happens to our sense of worry when we experience joy from an activity? When we experience the unmistakable sense of being alive we are also the most productive in service of our vision. Does this personal experience apply to organizations? Can we tell if an organization is joyful at first sight? What are the specific characteristics that create a context for joy for members and for people who interact with the organization?

THE CONTRADICTORY EXPERIENCE OF WORK AND JOY

Joy is fleeting; an organization is enduring. Joy is ephemeral; an organization has substance. Joy is impulsive; an organization is deliberate. Joy is a reward, which people in organizations do not often experience. The vast majority of people who work in organizations would probably confirm this observation. On the surface, joy and organizations seem to imply contradictory concepts.

Still, most of us work in organizations, whether they are industrial, agricultural, academic, governmental, technological, nonprofit, or anything in between. Working, especially working for an organization, is most of all about earning a living. It is a necessary, immediate, and constant element of life for the vast majority of us, and it feels like a burden. Joy, on the other hand, may be part of our lives, or it may not. Joy is serendipity, faith, magic; we all crave it, but achieve it only on rare occasions, if ever. Can the two converge? Can work itself ever be so fully engaging, that you become one with the task, and experience joy from its accomplishment—the simple act of doing it? Can the feeling of burden disappear from our everyday lives? Is it possible to create an organization that consciously promotes the experience of joy, yet at the same time is efficient, profitable, and competitive? We believe it is. It is possible for a few today, and it could be possible for the vast majority of us. Work and joy may appear antagonistic on the surface, but they are not at all contradictory. Quite the opposite is true: by becoming joyful, an organization can also become most effective in pursuing its vision and in enduring.

Nevertheless, joy is rarely part of our image of work. We have come to an age of increasing anxiety, reflected in our endless nostalgia for past times and other places we perceive to be happier, more joyful. While we try to manage our lack of satisfaction on a daily basis, we forget that it is we who have formed and who manage the organizations in which we spend most of our lives. That they should become the source of anxiety or joy, we believe, is our doing. Experiencing joy at work should not be the privilege of a select few. In order to initiate transforming stress into an experience of health and ultimately joy, we outline here an organizational philosophy and a way to put this philosophy into practice.

We establish organizations to fulfill a need. We provide a product or service. We work hard to make the provision of the product or service profitable or feasible for the organization. Yet, at the end of the day most of us feel overwhelmed. Working seems a significant sacrifice. Have you ever awakened with the unpleasant feeling of unwillingness to go to work? Have you ever told your friends that one of these days you will do something else and get a life? The contrast between intentions and outcome is striking.

How did we get into this situation in the first place? This was not our intention at all. As far as we can tell, neither was this the design of the founders and executives of the organization for which we work. We did not intend to "live" only after working hours, if then. We did not intend to operate an organization where employees feel alienated. There is great irony in this. We are miserable satisfying other people's needs all day long. In the limited time after working hours, we turn to satisfying our needs, requiring other peoples' suffering and sacrifice.

THE NEED FOR COMBINING JOY AND WORK

More and more people feel that this situation is not sustainable. They say, "I'm not going to go to work to sacrifice, to suffer 8, 10, or 16 hours a day. This happens to be my life, and my life takes place not only after working hours or during the weekend; my life takes place at all times. I cannot exclude working hours. I go to work not only to earn a living, but also to grow and develop. I want to contribute and feel useful."

They refuse to regard the greater part of their lives as an infringement on freedom, something to be avoided as much as possible. Instead of performing tasks against their will and thus making someone else's goal a reality, they are looking for an environment that will facilitate reaching their own intrinsic goals. If people do not find challenges, frequently run into conflicts in the organization, or accumulate negative experiences, they burn out and cannot reach these goals.

Widespread consciousness of these conditions makes it clear that healthy organizations within a healthy society satisfy a variety of human needs of their members as well as the needs of the customer and the organization. Yet, what does health have to do with joy? Health is a basic precondition for joy. If we are not healthy, we are preoccupied with our dysfunction, which prevents us from experiencing joy. The same is true for organizations. The concept of organizational health opens the black box of organizational operations and enables us to discover what prevents members of any organization from experiencing joy. Before we examine this further let us define this feeling with more precision. We know all too well what Dilbert is rebelling against; let us understand now what it is for which he longs.

WHAT IS JOY IN THE CONTEXT OF WORK?

When we think of joy, many of us struggle with articulating exactly what it is. Over time, most of us have lost the capacity to experience it. We define life goals in terms of happiness, satisfaction, but very rarely in terms of joy. How do we distinguish between satisfaction and joy?

In satisfaction, there is always a feeling of receiving, experiencing the plea-sure, whereas in joy there is no difference between the action and me. I can say, "I am eating this meal—so some of my senses are satisfied. But with joy, I forget myself and become one with the experience." One of the most obvious comparisons of joy is with music. When we listen to music, even if we are not experts, we may forget ourselves and become one with the beauti-ful melody. The quality of this experience is deeper than that of satisfaction. Joy is an inner experience that contributes to feeling alive, that makes life worthwhile.

It is more difficult to catch this feeling manifested in work. However, when you observe people closely, you find that whereas most people work because they feel that they have to, some people work with real dedication. The majority work not because they find work interesting, but out of necessity—they have to make a living. Still, some—at all levels of organizations from manual workers in factories to chief executives in boardrooms—work with real dedication. These dedicated people are of great interest to us, since through observing them, we can learn about the forgotten experience of joy.

My grandfather was a person who was extremely committed to his work. He was also a very independent person. After he retired from his job as a technician and supervisor, managing a pumping station on the banks of a river close by, he decided to become a beekeeper. He had his own workshop attached to his house. The workshop was very well equipped with quality tools, and he used to spend a lot of time in there. While working there, he would usually sing, smiling and submerging himself in songs from his childhood. He made hives for the bees, he made the frames, he cut the wood, he planed it, he put the wires through, and then he melted the wax on it. He did everything himself and he enjoyed it. If you looked at his workshop, you could see that everything was in order. He always left it clean and neat. If you observed him while working, singing, and smiling, you could tell that he was really enjoying himself. When something went wrong, of course, he got upset, but he corrected the mistake as best he could. He could do almost everything around the house, too. He was very happy and proud of everything he did; it was really a joy to be around him. As a small boy, I used to go to the workshop and work there with him. I learned a lot from him. I still remember him saying to me, "My dear grandson, you should remember that you qualify yourself by what you are giving out of your hands. Be careful and thorough with anything you do." He lived by his words.

My grandfather experienced joy when the frame was finally ready, and he looked at it with satisfaction. He also experienced joy from producing the frame, designing the intermediate steps, and completing it, in spite of any problems and resulting frustrations that might arise. Both types of joy are equally important. Both transcending previous achievement and the process of transcending itself can provide joy.

There is a remarkable similarity between the dedicated people of organizations and artists of all kinds. Artists have a strong inner vision they work toward, making it possible for other people to see this vision and interpret it. More likely than not, they get joy from work.

There is an art school just around the corner from us, and the sculpting courses are very popular. The studio has big windows facing the street, and what happens inside frequently draws a crowd of onlookers. While walking in front of the school, I often stop and peek through the window. One of the sculptors I recognize as a highly esteemed artist. The way I can differentiate him from the students is not because I know him, but because of his distinct way of handling his instruments. There is an unconscious gentleness about his way of working with the hammer, working it in the lightest way possible and using the fewest strokes. His students on the other hand have the tendency of handling the chisel and hammer more coarsely and roughly.

Dedicated people also work toward an inner vision, and they find that itself intrinsically rewarding. Working toward an inner vision makes people very conscious of quality. This inner vision is more than an immediate goal; it is a higher perspective. People with the capacity of joy have an internal aesthetic norm, which sets their goals to rise above and surpass the ordinary, resulting in an exhilarating feeling of transcendence. "Going beyond ordinary limits" is one of the Webster's dictionary's definitions of transcendence. Their goals originate from within the self, rather than being imposed by outside forces. It is transcendental in the sense that they always have a goal behind the goal, an internal assessment of the experiences by their inner norms. They do not just do what they are doing for the sake of being busy, but through their ideals they want to be connected to the purpose of the whole organization, and beyond the organization, to a purpose of the whole society, mankind, and sometimes even transcending that.

One of the clearest signs of experiencing joy is being immersed in the activity. When people experience joy, they are entirely absorbed in their activity. In joy, one forgets oneself; in joy, the person is one with the raw material, the instrument, and the vision. There is no sense of doing the activity. There is a sense of strength, alertness, and effortless control. One does not differentiate between oneself and the product or activity. One does not think of the activity in terms of working. Self-consciousness disappears.

The state of focused concentration, disregard of all sources of distraction, creates unsurpassable efficiency. People are able to sustain this involvement if they are truly paying attention to what is actually happening and handling their work purposefully. This deliberation is evident from their gentle rather than casual manner of working. The working material can be the hardest substance, stone or steel; they handle it with great care.

We were remodeling our home. One day, craftsmen came to put up wooden panels in our kitchen. One of them, seemingly the person in charge, walked around our kitchen examining and measuring everything with great precision. He asked us what we usually do in the kitchen, where we prepare the food and where we sit for breakfast. Having collected all the information they wanted, they proceeded to put up the panels. The craftsman in charge made holes in the panel, inserted the screws, and turned them gently, while his helper held the panel in position. When he finished a panel, he stepped back and looked at its impact and smiled. I was observing him continuously from a corner of the kitchen, and it occurred to me that during all of this, he did not use pressure at all. This made me nervous: "Are you sure the panels will stay attached to the wall?" I asked with my apprehension clearly detectable in my voice. He laughed and said, "Sir, I know my screws." Seeing the astonishment on my face, he added: "These screws require precisely six turns to attach securely. More pressure would unduly stress the panels and leave an unsightly mark."

The more skilled the person, the more he or she is able to handle the product with real gentleness. When you perform an activity with great skill, the energy loss reduces visibly. A skilled person tends to exploit the feeling of control, whereas the person who is learning and has not acquired the skill yet is aware of "doing it," or the desire of "wanting to do it."

Novices sit in the driver's seat with great deliberation. They grip the wheel tight with both hands. They change gears conscious of the steps they need to go through, rather than the need to coordinate those steps. They apply the rules for passing another car with visible awareness. A passenger can always tell if the driver is not very experienced. Other drivers have exceptional technical skills and are quick decision makers. They learn car handling and its way of reacting very quickly. They turn the wheel with their fingers only. They switch gears for the most efficient control. They exercise instinctive decision making while driving. A passenger can also tell when the driver is skilled.

Increasingly refined skills guided by a focused vision and inner standard lead to the powerful feeling of being in control. Since these originate deep in the individual's self, the worry about losing control dissolves. Therefore experiencing joy directly leads to great efficiency, as well as the feeling of liberty and self-fulfillment.

FOCUSED AND TRANSCENDENTAL JOY

We can distinguish between focused and transcendental experiences. Where one is so involved in the activity itself as to be completely submerged in it, we talk about focused joy. One visualizes the outcome while doing the activity and is not even aware of the activities being performed—becoming one with the activity itself.

Tightening screws can be a boring job. A skilled worker who knew his screws handled them with just the amount of pressure necessary, not more, nor less. While he was fixing the panels, he also had a larger purpose of decorating the room and making it more comfortable for a long time to come. He was not just drilling holes in the wall; his activity was part of achieving that larger purpose. As a person realizes that his or her current action is connected to a larger purpose, the person is experiencing transcendence. When, in addition to being submerged in an activity, we have a sense of contributing to a higher purpose that is transcendental, we experience transcendental joy.

Transcendence can be at higher and higher levels, as the well-known story of the quarrymen illustrates.

As they are laboring away in the quarry, a stranger asks three of the quarrymen why they are doing what they are doing. The first quarryman replies, "I cut stones, this is how I earn my living." The second quarryman replies, "Oh, I'm making a building." The first quarryman has a purpose, which is immediate and personal. The second quarryman has a feeling that he is doing something larger, carving stones that will form the walls of a building. The third quarryman gives yet another answer: "I'm building a cathedral."

The same applies to organizations. Making a profit is the most immediate purpose of a for-profit organization—similar to the first quarryman. Achieving this purpose consists of the immediate satisfaction of profit and dividend. It may not be joy, but simply satisfaction. In addition to being immersed in activity, in the case of a for-profit organization thinking in terms of profit, the next level of transcendence shows a sense of values: "Our profits are earned in a legitimate way. We have values. We provide quality to customers, every one of whom will recommend our product. Our employees are happy working here." This organization does not see itself as just a profit-making venture, but also as one that has a transcendental purpose. It may be considered as being at a higher level than the first organization, and it has a better chance of being joyful. Social service organizations, where values become institutionalized, often achieve this level. It is easier to learn to be immersed in an activity when you have a transcendent purpose in the first place than it is to develop and truly disseminate a higher purpose. Often it is the "managerial" rather than the "leadership" mind-set at a for-profit organization that is against the concept of values, saying that market forces should promote profit, not values. In spite of this common belief, market forces and values are not in conflict. Values help employees to rise above their function, and when the perspective increases, individuals can transcend.

Despite the fact that we think of an organization's purpose as being the matter of end goals, it is not just that; purpose, in fact, is a combination of means and ends. For example, organizations identify themselves by their end product, such as, "We are a company producing cleaning and personal care products, and we want to make profit by making and selling these." However, there is another aspect of their purpose: "We will make our profit from selling cleaning products, while taking care of people's health. We will not just sell these products but research and develop new ones paying special attention to their impact on the environment." Whenever the "how to get there" is translated into action, fulfilling the purpose has the capacity of providing transcendent goals to members of the organization. When employees feel that their work is contributing directly to a bigger purpose, the organization has mastered a big step on the way of becoming joyful.

It is easier to translate purpose into action while the organization is new and small. That is why start-ups more often exhibit the quality of having a transcendental goal about them, which is also one of their biggest attractions for new employees. When a transcendental purpose is not present in the organization, most people tend to feel that they are being exploited by the management. When transcendental purposes are present and internalized, people feel not "we are exploited," but rather "we are doing it together."

A truly mission-driven organization goes beyond the profit objective and has a higher and higher level of transcendent purposes. It can consider other stakeholders with a real sense of commitment. "We do not only seek to satisfy our customers, make a profit, and provide salary and opportunities to grow to our employees, but to increase employment in our community, provide a variety of social amenities, and ensure that our activity is sustaining the environment, not destroying it." This is a higher level of transcendence.

Truly mission-led organizations, by their very nature, often become institutions, benchmarks for other organizations. In an institution, employees experience a sense of importance from working in a wholly involved way to achieve the vision. We find that organizations that intend to become institutions are likely to become joyful organizations. Such joyful organizations in turn are admired by society.

I worked with a very successful company, which makes window treatments of all kinds. The entrepreneur himself is a very dedicated person. When he set up this factory in a village, one of his objectives was to provide employment to people there. He certainly wanted to make a profit. But equally important, he deliberately wanted to set his company up in this location. He trained villagers with a passion. Once, when I visited his factory, I saw a young employee discussing with him technical aspects of a machine. I asked this gentleman, "Is this young fellow an engineer?" He said, "No, he is not an engineer; he just graduated from high school." I said, "He obviously knows a great deal about the machine." He responded, "Oh, this is what everybody here has learned."

The founder had high standards. When he started the factory, he decided he would never give a bribe. That is a very, very rare thing in India. He said, "I will never give a bribe to anyone, and that includes an employee." He has never had to give a bribe, and he still succeeds in running the factory. In the beginning, the factory had an insufficient energy supply. The electric utility built a generator, a power substation near the factory out of admiration. In any other factory, you would have had to pay the people at the electricity department for that. In a variety of other ways, the founder has been able to reach his goals while keeping his high standards. He himself does not talk about all this with pride and a sense of self-achievement. He talks very, very humbly. He actually says, "People in this village are so attached, it is fun to work with them." He used the word "fun." I could not help but feel that it was a joyful organization.

INTERNALIZED PURPOSE AND VOLUNTARY INVOLVEMENT ARE PRECONDITIONS FOR A JOYFUL ORGANIZATION

If you have intrinsic motivation, you want to achieve your objectives, since this is very important to you. Your relationship with the organization that tries to fulfill the same purpose is voluntary. The more we see an opportunity for realizing ourselves, using our skills, developing, living up to our potential, the more we feel we are connected to the organization, the community, and society—that we are contributors, we matter, and we are important.

The feeling that we matter originates from different things for different people. One can experience joy through organizing and leading people to "build the cathedral." Alternatively, one can gain the same feeling from discovering innovative ways of putting the stones together. A third person can derive it from being part of a great team. A lot depends on how we answer the question, "Why am I doing what I am doing?"

In a joyful organization, we commit to doing our task. This is exercising rather than giving up our freedom. There is a purpose for our work, and there is a purpose we feel we serve through that work. Servicing internalized rather than externally forced goals reinforces the sense of self. When we reinforce our self, we feel in control, not helpless. We are involved, not alienated; we enjoy, rather than suffer.

In our view, if many people in the organization do not experience "mattering" and control, the organization cannot be a joyful one. It is a necessary, although not a sufficient, condition for the organization to have people who feel this way, to be joyful. The element of volunteering is fundamental. "I am not here because I have to be; I am in this organization because this is where I choose to be, where I want to be now."

Often people do not have the luxury to choose the type of work or organization they wish. They have to take the one that is available within the given circumstances. They take the job reluctantly and harbor negative feelings about it and about the organization. It is almost as if they are blaming the organization for their misfortune of having to work there. This attitude is self-destructive for the person and can have a negative effect on colleagues and for the working climate in the organization. This situation is definitely counterproductive for the creation of a joyful organization.

That is why it is important to help employees take responsibility for their own decisions. It is important to help them to understand that once they have made the decision to take the job—whatever the reason might have been— they are better off if they try to obtain the maximum for themselves including succeeding, gaining experience, improving the feeling of self-worth by being valuable contributors to their team, learning new things, and even trying to find enjoyable parts of their work. This has a lot to do with developing a positive attitude toward our activity, the people, and the organization around us. A team and a manager who are already having a positive working atmosphere can provide a good basis to develop the positive attitude and consequently joyful experiences at work.

Why do so few people in today's organizations experience joy? What is missing from these organizations? My grandfather had a lot of autonomy, deciding by himself, about all aspects of his work. He determined what was needed, when to do it, and how to do it. People working in organizations today typically do not have this kind of autonomy. They perform tasks given to them by others, and they believe they give up part of their freedom in order to do this. They perceive that the salary they receive is compensation for giving up autonomy. Freedom, however, is a very important part of human identity, which people fear losing. They only unwillingly allow somebody else to be in charge of their time, their life, and still feel bitter about it.

JOY FROM WORKING IN A TEAM

Most of us have some memorable experiences while working in a team. One of the clearest indicators of this experience is that we feel excited and more energized after a team meeting than before. We smile, we are happy with the result, and we feel very good about each other and ourselves. We feel attached, committed, worthwhile, and potent. We look forward to being together again to continue our project or start a new one if possible because we want to repeat the experience. These experiences reinforce our selves, our egos, but not to the detriment of others, because the others have similar feelings.

Having a joyful experience from teamwork has little to do with objective criteria such as the length of time the team members have known each other, or have been working together as a team, the size of the group, or the type of work (physical or intellectual) the team does. When we collected some of our personal examples of this experience we found that these indicators varied greatly. Some of these were concluding successfully a broad agenda with the executive team, working in the kitchen brigade in a 600-seat restaurant during lunch rush hour, and meeting a fellow organization development consultant for the first time and developing a jointly run workshop design. Others included working with family members on the family honey farm from early morning until late evening, creating a vision for a multi-billion-dollar company with the management team, and working in the production line as part of an autonomous work team.

In Table 1.1, we summarized the most important characteristics of a team where members experience joy and the opposite situation, in which something prevents that from happening. While reading it, the reader may recall personal experiences and compare the characteristics of the teams he or she participated in.

DO THOSE WHO ARE IN CHARGE EXPERIENCE JOY?

How do managers and leaders, who are supposed to direct and motivate people and usually do not work directly with basic materials, derive joy from their work?

Managers help organizations achieve their objectives with the minimally required energy, costs, and resources. They fight problems every day, develop and change processes that do not work, and manage all sorts of conflicts, challenges, and competition. Although this is one of the most overused phrases nowadays, it seems that managers are working in an increasingly complex and turbulent environment. We like the example of white-water rafting. The manager leads the boat and the crew through cliffs and rapids, in narrow valleys, and sometimes even through waterfalls. If the waterfall is too dangerous, the manager will instruct the crew to take the raft up on the riverside and carry it a little while, which may be much harder than rafting. The manager has to be able to give direction, coordinate the work of the crew, *and* be a member of the team. Meanwhile, the manager has to be in continuous touch with what is happening in the surroundings, with all his or her senses alive to be able to predict the unexpected.

Such a manager experiences joy when the team accomplishes its objectives. "We have done this together, and I had an important role leading the team through it." After the struggle there is a temporary slowdown. Soon, however, another set of rapids arrives, and the crew needs to be alert anew, to again fight the waves and turbulence. We think that those managers who find joy in the process of meeting the challenges are much more likely to be joyful. When a leader perceives challenges as headaches and focuses on the experience of "blood, sweat, and tears," fighting those difficulties can hardly provide a climate of joy for others. A leader who does not experience joy

Table 1.1
Joyful vs. Dysfunctional Teams

Characteristics of Joyful Teams	Characteristics Preventing Teams from Becoming Joyful
Once members are there, they want to be there and not somewhere else —voluntary participation. ⟷	Members are there because they feel they have to be.
Everybody in the team has a positive attitude. ⟷	Some members appear distant, critical, or skeptical; they withdraw, make faces, or otherwise express a negative attitude.
All members feel accepted, appreciated, valued, and welcomed by others. ⟷	Some members feel rejected, not valued.
There is a common objective that is important to everybody. ⟷	Members have differing objectives and priorities.
People feel good about themselves and compatible with the role they play within the team. ⟷	Some members are present only physically; their minds are somewhere else.
Team members openly express their thoughts and feelings. ⟷	Team members hesitate to reveal their real thoughts and feelings.
When developing something new, members build on each other's ideas. ⟷	Negative comments are common. People phrase ideas as opposing previous ones.
There is an informal work environment; everybody focuses on the task at hand and not on formalities. There is flexible use of different methods. ⟷	There is a closely controlled, formal, rigid, structured work environment where procedures are to be strictly followed.
The climate is nonjudgmental, cooperative, supportive, and balanced between focused work and using sense of humor. ⟷	There is a judgmental, oversensitive, win-lose climate. Rivalry is common.
There is a feeling of "WE-ness." ⟷	The focus is on egos.
There are feelings of being productive, meeting challenges, overperforming, discovering something new, and knowing/feeling "We have done it as a team." ⟷	There are feelings of being stuck, not getting anywhere, circling around, and being unproductive.

himself or herself through the journey is unlikely to provide or even allow a joyful climate. One of the most important issues for a joyful organization is how its leaders can experience joy under difficult circumstances. The more joy they can experience, the more likely they are to help and create circumstances under which people can also experience joy.

A JOYFUL ORGANIZATION IS A CONTEXT OF JOY FOR OTHERS

Joy in an organization has another quality: it is "contagious." When members of the organization have a sense of "we are doing it together," the organization is likely to be much more productive, since it makes people feel that they belong. Where people belong, they contribute their best. A joyful organization is also a context for joy for other people who are associated with it in various ways, such as suppliers, visitors, regulators, and constituencies. It is an organization that spreads joy. It makes people who come into contact with the organization motivated to contribute to it. It makes the organization's relation to the environment more harmonious. When we leave as a visitor, we feel recharged. We think of ways to take forward the joyful organization. We also become motivated to create a similar environment in the organization of which we are members. People who have contact with a joyful organization also experience joy.

Employees in a joyful organization understand the purpose and the vision that are internal to them. Since they operate with an internal understanding of the organization's vision, they work out the most efficient way to move toward that purpose. While working, every member of the organization is doing his or her job with the awareness that all the other members are doing their part in order to reach the common vision. This provides a feeling of togetherness and solidarity: "I'm part of something greater, I'm creating something important." A joyful organization's people are happy to go to work.

On the rare occasion when I go to our office on Sunday morning, when nobody is there, I open the door and a good feeling comes over me. It's a very ordinary office and there is nothing particularly special about it. But, I have a good feeling walking in. There is my work, the memories of struggles and fun with my colleagues, and there are my mementoes from different clients I've been working with. Looking at them fills me with a good feeling.

In a joyful organization there is an attitude of discovering things. People enjoy their work similar to children who enjoy playing. There is a climate of discovery, experimentation, creativity, and recognition. It is okay to experiment and even to fail, as it is customary to be appreciated if you succeed. Walk into this organization and you see people smiling, though at the same time they work seriously and are involved in their work. You can hear the laughter of people frequently making jokes. At any level, in any meeting, they are pulling each other's leg. There is a relaxed atmosphere, humor, and easy manners. Work is not associated with sacrifice and suffering, but with an emotionally balanced, inspiring atmosphere.

A joyful organization is a productive one. There is an overall feeling of potency, supported by experience. Members go through a lot, solve all sorts of problems, develop new things together, and this experience gives them a tangible sense of "Yes, we are productive." In the face of adversity this feeling indeed assists the organization in overcoming it in more ways than one. Productivity is also bolstered by the fact that a joyful organization is transparent. Transparency is not limited to clear roles and rules of operations, but includes the availability of information to members. An organization that is not healthy tends to be secretive.

Members of a joyful organization are very proud of its results. Some people may argue that they are idealistic, but their response is that ideal things should be made practical. When ideal things are made practical, they inspire pride and commitment. Members will be committed to their results, and the process of pursuing them—as opposed to being committed to an organization. Commitment does not originate from "niceness," but from a set of tightly knit criteria.

POTENTIAL DANGERS IN JOY

While we are promoting joy, it is also necessary to look at some potential dangers in joy. Very often people use the concept of joy as a way to escape. If they become captive in it, joy is a way to escape from troubles of reality. You may rise to a transcendental level of joy, not wanting to ever be again at a mundane level, to have to start again in order to repeat the experience. In this case, very often you become blind to reality. Whether the activity that led to the joyful experience is still relevant or not is forgotten, because you are "in it." While having joy is fundamental for the self, being blinded by joy can be dangerous. It is similar to the process of using a narcotic. We consider it necessary in the "reality" of an organization that people be encouraged to occasionally climb down from that transcendent level to a lower level, examine the world, and cope with the ambiguities of life before once again experiencing joy. This coming in and out of joy is very important because, in the process, our capacity to experience joy also increases.

CHAPTER 2

Successful, Healthy, or Joyful?

If it is so desirable, why is it so rare that people call an organization joyful? What do we mean by successful? What is the difference among a successful, a healthy, and a joyful organization? If an organization is a living system, what functions does it need to have before it can be considered "alive?" How long can an organization survive with one or more of these functionality criteria unsatisfied? Why are we necessarily preoccupied with restoring functionality before we turn our attention toward how best to pursue the organizational vision? What do we sense when a function is not meeting requirements? How do we define an organizational disease? Do diseases have common causes? What happens when an organization satisfies—to a high degree— all organizational health criteria? Is it only a healthy organization that can become an environment for joy?

A SUCCESSFUL ORGANIZATION IS NOT NECESSARILY HEALTHY

Experiencing joy inherently assumes that the individual has a certain level of physical and mental health. When people are preoccupied with fighting an acute disease, they first focus on restoring their operational ability, not on pushing the limits of self-realization. Our analogy of individual and organizational behavior indicates that a joyful organization is a healthy organization. Yet, people do not address organizational health directly; when they characterize organizations, they talk about successful ones. What are the differences between a successful and a healthy organization? Is there any difference?

To enable us to characterize organizations in a meaningful way, we begin with defining the nature of organizations. People create organizations in order to facilitate the achievement of a set of objectives, objectives that can be achieved only by an organization. (If we could meet those objectives ourselves, why build an organization?) Once we have decided to create an organization, the following four fundamental issues need to be considered, consciously or unconsciously:

• Organizations aim to satisfy the specific needs of a select group of people, with the hope of receiving a reasonable reward for their activities. Customers—whether they pay or not—legitimize the existence of any organization.

• An organization is always a collection of people, not a collection of objectives. Not just those who establish the organization, but those who join it as well, have their own agendas—existential, social, and psychological—related to what they want to see accomplished within the context of the particular organization. Life for every human being inherently comprises numerous inseparable aspects. Being the member of an organization is only one of these aspects. By every act they engage in, individuals manage these multiple aspects simultaneously, and this requires that they develop purposes of their own. Members have to realize their own objectives in joining an organization, not only the objectives of the organization.

• Only when certain resources are available can an organization start to operate, and only if the organization uses resources efficiently will it be able to survive over time. The very concept of an organization is to bring order in the pursuit of its goals, to organize itself efficiently.

• Every organization has to exist, succeed, and survive in a given, although not unchangeable, environment.

WHEN DO WE CALL AN ORGANIZATION SUCCESSFUL?

When we call an organization successful, we directly refer to its effectiveness and efficiency of using resources, and perhaps indirectly, to its ability to attract customers. Both of these characteristics are relative. The concept of success assumes the existence of a benchmark, a standard, compared to which one is successful. Peers usually serve as a reference group and one defines success as exceeding someone else's performance. Thus, success necessarily implies comparison and competition. The success of organizations is measured by financial results almost exclusively. If an organization achieves profit, that is, its revenues from customers exceed—or in the case of a nonprofit, equal—expenses, it is widely considered successful. If the profit is above industry average, and/or exceeds analyst expectations, it is considered even highly successful. Other indicators can complement the profit measure, for example, revenue per employee, productivity, market share, or price earnings ratio. These measures further scale the efficiency with which resources are applied to fulfilling the objectives and the growth of the organization. The question we would like to ask is this, "Does financial success, indicated by the above measures, necessarily imply organizational health?" By our definition, it does not. Examples abound of financially successful organizations, visibly unhealthy to an observer, suffering from various organizational problems.

Measuring success alone has a serious drawback when considered from the point of view of joy, namely, that it lacks the concept of fulfilling internal ideals, surpassing ourselves, by setting challenges or developing skills, and improving competencies. In its purest form, competition forces individuals to focus on trying to beat others rather than to live up to their own potentials. When competing or continually focusing on others—including developing a negative or destructive attitude toward our competitors—we easily lose sight of our internal transcendent purposes, which have the capacity to bring joy to our daily activities. The same applies to organizations. Focusing on a vision and realizing part of it day by day while continually monitoring our environment, including the competition, is characteristic of a healthy organization.

ORGANIZATIONAL HEALTH IS A HOLISTIC CONDITION

Our analogy of individuals and organizations suggests that organizational health is a holistic condition, the coexistence of numerous aspects of organizational functionality. This definition looks simple, but on a second look raises many questions. What are the main aspects of organizational functionality? Does health mean the total absence of dysfunctional activities? Are there any indicators, preferably measurable, to define health?

The nature of organizations implies several dimensions in which functionality should be considered in order to assess the state of organizational health. By our definition, an organization can be considered healthy if the following statements can characterize its functionality:

- A healthy organization satisfies customer needs by providing great value for the customer and thus earns legitimacy for its existence and the ability to maintain itself as a going concern via the continuous stream of revenues,

- A healthy organization satisfies the needs of its members by creating an environment where members develop (grow) and believe that they matter and so fulfill their individual objectives while they realize the objectives of the organization,

- A healthy organization satisfies economic requirements (financial benchmarks such as profitability imposed mainly by markets and regulators) by using resources most efficiently and effectively in its pursuit of objectives,

- A healthy organization maintains a balance between these three fundamental objectives by developing a structure and a culture that encourage, considering all three simultaneously when making decisions,

- A healthy organization grows and develops over time, increasing its reach and/or ability to handle complex situations, and

- A healthy organization lives in harmony with its natural social and economical environment. See Figure 2.1.

We define organizational health as the holistic condition of these six main criteria being satisfied to a high degree concurrently. Naturally, satisfying

Figure 2.1
The Model of a Healthy Organization

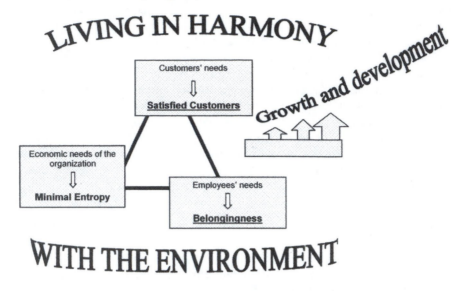

these is not a binary, yes, no, choice but a question of degree. The objective of an attempted "assessment" is not the identification of this degree to minute detail; instead it is to indicate what may need to be addressed in order to build a healthier organization.

When an organization can be described as vigorous and potent, satisfying to a high degree each of these organizational health criteria, a new set of choices appears. At this level, the attention of members can now turn toward how best to pursue objectives, because they are not preoccupied with restoring functionality. It is in this environment that experiencing joy becomes a possibility.

The aspects of organizational health criteria, their detailed descriptions, and their relationships are the subjects of the next chapters. As we draw up a detailed picture of a healthy organization, we offer our interpretations of characteristics of health, emphasizing those we found particularly curious and even counterintuitive. We illustrate how each of the characteristics unfolds, and we describe situations in which one or more health criteria are not sufficiently satisfied. This raises another aspect of organizational health: dynamic condition.

HEALTH IS SOLVING PROBLEMS BEFORE THEY BECOME ACUTE

We can extend our definition of organizational health to include the following abilities:

- to cope with events that have a negative impact whether occurring inside and/or outside the organization and
- to exploit opportunities sufficiently rapidly in such a way that diversion from pursuing the purposes of the organization and/or dissatisfaction of stakeholders is not persistent and recurrent.

This means that if the organization can master internal and external resources to solve problems so that not only are they solved for the time being, but also so that they do not deepen or recur, we consider the organization healthy. In a healthy organization, problem-solving mechanisms work automatically, similarly to the immune system in physiology. When the problem-solving mechanisms are absent, weakened, or slow in response, problems occur, persist, or recur, wasting energy and resources in a preoccupation with short-term and partial remedies, not main purposes. We call this phenomenon organizational disease. We define organizational diseases as situations in which

- part(s) of the organization do not fulfill their functions according to the requirements,
- some of the organization's processes persistently fail to meet requirements, and
- one or more of the fundamental objectives are repeatedly neglected in the decision-making process.

WHEN PROBLEMS BECOME ACUTE, THEY BECOME ORGANIZATIONAL DISEASES

In order to understand the state of health of an organization, it is necessary to understand how that particular organization functions. However, we must also compare the identified symptoms of ill-health to a typology of organizational diseases, in the absence of which the diagnosis of the state of health becomes a random collection of information. Typology associates the disease with the following:

- the part of the organization where the malfunction is located,
- the location where the effect of malfunction is mainly felt, or
- the structures and systems that tend to perpetuate the problem.

If the organization is oblivious to these problems, they become acute. Acute problems radiate outward to related areas of operations, decreasing functionality exponentially. In this book, our objective is to try to explore how organizational health and diseases can be analytically dealt with, not to be exhaustive in our details of diseases and attempting to list all of them. We encourage readers to refine the following classification by their experiences and ideas.

ORGANIZATIONAL DISEASES HAVE OBSERVABLE SYMPTOMS

As problems become recurrent, typical behavior manifests in organizations. We call observable behavior patterns associated with problems, symptoms. Our diagnosis of organizational health consists of observing the various symptoms and classifying them similarly to diseases of the human body. Symptoms of organizational diseases must appear together to constitute the disease. Malaria, for example, is identified from periodic attacks of chills and fever and loss of energy together; high temperature alone will not indicate malaria. A combination of symptoms forms a syndrome, which uniquely characterize a disease. Diagnosis of organizational health entails a focused collection of data for the purpose of identifying and treating organizational diseases. To treat a disease, after ascertaining the nature of it, one must determine its cause. To be able to state that a cause renders an organizational disease, we should be able to see that whenever the cause happens, the disease happens. The malaria organism generates the chills, fever, and loss of energy; without infection by this parasite the symptoms are not likely to occur together.

THE CAUSES OF ORGANIZATIONAL DISEASES AND THEIR ORIGINS

If our final goal is to prevent or address dysfunctional activities in our organization, a diagnostic understanding of the causes of the diseases and their origins is also necessary. To systematize the treatment of a disease we must clarify its cause. As we see later, a number of structural-, cultural-, and leadership-related characteristics of the organization or the surrounding environment can be identified as a cause. Examples range from how the different levels of the organization cooperate to how predictable a specific part of the environment is. To facilitate the treatment of a disease we must clarify the origin of the cause as well. We found that causes of organizational diseases have three most typical origins.

The first origin we call "genetic." When the origin of a disease is genetic, the cause of a disease can be traced to the character, the personality, and the consequent belief system of the key players who had established or been the leaders of the organization. Although this process involves a plethora of probabilistic outcomes, the structure and culture of an organization can and often does astutely reflect the founders' belief systems, and the specific characteristics of their individual personalities. Furthermore, certain sets of beliefs are likely to lead to certain structural or cultural causes, provoking the appearance of corresponding symptoms and thus diseases. We show how leaders' beliefs lead to organizational health or diseases through examples at the end of the leadership chapter (Chapter 10).

The second origin is "birth related." Trauma, shock, or difficulties during the period in which the organization is brought to life, as during delivery, can create long-lasting effects. Founders mobilize resources when they establish an organization. Sometimes the resources prove to be inadequate for the purpose. Inadequacy of resources during the early period of getting established can have a long-lasting influence on the culture and structure of the organization. When this situation occurs, it results in causes that provoke a certain kind of symptoms and behavior patterns from the members of the organization. These behavior patterns are likely to influence the organization for a long time to come even if the shortage of resources has long since been resolved. For example, a shortage of financial resources leads to unwarranted decision-making power of the finance department long after the critical phase in the life of the organization is over.

The third origin of diseases is "environmental." Factors external to the organization, such as circumstances defined by the surrounding society and its cultural norms, the market, and the regulatory system impact the structure and culture of an organization. If the environment of an organization facilitates, for example, corrupt transactions, similar practices are likely to occur in organizations as well. These external factors, either the general environment or specific inputs from the environment, can have a detrimental and long-lasting impact on an organization.

Later in the book we describe several organizational diseases, including their definitions, symptoms, causes, and origins. For every disease we also identify what other related diseases are likely to occur together with that particular primary disease. However, our list is not exhaustive, and we focus on diseases that occur frequently and are familiar to most people. We expect that readers will be able to identify more diseases and disease clusters they have experienced firsthand. Our hope is that applying the framework will lead to better analysis and improvement of health.

To help the readers extract practical applications from the book—perhaps for their own organizations—after each disease we have provided a table that summarizes systematically the possible causes by three categories and consequently a series of alternative actions to consider in treating the given disease. Every organization is individual in some ways, so every cure and remedy must be too. Still, what these tables include could guide anyone who wants to begin working in a healthier and a more joyful organization. This framework, as both a diagnostic tool and a tool kit to improve organizational health, has been instrumental in bringing about positive change in the wide variety of organizations with which we have worked.

THE RELATIONSHIP BETWEEN HEALTH AND JOY

As we have discussed, organizational health is a precondition of developing a joyful organization. This of course does not mean that members of an organization suffering from acute organizational diseases cannot—even if only temporarily or partially—experience joy from work. However, this experience will be the exception rather than a characteristic of the organization. Members of an organization suffering from recurring and acute organizational diseases often get weary and cynical in the daily fight of trying to restore functionality, losing hope that these problems will ever be resolved. This state of mind disfavors un-self-conscious, devoted, dedicated, and liberated work.

In an organization that satisfies the health criteria in all dimensions to a certain high degree, and where members believe in a common vision, a transcendent purpose important for them as individuals, the conditions exist for experiencing joy from work on a more frequent basis. Members can focus their energies on performing their tasks, and they do so in a devoted way, which in turn increases their self-respect in a virtuous cycle, and then the feeling of success and joy can then be experienced through everyday work.

Organizational health is a necessary but by no means sufficient condition for developing a joyful organization. It is also required that the executives of an organization deliberately articulate the objective of becoming one. It is the widely recognized role of executives to ensure that the mechanisms through which members develop the shared transcendent purpose are in place. They also consciously or unconsciously influence whether work conditions make it possible for individuals to perform their tasks in a way as described above. Thus through these two influences, executives determine if the members of the organization can feel valuable and experience joy through work by continuously experiencing how much value they add through their daily contribution.

Since the first and most complex exercise is to create and maintain organizational health, we focus on this step in the following chapters.

PART II
_____

The Fundamentals of
Organizational Health

CHAPTER 3

Balancing the Three Fundamental Objectives of Organizations

What are the three main objectives of organizations? How do these objectives manifest themselves in everyday decision making? What happens when one objective is emphasized at the expense of the other(s)? How does treating customers too well take away from financial success and employee satisfaction? How does focusing on financial needs leave customers and employees dissatisfied? Does pampering employees lead to unsatisfied customers and financial obligations?

Why do we find balance so elusive?

OBJECTIVES OF ORGANIZATIONS

Over the last two decades we asked managers to tell us about the most important objectives of their organizations. We asked them to ignore the formal mission statement, the purpose of the organization described in the strategic plan. We encouraged them to tell us what they personally considered the most important actual objectives—even if it was politically incorrect. Some managers mentioned minor objectives, such as finishing the last investment project successfully, but most asserted more fundamental ones. The answers can be grouped into three categories.

Most managers' answers included a reference to customer satisfaction in the form of providing high-quality service or products, great value, timely delivery, or simply meeting the true needs of customers.

Managers also frequently responded that financial success is the ultimate objective of their organizations. Some answers were limited to making profit; others aimed to provide a good return on investment for owners and stockholders. Even executives of nonprofit organizations we questioned expressed the importance of efficient resource utilization as a basic objective; society was not indifferent to the cost they absorbed providing their services. This second group of answers can be summarized as meeting the economic needs of the organization.

Finally, managers told us about organizational objectives concerning the people working for the organizations. They explained that the organizations aim to retain members who invest their energy into achieving the objectives of the organizations by rewarding them for their contributions.

However, answers related to this last basic objective were the least frequent and least directly expressed. We found that articulation of the organizational objective of satisfying employee needs is particularly influenced by how current management thinking reflects existing social values.

Providing attractive products or services (customer needs) and operating in an efficient manner and providing a good return on investment (economic needs) are widely perceived as more immediate needs than fulfilling employee needs. Managers consider the consequences of not fulfilling the first two objectives as a straightforward short-term problem, while the consequences of not fulfilling the latter are less apparent. It is not surprising, therefore, that managers will more readily articulate customer and financial performance-related objectives.

Looking at these answers we also found that the way fundamental organizational objectives are articulated is susceptible to socioeconomic and cultural interpretations.

Eastern European managers of the 1980s often told us that the fundamental objective of their organization is to provide the highest possible compensation for employees: "provide higher salary than other companies," "supply jobs for the employees," "give more to the employees than any other company," and "provide salary increases exceeding the inflation rate for the employees." During the 1980s, before the social-political changes in Central and Eastern Europe, political slogans emphasized workers' rights and welfare. In the so-called "shortage economy" the "market" is driven by supply; therefore, customer satisfaction does not appear as a direct objective for economic units. Neither does state ownership enforce effective resource allocation, so the financial objective of an organization is limited to complying with regulations. In this political and economic environment, the stated objectives of an "enterprise" demonstrated the cultural bias in how the organizations' objectives are articulated. Fast forward to the 1990s to a demand-driven market economy in Eastern Europe and find that profitability and productivity increase have become by far the most emphasized objectives, with customer satisfaction slightly behind but employee needs barely mentioned.

When we asked American managers what the true objectives of their organization were, they consistently emphasized customer satisfaction and profitability and return on investment. In most cases, they entirely neglected to articulate any objective related to employee satisfaction. However, they would occasionally mention operating in a meritocracy—up or out—as a basic objective of their organization.

THE THREE FUNDAMENTAL OBJECTIVES

We call the three categories into which all answers can be classified the fundamental objectives of organizations. The three fundamental objectives of every organization can be depicted in a triangle. Each corner of the triangle stands for a fundamental objective. Customers have needs, and, having consumed goods or services, they evaluate their level of satisfaction. The market and its regulations in general, owners and shareholders in specific, define the standards of satisfying the economic needs of an organization. The social environment and the employees themselves define their expectations and the level of satisfaction they get from working in the organization.

BALANCING THE THREE FUNDAMENTAL OBJECTIVES

We define the first criterion of organizational health as satisfying the three fundamental objectives in a balanced way over time. No single objective has exclusive priority within an organization's goal hierarchy; therefore, the three fundamental objectives should be satisfied simultaneously. See Figure 3.1.

Why is the continuous balancing of all three objectives of organizations so important? Quite simply, emphasizing one of the basic objectives can happen only to the detriment of the others, and this necessarily results in an imbalance, thereby reducing the performing ability of the organization. When satisfying any one or two of these basic objectives is overemphasized at the expense of the other(s), the actualization of the other(s) will suffer and this over time will start propelling the organization in a downward spiral, toward

Figure 3.1
Fundamental Needs

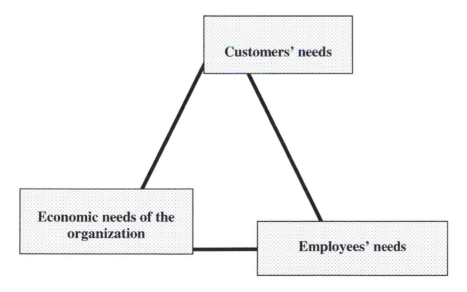

disintegration in the extreme case. Let us examine each objective to see how the interconnectedness of them renders the lack of balance detrimental to the organization.

THE CUSTOMER NEEDS CORNER

Regardless of whether the organization provides products or services for profit or not for profit, there must be customers or clients behind it. All organizations, business, not for profit, even religious ones offering their services to satisfy society's need for spirituality, aim to satisfy needs that exist independently of the organization and are outside the organization's boundaries. Employees of car manufacturing plants do not produce cars for themselves, but for all those who need personal transportation. Effective satisfaction of outside needs justifies the existence of an organization. This objective applies to subunits or departments of an organization, as well as for the individual members. In this "chain" all links provide a product or service to their external (or internal within the bigger organization) customers, which legitimizes their existence within the organization.

In most cases customers pay for the goods and services, whether in the form of paying a price or providing a contribution. In the case of not-for-profit organizations, other organizations may also provide funds for the organization. This revenue is the source of resources necessary for operations, development, and growth for a going concern. If the number of customers or amount of revenue provided by them is insufficient, the organization loses not only its raison d'etre, but over time, its ability to operate as well. The process of matching product features, quality, and price to meet customer requirements is a trial-and-error process. It is possible that the matching process takes several attempts before it succeeds in finding the right constellation of features satisfying the customer need. However, if an organization completely neglects the need of customers or does not continuously strive to make its products attractive to customers, it will not survive.

CUSTOMER-RELATED DISEASES OF THE LACK OF BALANCE

See Figure 3.2.

Disease: Customer Exploitation

It is the customers' responsibility to fight for the value they need.

Description

Customers are perceived primarily as an income source, a means to an end. This attitude results in an exploitative approach toward customers, serving the overall goal of becoming rich in a short time. When this culture

Figure 3.2
Satisfied Customers

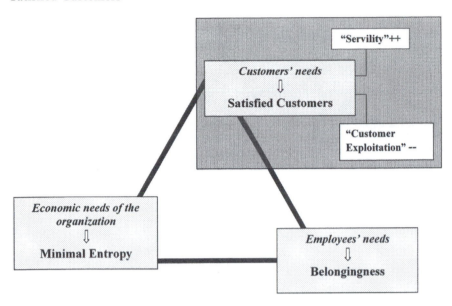

predominates, it is likely that the exploitative approach is not limited to customers, but is extended to other stakeholders as well. The following statement summarizes the philosophy of the organization suffering from customer exploitation: "It is the customers' responsibility to fight for the value they need. Let's gain the most, while we give them the least we can get by with."

Symptoms

- A high percentage of the product or service is rejected.
- The number of quality complaints is high.
- Delivery problems increase above target, industry average, or as compared to a previous period.
- There are comparatively few repeat customers.
- There are reported conflicts, debates, and fights with the customers.
- Members of the organization are constantly criticizing the customers, telling nasty jokes and stories about the customers with zeal. The stories indicate that customers are a burden or "a pain in the neck."
- Customers are late or hesitant to transfer payment for services or products, indicating that they are not motivated to keep up a good relationship with the organization.
- Customers have a negative image of the exploitative organization, they do not think much of the organization as a provider of a product or service, and they turn to it by

necessity rather than by choice. Government agencies and organizations in monopolistic situations typically exhibit this symptom.

• Only the marketing or frontline personnel address customer issues; the rest of the organization has no incentive to do so, perceiving customer satisfaction as not their responsibility. Customer issues are not disseminated throughout the organization.

• The organization spends resources to make "unproved," misleading, or downright false promises to the customers through advertising, resulting in disappointment.

Cause

• The organization consciously defines its relationship with the customers as a purely transactional relationship, one with a short time frame. There is no long-term thinking. Customers therefore are perceived as adversaries or enemies, with whom the organization needs to fight a battle.

Origins

• The genetic origin is that the founder or executive is selfish and an opportunist who established profiting from exploiting the customer as the organization's primary motive. Therefore the prevailing belief is that the organization cannot trust the customer, who is there to exploit the organization, so it also has the right to exploit the customer in turn. Another genetic origin could be the anxiety of the founders for being taken advantage of by customers, in which case they overcompensate for feeling vulnerable.

• The birth-related origin is that during the first phase of the organizational life, economic regulation or political legislation provided easy sales through establishing a monopolistic position. Even if regulatory circumstances have changed, the behavior of the organization and its members remains.

• The environmental origin is that a shortage exists in the market of the particular product or service the organization is providing, due either to the originality of the product or limited supply. The organization may get along with this disease for a while, before other suppliers are able to catch up and thus change the environment. Another environmentally rooted origin can be if taking advantage of others is a common practice in the culture of the broader society.

This disease often occurs together with others such as Money Mania, Shortsightedness, and Aggressive Approach to the Environment.

A structured list of causes and possible actions for improvements for this disease can be seen in Table 3.1.

Consider the opposite situation, when satisfying customers' needs predominates decision making at the expense of the financial well-being of the company and/or satisfying employee needs. Operating costs will rise due to indiscriminate spending. The product may originally have been high quality, but following this path the organization eventually will run out of resources to develop it further. Similarly, resources to meet compensation standards for employees will decrease, resulting in low morale and a high turnover.

Table 3.1
Customer Exploitation

Structure of Causes	Possible Causes	Possible Actions for Improvement
Personal, Leadership Related	1. Management's attitude is purely profit centered. 2. Management does not pay attention to customers and is not interested in finding out the needs and considerations of customers. 3. Management/employees look at customers as adversaries and at the transactions with them as a win-lose battle.	*Executive Coaching, Training Workshop, and/or Other:* • Conduct market surveys and feed back the results. Benchmark the organization against competition and show the possible losses and negative consequences if the organization does not improve its relationship/attitude toward customers. • Create learning occasions where management/employees can see how a win-lose approach tends to end up at lose-lose. Help them to redefine their attitude/relationship with customers to win-win. • Hire/promote managers to key positions who are well known for their customer-oriented approach.
Organizational, Operational	1. The most important objective is growth, the short-term increase of profit. 2. The customers are perceived as a burden, as a source of frustration.	*Coaching, Training Workshop, and/or Other:* • Start a systematic cultural turnaround in the organization for customer focus and involve a broad range of employees in it.

Table 3.1 (continued)

Structure of Causes	Possible Causes	Possible Actions for Improvement
	3. The prevailing values of the organization express that the marketplace is a battlefield, where winning at any cost is the final objective. 4. Past successes make people overconfident; expecting customers to provide the revenue for the organization, regardless of how much the given product or services meet their needs. 5. Incentive system focuses exclusively on short-term profit results.	• Invite customers to the organization so that management and employees can hear directly from the source of feedback. • Assess customer satisfaction; share the results across the organization, followed by specific action steps to improve the results. • Analyze reasons for loosing customers. • Create opportunities for employees responsible for customer relations to express their opinions and to improve those relations; restructure customer relations. • Reconsider the incentive system putting more emphasis on customer satisfaction and long-term results.
External, Market Related	1. Monopoly, or sellers' market, which has led to overconfidence. 2. Pressure for short-term profitability is too high from investors.	*Interventions:* • Demonstrate how the low image and/or customer orientation of the organization can harm profitability, shareholder value.

Ultimately, the quality of the product will suffer as well. The accumulating problems will threaten the existence of the organization as a whole.

Disease: Servility

Servility entails trying to get the order and keep the customer whatever it takes and subordinating to customers' wishes by disregarding the business model, thus providing benefit to the customers alone.

Description

The opposite disease of Customer Exploitation is Servility, focusing on customer needs at the expense of the organization's financial—and/or the employees'—needs. The extreme philosophy of a slavish organization can be summarized as "never confront a customer, never turn down any business, no matter what it takes."

Symptoms

- Employees hesitate to differ with the customer, even if it would be in the customer's best, although perhaps not explicit, interest. Instead of a "service provider attitude," manifested in treating the customer as a partner, the prevailing culture enforces a "servant attitude" toward customers.

- The organization urges employees to stretch resources and efforts to meet changes in customer demand, which the organization seeks to accommodate at any price. This manifests, for example, in modifying the product, changing the service, and changing the deadline.

- Unethical practices can spread in slavish organizations in order to attract more customers. Bidding or competing for an order is a typical situation, in which temptation to use questionable means occurs in order to gain customer orders. Executives may rationalize questionable practices to get customers by saying, "If our organization won't do it, another will," or "every organization follows that practice, so we have to as well."

- Employees exhibit eagerness to overspend on the product or the services with respect to the original budget.

- In order to get and keep customers, employees give unreasonable discounts and advantages, which are financially not acceptable and lead to losses.

- Overspending on sales rather than on marketing occurs, emphasizing accommodation of customers' whims rather than communication of the value the product provides.

- There is a recurring feeling that transactions are not beneficial for the organization. This springs from the practice of overstretching employees, budget, and other resources in order to keep the customers.

- The organization finds it difficult to take a strong stand when necessary, such as when collecting outstanding bills.

Causes

- Members of the organization believe that the organization has to try everything to keep customers out of fear of losing them and to get enough contracts to keep the business going.
- The single most important objective of the organization is growth, overriding understanding customers' needs or improving the competitive position of the organization. Members of the organization—especially in sales—do not really concern themselves with the particulars of a contract, but with winning it. Consulting and software companies or advertising agencies, for example, are periodically prone to this disease, due to the quickly changing desirability of their products for the customers while the requirement of their showing financial growth is constant.

A multinational data processing service provider experienced significant margin decline on its primary product during the early 1990s. In order to expand activities into higher margin areas, based on the recommendation of a highly regarded strategy-consulting firm, the board of directors decided to channel substantial resources into establishing a management consulting arm. Counting on synergy from providing technology solutions and management advice, they claimed that the new group would redefine management consulting. The resources invested into making this vision a reality were in line with the grandness of it. The company went on an unprecedented acquisition and hiring spree, bringing together thousands of management consulting practitioners from almost as many disciplines in a few months' time. Already in the first quarter, the pressure was on to counterbalance the massive expense of acquisitions and employee compensation with at least some revenue. The chase for clients had begun and no engagement was too small to fall below the radar. The time the highly compensated principals spent on bidding for engagements often cost more than the expected revenue from the assignment. No engagement was too unusual to be considered either. In one case, about a hundred highly educated consultants staffed a call center for six months. In another case, consultants were "rented out" to a client, to participate in rolling out a new product to third parties. Consultants remarked to management that this position compromised them by confusing the role of an independent consultant with that of a third-party salesperson. This, in their opinion could possibly have led to a conflict of interest, as well as diluted the image of the company in the eyes of a potential customer base. However, as long as the revenue came from the engagement, even client letters indicating the seriousness of the conflict were ignored.

The lack of unified corporate culture and diverse but unmatched expertise led to similarly random sales efforts partnering with the data processing arm. In summary providing any kind of consulting service that any prospective client was willing to pay for was considered. With time the focus shifted from developing the world's largest management consulting business to hitting revenue targets at any cost. As part of an established publicly traded company, it was not long before the unit could not maintain its expansive employee base and indiscriminate pursuing of clients. It was dissolved (at great expense though with public relations intact) through the acquisition of a well-established name in the consulting business. Interestingly many of the principals from the acquired consulting company went along enthusiastically with the original vision. This time revolutionizing the consulting business was attempted with a much reduced employee base as well as an effort to keep the continuity in the

Table 3.2
Servility

Structure of Causes	Possible Causes	Possible Actions for Improvement
Personal, Leadership Related	1. People in the company are afraid that they will lose customers or lose out in the competition. 2. Low self-esteem, including the products/ services or the performance of the organization. ("We are not good enough; others are better than we are.") 3. Some key executives provide the primary example of considering customers and acquiring new customers as an absolute priority, at any cost.	*Executive Coaching, Training Workshop, and/or Other:* • Help key executives to face the cultural and financial consequences of their servile attitude toward customers and to overcome it. • Participate in programs that help to boost self-confidence, assertive behavior. • Select inspiring leader(s) for key positions who can boost morale and self-confidence across the organization.
Organizational, Operational	1. The organizational culture explicitly or implicitly pushes for accommodating customer wishes, desires at any price. 2. The most important objective is growth, increased revenues, acquiring new business, customers, markets, and orders; and this influences the behavior of employees. 3. Financial conditions do not have enough weight in contracts. 4. Lack of necessary understanding of the real strengths and weaknesses of the organization.	*Coaching, Training Workshop, and/or Other:* • Strengthen the financial analyses and feedback on profitability by customer groups, products, sales activity, and so forth, where employees can clearly see how much resources they have invested and how much return the company had on specific business. Create forums where different parts of the organization can face these hard data and facilitate the process to make the necessary corrective actions.

Table 3.2 (continued)

Structure of Causes	Possible Causes	Possible Actions for Improvement
	5. Some previous failure related to customers affected the organization significantly and is continuing to have an effect in the form of overdone carefulness. 6. The main focus of the Evaluation/Bonus System is to get and satisfy customer orders at any price.	• Make it explicit what the organization can or cannot provide to address customer complaints and empower employees to stay within these boundaries. • Review personal incentives in the performance evaluation system, improve sales and efficiency-related criteria, including profitability. • Improve negotiation skills, polite but assertive communication techniques, and so forth.
External, Market Related	1. The increasing competition forces the organization to undercut prices or over-stretch resources just to get/keep customers.	*Interventions:* • Strengthen marketing activity; increase the value of the product as perceived by the customer. • Bring the customer closer; provide a sense of the conditions and costs of internal operations. • Review contracts, clarify and provide details to conditions. • Prioritize customers. • Assess competition.

acquired business to ensure revenue flow. However, in ten years' time the consulting company called it quits and silently parted ways from the data processing company.

Origins

- The genetic origin is that founders or key players fear losing or getting an insufficient number of customers and spread this culture across the organization. This fear stems from low self-esteem, the perpetual fear of not being good enough.

- The birth origin is that when the organization was brought to life, it had to struggle to get orders. When it is a question of survival, it becomes imprinted in the members' consciousness and this imprint remains, even after the situation has changed.

- The environmental origin is a shift from a sellers' market to a buyers' market, the sudden appearance of alternative providers, and the subsequent drop in orders can be factors.

This disease often occurs together with Negligence of Financial Matters.

A structured list of causes and possible actions for improvements for this disease can be seen in Table 3.2.

THE EMPLOYEE NEED CORNER

The majority of people in most societies of today's world spend a significant part of their time (if not the most significant part) in organizations. We perform our duties directly or indirectly to satisfy an inside or outside customer at the highest level possible. We also have to perform this in the most effective and efficient way possible to meet the economic needs of the organization. We are expected to focus our energies to comply with these two criteria. We do so to the best of our abilities, while at the same time we constantly face a question so forceful it is impossible to ignore: How do we feel while we are performing those duties? Do we feel like victims, under constant pressure to satisfy customers and do it ever more efficiently; or do we feel that during this process we ourselves grow and develop, finding satisfaction and experience joy in performing our duties?

Immanuel Kant, the German philosopher, said, "No man must be the means for the ends of another man." In a healthy organization as well as in a healthy society, members are not simply parts of a machine serving customers and organizational economic demands, to be exploited and then discarded. Satisfying the needs and objectives of its members as fully as possible is an equal objective of the organization.

Let us assume for a second that this is not true. Every member of an organization endeavors only to fulfill instructions and switches off his or her social and self-realization needs. Let us further assume that this organization fully satisfies the needs of its consumers. Members of this organization alienate themselves for the purpose of satisfying those who consume the products and services produced by them. They are limited to satisfying their own needs to the restricted time after work, through consumption. Is this scenario probable?

We are the ones who work to satisfy other people's needs, and our needs are satisfied by the result of other people's work. We spend the majority of our waking hours at work, and it is impossible to suspend life while we are there. Life cannot be split into a consuming and a serving part, and neither can society, since we ourselves make up both. It is an unhappy society where people perform their work and duties bitterly, in alienated circumstances, spending the most significant portion of their waking hours being unhappy.

EMPLOYEE-RELATED DISEASES OF THE LACK OF BALANCE

See Figure 3.3.

Disease: Alienation

They abuse you so abuse them in return. Hang on for payday. Employees are treated as a means to the organization's end.

Description

The prevailing belief of executives of an organization suffering from alienation is that employees are the means to the end of the organization. Members of the organization, unable to satisfy their needs for growth and belonging, become estranged. Their capacity to function beneficially for the

Figure 3.3
Belongingness

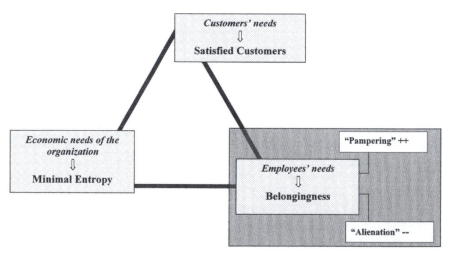

organization and to add value decreases. Employees, who have marketable skills, leave. The feeling that they cannot afford to leave paralyzes others.

Symptoms

- High turnover, above industry standards or increasing in comparison to the previous periods.
- High sick leave.
- Quality problems, with a high waste production and a high rejection rate.
- Members block each other's work deliberately, or out of negligence.
  A typical conflict area is a work situation where system thinking is required, for example, the shift turn. If operation of a machine indicates problems, instead of trying to prevent them, workers let the next shift handle it, even if by then it costs more time and money since the problems accumulate. The telling sign is the passive, negative attitude expressed by the employees of the shift where the problem occurred. Sometimes it is underlined by the rivalry among shifts; sometimes it is management that starts the rivalry.
- Strikes.
- Gossiping is rampant within the organization, spreading false information.
- People tend to take long breaks whenever they can.
- Destructive, unfounded rumors circulate within the organization.
- Contracts not fully expressing the interest of the firm get approved.
- Employees pretend to work hard when the boss comes and slow down or go for a break when the boss leaves.
- People pretend to work without producing any expected result, any real value (people comment on "work-like" behavior or defend themselves by saying "they pretend to pay, we pretend to work").
- Employees come late and leave early.
- Employees steal supplies and corporate assets.
- Employees sabotage work.
- Psychosomatic syndromes are common among the employees. People have headaches, stomach problems, or similar symptoms, suggesting that their mental health is not satisfactory
- Passivity, pessimism, disillusionment, frustration, and apathy are manifested in the general attitude of employees, showing interest neither in improvements nor in solving problems.
- Employees frequently cover up issues.
- Individuals hide; if necessary they turn to faking.
- Employees mislead executives or other employees.
- Politicking is rampant in the organization.
- When people talk about the organization they use the phrase "The company," not "My company."
- People criticize the company extensively.

- There are strong signs of distinction between management and employees (two absolutely different castes within the organization). Typically the language reflects this division as in "we" and "they."
- Low productivity.
- Increasing overtime payment. There may be two types:

  1. Either people do not work efficiently enough during working hours because by working overtime they can get extra pay or
  2. The organization deliberately underestimates the necessary workforce or would rather have people working overtime.

Causes

- Alienation results when people are taken for granted and are being treated as machines. The culture of the organization lacks aspects of nurturing and caring, as efficiency and profitability are overriding concerns. If the top management's behavior alienates employees, managers at various lower levels also tend to repeat that behavior pattern, intensifying alienation. The organization may expect loyalty from its employees, but fails to be loyal to them.
- Management has insufficient people skills. They are technocrats and their understanding of human dynamics is limited.

Origins

- The genetic origin is that key executives believe that people are not to be trusted. Therefore employees are considered the means to an end. Management is considered to be the brain, which directs, and the rest of the organization is supposed to obey and perform tasks. This is the most likely origin. People who share this belief system tend to get promoted and occupy managerial positions.
- The birth-related origin is that when the organization was founded, possibly due to high local unemployment, people were glad to take a position, any position, rather than choosing a position matching their interests. The organization could ignore people's needs because of the oversupply.
- The environmental origin is that when the broader environment is very competitive and exploitative in nature, then people will more easily see opportunities to exploit others.

This disease often occurs together with Money Mania or with Negligence of Financial Matters and with Organizational Paranoia, Insensitivity to Problems, Self-Centered Leadership, and Joyless Organization.

A structured list of causes and possible actions for improvements for this disease can be seen in Table 3.3.

Human beings are social creatures, and the most characteristic feature of human nature is the requirement that an individual's contribution be recognized and be considered important by others. If we perceive that we do not make a difference, we do not even feel aware of the fact that we are alive. When we experience the opposite, we burst with life and energy. It is

Table 3.3
Alienation

Structure of Causes	Possible Causes	Possible Actions for Improvement

Personal, Leadership Related	• Technocratic management. Employees are regarded only as a means to the end, as cost factor.
	
	 • Poor interpersonal skills of managers. Lack of understanding of the importance of the human factor in the success of an organization.
	
	 • Overcentralized leadership. All decision-making power and control is centralized on the top; others do not feel involved.
	
	 • Lack of attractive vision of the future. Members do not see the objective of their work and do not feel their contribution is valuable.
	
	 • An "everybody-is-replaceable" attitude is expressed by management toward employees.
	
	 • Leadership style is too critical—very little positive feedback or reinforcement.
		Executive Coaching, Training Workshop, and/or Other:
		
		 • Help the managers to be able to see the following:
		
		   • The impact of their own behavior/attitude for employees commitment and performance,
		
		   • How their beliefs about employees shape the employee's behavior, and
		
		   • How they can change employees' commitment and performance by changing their own believes, attitudes, and behaviors toward employees.
		
		 • Provide various joint programs for key executives/managers and employees where they can experience each other as human beings and can see the positive value in each other.
		
		 • Provide development programs for managers to improve interpersonal skills, participatory leadership style, empowerment, delegation, and so forth.

Table 3.3 (continued)

Structure of Causes	Possible Causes	Possible Actions for Improvement
		• Develop a shared, attractive vision for the organization followed by a persistent implementation with the active participation of the employees. • Put some leaders in key positions, where they can be positive role models for others.
Organizational, Operational	1. This is a highly hierarchical organization. The layers are rigid as in a caste system. Status symbols underline the hierarchy even more. 2. There is not much interaction among the different layers of the organization; there is mostly one-way communication. 3. Frequently ones look to see who is at fault (blame-game culture). 4. None or too few actions for developing the "we are a team" feeling exist. Employees and departments are working in isolation. 5. Unethical behavior exists, so members of the organization try to personally separate themselves from the organization's activity.	*Coaching, Training Workshop, and/or Other:* • Develop a shared organizational vision including aspects related to employees' concerns. • Analyze the impact of leadership and organizational culture, reflect on the actual situation, and define changes together where necessary. • Help develop missing systems and units that will increase involvement and buy-in, such as the information system, promotion criteria, training and development, incentive system, and so forth.

Structure of Causes	Possible Causes	Possible Actions for Improvement
	6. Unreasonable treatment of employees exists (compensation, work-related expectations, demands, and so forth.) 7. Employees words, concerns, and perspectives are not listened to.	• Conduct an employee satisfaction survey and follow up with specific actions to improve results. • Institutionalize forums where employees' concerns can be articulated and listened to. Have follow-up actions when necessary. • Break down the walls among hierarchical layers and among different departments by organizing joint activities and projects, with a rotating leadership function, creating common physical areas where people have a chance to meet and interact with one another. • Provide community strengthening programs within the organization.
External, Market Related	1. A high level of unemployment exists, so there is no pressure on employers to keep their existing employees because they can find new ones easily. 2. An alienated society exists, which is the general pattern people are used to.	*Interventions:* • Analyze the cost of quitting, hiring, and training new employees. Invest part of this money to gain more commitment from existing employees. • Develop a mutually respectful, caring, and productive culture, which, as a contrast to the other ones, would attract excellent people wanting to work for this organization and would produce outstanding results.

not our breathing and heartbeat that make us feel human; it is how we inter-act with the world and our impact on it. If we do not feel that our contribu-tion makes a difference, our relationship to the organization is reduced to the transaction of getting the most for the least effort. In this situation, people perform only at the minimum level they can get by with, instead of giving what they could have given based on their knowledge, skills, and potential. Therefore, an organization can attain higher consumer satisfaction not by suspending individual motivation, but by encouraging individual efforts through satisfying employees' varying financial and psychological needs.

People fulfill the most of their potential where they feel they belong. We discuss what makes up this feeling in detail in the Belongingness chapter (Chapter 4). Let it suffice to say here that beyond the fair and motivating material compensation, it is the opportunity to satisfy our most basic and important human needs that influences how much we feel we belong.

Naturally, satisfying these needs cannot obstruct satisfying the customers or the economic needs of the organization. Rather, it is the other way around as the latter actually get realized through experiencing success in the former. The organization in which this balance does not exist and where customer and economic needs are repeatedly ignored during decision making in favor of the interest of individual members suffers from the Pampering disease. In this case, focusing exclusively on the needs of members starts a downward spiral. Satisfying member needs at the expense of efficient operations leads to unsatisfactory economic indicators. Consistently putting member interests over those of the customers will result in an unhappy if not a decreasing cus-tomer base. Over time both impacts are strong enough to destroy the further basis for pampering, and eventually, the existence of the organization.

Disease: Pampering

Members of the club are always right and confronting them is not right, even if problems remain.

Description

When organizations focus too much on the individual needs of their own members—either management or a broader segment of employees—and neglect other fundamental objectives of the organization, they suffer from "Pampering." At their most extreme, pampering symptoms, like cancerous cells, feed on themselves, sapping energy and resources away from satisfying the customer and the financial needs of the organization.

Symptoms
• When an employee's performance is problematic, managers feel reluctant to take action. Punishment remains a verbal threat at most, without practical consequences.

Table 3.4
Pampering

Structure of Causes	Possible Causes	Possible Actions for Improvements
Personal, Leadership Related	1. Harmonious and pleasant atmosphere is more important than performance; performance-related feedback is nonexistent or is designed to be conflict avoiding. 2. A lack of result orientation in leadership exists. 3. Middle management members regard themselves as representatives of employees' interests. 4. Key executives are unable or unwilling to make necessary decisions that may have a negative impact on people. 5. Executives are bad examples, since they do not face consequences when their performance is not up to expectations.	*Executive Coaching, Training Workshop, and/or Other:* • Map personal relationships among executives to facilitate confrontation and feedback. • Practice giving critical and developmental feedback. • Practice assertive communication and conflict management. • Provide a more conscious leadership role (for example, synchronize personal and organizational objectives, share information, and provide clear evaluation of members). • Make sure that both task- and people-oriented executives are represented and that all of them have learned to practice both orientations.
Organizational, Operational	1. The organization does not have clear expectations toward people, does not identify challenging objectives, or these are not communicated effectively.	*Coaching, Training Workshop, and/or Other:* • Develop human resource (HR) systems: performance evaluation, information,

Table 3.4 (continued)

Structure of Causes	Possible Causes	Possible Actions for Improvements
	2. There is a lack of meaningful or sufficient performance evaluation. 3. There is a lack of a sufficient incentive system, which would tie awards to performance and attach consequences to underperformance. 4. There is a fear that nobody else can do the work, that some people are irreplaceable.	hiring, succession planning, motivation, and incentives. Improve HR activity in areas where there is a lack of available qualified employees. • Develop a detailed management competence system and apply it at hiring, promotion, and performance evaluation. • To increase awareness of personal responsibility, map the financial consequences of different actions and decisions; show the cost of inefficiencies involved.
External, Market Related	• The organization can afford to operate like this due to a monopolistic situation, ample resources available, and lack of pressure from the environment.	*Interventions:* • Implement market assessment, competitive analysis, and benchmarking to show the danger of remaining like this.

- People avoid giving negative feedback to avoid confrontation. The organization's culture discourages confronting employees with problematic behavior.

- When conflicting interests are present, individual needs usually take priority over organizational needs. When sacrifices are needed to handle a crisis, people are unwilling to make these sacrifices in the interest of the organization.

- Executives often delay making hard decisions that have negative consequences for individuals. The most notorious example is when demand consistently declines for a product, production cannot be sustained, and the respective plants should be shut down. Though executives see the situation, they refrain from taking action, perceiving it to be too hard on employees, as well as not wanting to face conflict (naturally, government regulations and the strength of the unions define significantly what can be considered avoiding conflict in these circumstances).

- There is a lack of discipline. Employees may arrive late or leave early. They try to adjust conditions to their own convenience, rather than consider how they can optimize processes for the organization and for customers.

- There are no negative consequences for an individual for consistently dysfunctional behavior. For example, no consequences follow when people do not meet deadlines or when somebody repeatedly makes the same mistake. There is no learning, and there are no changes.

- In case of conflicts with customers, the organization supports employees against customers, blaming the customer instead of working out a mutually beneficial solution.

- Management and/or employees are more eager to satisfy their own needs, such as better working conditions, than to meet the needs of their customers and the organization.

- The organization spends too much time, energy, and resources on arranging and administering personal issues and benefits that have no relation to performance. While it is difficult to establish a scale to measure this symptom, it is always possible to compare with other organizations.

- There are either no clear individual performance indicators or they are not consistently applied.

- Business trips are not quite legitimized by business purposes. People spend easily, finding some excuse for it, without considering the costs and benefit of the trips for the organization.

- In the name of involvement, there are far too many, typically ineffective meetings held, because executives want to be sure that everybody understands the issue and everybody has a say. Beyond a certain point, these meetings decrease the efficiency of operations, and even employees get tired of them.

Causes

- People orientation overrules task/result orientation in the existing culture, even if indiscriminately accommodating people has been proven problematic over the long term.

Origins

- The genetic origin is that executives are personally afraid of rejection, of not being loved, or of being abandoned. Some executives have a hard time accepting the fact that people leave. They may feel that the organization is a family, and they have to take care of its people no matter what. This leads to overprotectiveness and leaving hard questions about accomplishments unasked. One of the belief systems, which can lead to this disease, professes, "The organization is for the individual." Members created the organization for themselves, wanting the organization to serve them, rather than them serving the organizational purposes.

- The birth-related origin is that in the early stage of the life cycle of the organization key people leave, producing a vacuum, which may create massive shock and survival problems for the organization. The use of difficult-to-replace special experts at the start-up phase may also lead to this disease.

- The environmental origin is that the organization is in a very favorable situation in the market, perhaps the result of a sellers' market. In any case when the market is booming and it seems there is an endless source for revenue, there is a tendency for organizations to become lazy, comfortable, and fat. They hire new people because existing employees do not want to overwork. These organizations have a hard time when the situation changes and more competition arises. They have to reconsider their whole operation, their internal culture, and may need to develop new structures. Demanding more from people unused to demands or critical comments is problematic. Government organizations are more likely to have this type of disease than are profit-oriented organizations. It is often the case in governmental organizations that resources are provided while the performance criteria are fuzzy and not consistently enforced. There may also be scarcity in the labor market so the organization is afraid of losing its people.

This disease often occurs together with Negligence of Financial Matters and Suboptimizing.

A structured list of causes and possible actions for improvements for this disease can be seen in Table 3.4.

THE ECONOMIC-NEED CORNER

The very concept of an organization is to bring order in the pursuing of its goals. The founders of the organization define the common goals and the means of getting there. The means, for example, can be the structure, the roles that different units play in the structure, the procedures they follow, and the systems they use for coordination of the activities, culture, and style. The main aspiration of an organization is to organize itself in the most efficient way to achieve its objectives by using the least resources. This in turn means that all input received from the environment is processed with a minimum loss of energy while output is the closest to the desired one. Being organized as a system, using common methods through which order is created, makes an organization what it is.

In other words, it is every organization's objective to operate in the most effective and efficient way in the circumstances, absorbing minimum resources. The incentive to do so is not limited to the necessity of providing a good return on the investment but also to make the products or services competitive, to reinvest profit to fund further growth, as well as for technical and human development. Neglecting this objective inevitably leads to insufficient resources to invest in the future, undermining the investor's interest as well.

ECONOMIC NEEDS–RELATED DISEASES

See Figure 3.4.

Disease: Negligence of Financial Matters

Little attention is paid to financial matters, leading to chronic problems.

Description

An organization suffering from negligence ignores the financial aspects of decisions. People in the organization are just not interested and do not put enough emphasis on or pay enough attention to the financial consequences of their activities. Negligence leads to waste and inefficient allocation of

Figure 3.4
Minimal Entropy

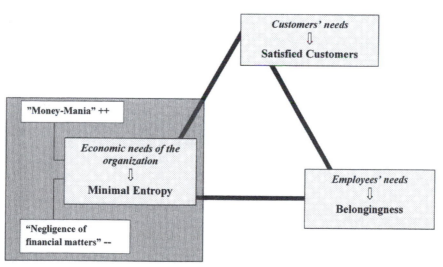

resources that eventually puts the financial stability of the organization at risk.

Symptoms

- The organization is prone to overspending. From time to time this organization spends more than is necessary, more than it can afford, or more than other similar organizations spend.

- A negligent organization is likely to have a higher loan ratio, as well as higher interest payments due to the lack of accurate planning and controlling.

- Negligent organizations are frequently surprised by the occurrence of financial problems, such as a loss, a significant drop in revenues, or an increase in inventory.

- Cash crunches are frequent, which means a continuous shortage of working capital. Suppliers are lining up waiting to get paid. The organization may even lose its best suppliers and vendors due to late payments.

- The return on investment is lower than the average in the industry or than the interest rate of the loans to be repaid.

- The value of the shares in the stock market falls below the issue price.

- Some negligent organizations are forced out of business because they do not pay their taxes or file reports professionally. The accumulated amount of taxes and penalties may be so high that they have difficulties paying them.

- Finance does not have a say in major decisions. Finance's role is limited to "recording events." Finance professionals are considered bookkeepers or clerks.

- Typically these organizations have underdeveloped intraorganization information systems. The executives have difficulties keeping track of how the organization is doing financially and of the financial situation of the different departments. For example, if the organization produces a variety of products, they cannot distinguish profitable and unprofitable parts of the operation. If the operation is divided among different locations, the integration of functions among locations is weak.

- The nonfinancial areas are not aware of the financial implications of decisions and may make unnecessarily costly decisions whose implications become clear only much later.

Causes

- One of the causes of this disease is that a financially negligent organization is absorbed in purely producing the product or the service it is providing. Employees share the vision and consider their vision more worthy than that of other organizations. They love to perform their activity, almost as though it was the hobby of the members. Members can be strong technocrats, buying the best machinery, the best equipment and materials available to work with. They try to be the best provider of the service or product in the market, and in doing so they go beyond the reasonable effort to provide the goods or services. Nonprofit organizations and science-related product or service providers might be liable to have similar problems, because their objectives related to customer value-added and employee needs are likely to override financial objectives.

- Another potential cause of this disease is the lack of the necessary financial competencies among employees. Executives think it is unimportant, or too expensive, to hire finance professionals for operations at the start-up stage.

Origins

- The genetic origin is that founders have a strong personal commitment to their activity, clients, or product. It may also happen that their business interest and/or education is lower than the average. Consequently, in these organizations you will find strong commitment to work, enthusiastic employees, but limited financial expertise.
- The birth-related origin is that ample funding was easily available for the organization. The organization may have attracted foundations, government attention, or venture capital interest at its inception; therefore, it has no strong incentive to develop sufficient consciousness of financial consequences of decisions. When consciousness of financial consequences has not become a part of the culture, it is very difficult to implement proper financial control systems later.
- The environmental origin is that an abundance of resources is available in the financial market. When money is cheap for a certain sector or type of activity, organizations are more tempted to operate without tested business models. After the money market tightens up, these organizations may not be able to adapt to the change and find themselves in trouble.

This disease often occurs together with Pampering and Suboptimizing.

A structured list of causes and possible actions for improvements for this disease can be seen in Table 3.5.

On the other hand, overemphasizing the financial aspects of every decision disregards the interest of the very people who make up the organization, and who are expected to meaningfully contribute to satisfying consumer needs. This perspective leads to a limited commitment to the results of the work and to involvement in work and negatively impacts the quality of the product. Similarly, an overt attempt to give the bare minimum to customers leads to customers feeling exploited or in serious cases even cheated, and consequently the level of customer satisfaction decreases. Customers feel dissatisfied, employees abused, and eventually profitability as well will decrease.

Disease: Money Mania

The single focus is on financial results.

Description

An organization suffering from Money Mania focuses on the financial aspects of decision making at the expense of customer and/or employee needs. The main objective for the organization is to operate with minimal cost resources, while maximizing short-term profit. Executives scrutinize

Table 3.5
Negligence of Financial Matters

Structure of Causes	Possible Causes	Possible Actions for Improvement
Personal, Leadership Related	• Present successes go to management's head. • Production and the product or service are important and costs and finances are considered unimportant. • In the mind of people in key management positions finance is a necessary evil and is not important.	***Executive Coaching, Training Workshop, and/or Other:*** • Analyze together the long-term consequences of neglecting the financial issues with leadership. • Clarify all the main areas of responsibilities of managers and why financial control should necessarily be part of it.
Organizational, Operational	1. Too much of a mission- or expertise-oriented organization → finances are just tolerated (e.g., some nonprofit organizations). The product/service is what really matters; they do not care much about costs and expenses. 2. The financial department has little impact on the organization ▪ because of problems with appropriate financial expertise ▪ and opinions or advice from the financial department is ignored.	***Coaching, Training Workshop, and/or Other:*** • Increase financial expertise and skills in the organization (training). • Increase expertise in basic economics and finances: ▪ Share information about the financial position of the company (revenue, profitability, cost efficiency, market prices, and so forth); present benchmarks.

Structure of Causes	Possible Causes	Possible Actions for Improvement
	3. Financial decisions are too decentralized without the necessary control and information systems being in place providing appropriate data.	■ Involve others than those in the financial departments more intensely in analyzing cost efficiency in defining related responsibilities and authorities. Strengthen the business approach based on trust within the organization. Support these efforts by a clear and simple financial controlling system.
	4. Financial information is considered confidential; few employees know real numbers, so they do not care.	
	5. The different departments are expected only to perform their duties without controlling their costs.	• Clarify and make people more aware of what is considered "value" and "value addition" in the organization. → Who are the ones who can say that value has been added or not?
		• Develop an appropriate financial information system involving all indicated people.
		■ Be prepared for resistance → organize forums to deal with the issues.
		■ Make efforts to avoid the opposite disease (Money Mania).
		■ After the necessary preparations, evaluate the activities of the different departments from the financial perspective.

Table 3.5 (continued)

Structure of Causes	Possible Causes	Possible Actions for Improvement
		■ It is important to distribute information and strengthen this business-minded approach in as many forums as possible. ■ Assess areas where operations can save money and implement. ■ Analyze return before and after every investment.

External, Market Related	• The following items contribute to successful operations:
	
	  ■ Increasing market demand,
	  ■ Increasing revenue,
	  ■ High profitability,
	  ■ Monopolistic situation, and
	  ■ Availability of resources.
	
	• Owners defend and protect the organization; market effects barely touch the organization.
		Interventions
		
		• Create a sense of urgency in financial issues in employees and owners:
		
		  ■ Explain how competition will increase,
		  ■ Explain how the market will saturate,
		  ■ Explain how resources will dry out, and so forth.

operation processes with little or no attention paid to the value added for customer or employee development and morale. There is no credible, shared vision of the organization beyond some financial, economic, and profit targets.

Symptoms

- Cost-reduction campaigns are in effect time after time across the organization.
- Necessary investments such as machinery replacements are delayed until the last minute or even beyond.
- Functions other than finance have comparatively small budgets and control, at the most a fraction of the overall budget.
- Departments almost exclusively are evaluated on their ability to generate revenues; profit centers are favored to cost centers.
- Executives overemphasize short-term results, continuously checking current-day performance.
- In management meetings, particularly at the executive management level, substantial time is spent on evaluating how various departments are doing against budgets. If a department is overspending, lengthy reports have to be written and special investigations may take place. Budgetary issues are the main concern of top management.
- Negotiations with suppliers involve executives and are tedious. Supplier contracts are for the short term. Switching of suppliers for price discounts is frequent.
- Every effort is made to minimize cost; salary increases and rewards are minimal. Employees resent this practice and turnover is high. Complaining about the level of compensation is frequent, and exit interviews may reveal that higher income is a frequently named reason for leaving.

A multinational company wanted to minimize labor cost as much as possible. For hiring new people, the company used a local government agency, whose task was to keep a record of unemployed people. The government gave tax relief for each employee hired through this agency. The new employees worked for a lower wage during a probation period, after which their contract was not extended. By letting employees go after a short period and hiring new formerly unemployed employees, the benefits paid by the agency accumulated, minimizing labor costs. Not surprisingly, the company was notorious for its low morale and had no respect among local residents. Employees with a long tenure also started to leave as soon as they found alternatives.

- Benefit packages are kept to the minimum allowed by regulations.
- The finance function is perceived as a "profit producer." There is considerable effort invested in the representation of financial data in a favorable way.

One of our clients used to have a telling ritual every year. Toward the fourth quarter, the possibility of not meeting the yearly profit targets looms large. Managers look at the expenses of production, training, marketing, and sales, and suddenly they realize that the profit target will be missed. They start to squeeze the organization, with short-term measures, but without the desired effect. During the last few weeks, the finance department takes over, moves money around to come up with the desired profit numbers, and becomes the hero of the organization.

- The finance function is the most powerful one across the organization. The Chief Financial Officer (CFO) is the formal or informal deputy of the Chief Executive Officer (CEO), having a powerful position in the organization.
- The finance department must approve expenditures and thus controls all activities. Other departments have to fill out long requisition forms, giving a detailed rationale for the expenditure. The finance department examines the submitted forms, compares them with the budget, and sends them back after having been reviewed by multiple people consuming much time.
- Finance plays a controlling role in other departments' decisions. It need not be said that in these organizations finance is not the most popular unit, albeit the most powerful.

At the same organization mentioned above, when the marketing department decides on advertising, during the decision-making process the head of finance will show up and make comments. She approves or disapproves the commercials, although advertising is clearly not falling in her area of expertise. Because she controls the budget and the CEO trusts her, she can overpower professional decisions of other departments.

Causes

- Money is perceived almost as the only value, which matters to such an extent that it overpowers other values, for example, value addition for customers and value creation by employees.

Origins

- The genetic origin is that the entrepreneur's overriding objective in founding the organization was simply to make money.
- The birth-related origin is that at its beginning, the organization had major financial problems and/or a lack of financial resources. If from the beginning the organization struggled to survive, it becomes imprinted in the culture—no matter how unconscious or subconscious it is—which is carried on in the later life cycles of the organization.
- The environmental origin is that there is a lack of financial resources in the market, typical in emerging markets or economies in transition.

During the late 1980s in Hungary, financial regulations were fundamentally changed to reflect market conditions. For the first time in 50 years, companies started to have liquidity problems and meet bankruptcy requirements. Immediate problems of working capital and cash flow management led to a halt in transactions at a significant portion of enterprises across the whole country. Unable to pay, companies instructed banks to queue suppliers to get compensation for their products or services. Each company accumulated a long list of payables due, which obligations they were unable to fulfill, as well as a list of collectibles they were unable to obtain. Current accounts were "frozen." A nationwide liquidity crisis threatened. Under these circumstances, organizations became extremely focused on cash flow management. Banks circulated lists of payables and collectibles among each other, trying to match and "cancel" out collectibles and payables as a clearing center.

This disease often occurs together with Customer Exploitation, Aggressive Approach to the Environment, Alienation, Shortsightedness, and Workaholism.

A structured list of causes and possible actions for improvements for this disease can be seen in Table 3.6.

These extreme examples illustrate the necessity of keeping a balance among the three fundamental organizational objectives. We have repeatedly seen that even a much less drastic imbalance of the three objectives has a significant negative impact on the organization, leading to organizational diseases, the fighting of which then absorbs the energies of members. There is little chance for joy in those circumstances. The bottom line is that a healthy organization simultaneously looks after its three fundamental objectives—satisfying customer needs, financial needs of the organization, and employee needs—and keeps them in balance.

This model applies not only to an organization as a whole, but to different subgroups within it as well. For instance, let us consider an information technology department, serving mostly internal customers. The company considers it worthwhile to spend some of its resources on the services this department provides. Unless it satisfies customers, partly or wholly outsourcing this unit's function will be considered. The department has to be cost-efficient; otherwise, if it is spending too much providing the service, it does not serve the best interest of the company. Yet in the meanwhile, it has to be ensured that people working within the department develop. The triangle model of fundamental objectives applies at the organizational, the departmental, and even at the individual level. We put the emphasis in the case of the balancing of fundamental objectives over the long term. From time to time, under changing circumstances, one of the objectives may receive a higher priority than the other two. Over a longer period, however, if decision making consistently ignores one or two of the objectives, organizational health is impacted and, hence, the organization's ability to maintain its existence.

FACTORS DISTORTING THE CODEPENDENCY OF OBJECTIVES

Although the above may seem evident, our experience shows that when questioned, most managers and executives do not identify the codependency of the three main objectives. Instead they emphasize one or perhaps two of the three. This is not a coincidence, but results from the specific nature of

Table 3.6
Money Mania

Structure of Causes	Possible Causes	Possible Actions for Improvements
Personal Leadership Related	1. The CEO has a strong background and experience in finance, and the corporate culture reflects that. 2. Management has an overall miserly attitude.	*Executive Coaching, Training Workshop, and/or Other:* • Employ leadership coaching, strengthening leadership values beyond those of solid financial management • Increase management skills related to other than financial areas. • Confront leadership with the consequences/impact of a stingy attitude on employees and business in general.
Organizational, Operational	1. Changing to a new system when previously not focusing on financial implications; for example, introducing controlling into corporate processes can in itself give people the sense of Money Mania. 2. The CFO has the strongest power base in the organization (for example, an expatriate in the multinational company; having direct relationship with the regional financial director, strong informal connection to	*Coaching, Training Workshop, and/or Other:* • Provide cross-functional training to integrate the financial function with the other organizational units: ■ To better understand the impact of financially motivated decisions on different organizational units. Provide feedback about financial decisions, both positive

Structure of Causes	Possible Causes	Possible Actions for Improvements
	owners, lack of trust toward locals or other departments).	and negative impacts on other units of the organization. ■ Allow members of the finance department to explain their point of view. ■ Strengthen informal relationships, create and increase trust, and increase efficiency of cooperation. • Develop cross-functional projects, workshops, and programs to "educate each other." • The examples set by the CEO and the CFO are critical in rolling out these programs and making them effective.
External, Market Related	1. Management performance is singularly or primarily measured in short-term financial results, for example, quarterly reports. 2. There are financial difficulties or increased competitiveness on the market as depicted by the following: ■ price-war, cost-reduction pressure,	*Interventions:* • Change the incentives of the executives so that they are rewarded for the long-term increase of the value. • Increase the basic financial understanding of employees:

Table 3.6 (continued)

Structure of Causes	Possible Causes	Possible Actions for Improvements
	<ul><li>decreasing revenue growth or profitability,</li><li>decreasing demand,</li><li>macroeconomic indicator changes, for example, exchange rate changes, and</li><li>end of market dominance.</li></ul>3. Management attempts to satisfy extreme financial expectations of owners.	<ul><li>Provide times of information sharing about the financial situation of the organization (revenue, profitability, cost efficiency, market prices, and so forth), benchmarking other organizations.</li><li>Involve nonfinance functional units more intensely in budgeting and cost management and support the above changes by a transparent controlling system.</li></ul> • Clarify what is considered a "value" within the organization; identify who or what decides when there is a value-adding activity? Train with tailor-made examples for the organization. • Clearly show a return on investment (into assets, markets, R&D, or individuals) for investors. • Provide stronger, more assertive, and more convincing presentations to bosses, the board of directors, and investors that better address their issues and concerns. Provide better communication of long-term interests and incentives for them.

the way we think, as well as from the economic and social environment surrounding the managers and executives. The most important social and economic factors influencing the lack of recognition of the balance among the three main objectives are as follows:

Impact of Social Values

• The stronger the accumulation of material wealth and becoming rich quickly are regarded as a value, the more likely it is that owners and executives will tend to overemphasize the economic aspects of organizational operations at the expense of customer and employee satisfaction. As the drive for profitability overrides the objective of satisfying employees and customers, the attempt to minimize costs leads to treating employees as if they are replaceable, and the attempt to maximize revenues leads to exploiting customers through win-lose transactions.

• The more people are socialized to care only about themselves, the more they apply the attitude of extreme individualism in organizations. This approach, however, contrary to the intent of individuals practicing it, leads to suboptimizing sections of the organization in their own interest at the expense of optimizing the greater system. For the organization, the natural consequence is the well-recognizable establishment of the so-called "zero sum games," of which the long-term predictable outcome is the "lose-lose" position.

Impact of the Market Mechanisms

• The more competition and free trade characterize the market environment, the less likely is customer satisfaction to be ignored. Monopolistic situations or protectionism practices of any kind limit customer choice. This, in turn, is likely to effect a situation where organizations or units have less incentive to consider the satisfaction of their customers, instead organizing circumstances to their own convenience and disregarding customer interest.

Impact of Discontinuities on the Time Horizon

• Instability in the social and economic environments and the acceleration of changes and discontinuities urge the overemphasizing of short-term return on investment, without regard to future consequences. Customer and employee satisfaction is sacrificed for more immediate profit objectives.

MECHANISMS OF ACHIEVING BALANCE

To satisfy the health criterion of balancing the fundamental objectives, an organization should develop systems, structures, procedures, and a culture that make it possible to harmoniously satisfy all three objectives, as well as take into consideration that needs are dynamic. These organizational systems detect changing requirements and adjust operations accordingly, while preserving the balance through holistic decision making. This requires that an attitude of developing, learning, and changing be widely shared across a healthy organization.

CHAPTER 4

The Feeling of Belongingness

Why do organizations have to satisfy the needs of their members? Are the interests of the organization and the individuals compatible?

What do people want from belonging to an organization? Why do people form, join, and leave organizations? Who is the owner of an organization? What happens when members are considered as replaceable instruments of reaching organizational objectives? What is the difference between performing a function and fulfilling a purpose? Why are opportunities to express our judgment, feelings, and intellectual capacity inherent in fulfilling a purpose? How do mattering and autonomy give us our sense of identity? Why is it that every one of us still wants to be able to say "we" as well as "I"?

SATISFYING MEMBERS' NEEDS INFLUENCES JOY AT WORK DIRECTLY

We start our discussion of the three fundamental objectives of organizations with satisfying members' needs, in other words, the level of belongingness. Belongingness, similar to joy, is a feeling, and thus satisfying the needs of members is the organizational objective that is usually the least analyzed objective. At the same time the level of belongingness has the most direct influence on whether the members of the organization experience joy through their work or not. People's experiences of joy at work depend directly on the quality and characteristics of their life spent in the organization. To satisfy their needs for belongingness therefore has a distinguished position from the perspective of building a joyful organization.

The other two fundamental objectives—satisfying customers and operating with a minimal level of entropy—are easier to quantify and therefore have traditionally been better analyzed. They have an indirect effect on building a joyful organization. The transcendent objective of the organization ties the fundamental objective of satisfying the customer to being joyful. However, satisfied customers in themselves will not cause an organization to be joyful. Similarly, operating with minimal entropy does not necessarily result in a more joyful organization. The existence of a high level of entropy obstructs the development of a joyful organization. If an organization is not healthy, joy will be a less likely experience for its members. When it is the fundamental needs of the members that are the least healthy aspect, the joyful experience will be diminished to a higher degree.

AN ORGANIZATION IS THE COMMUNITY OF ITS MEMBERS

Organizations are creations of people. It is necessary to understand what determines individuals' behaviors to gain an insight into why and how people form, join, contribute to, and leave organizations. We often find that even problems, which at first appear to have a technological or technical nature, have their root causes in the character and the behavior of the individuals involved.

Another important behavior-related aspect of an organization's existence is that once people have established it, they tend to try to keep it alive, even if the original objective becomes irrelevant or superfluous. Members will likely attempt to identify different objectives they consider important and tenable by the resources of the organization. They will try to stick together, carry on with their own agendas and the organization's new agenda, to survive as an entity. In this sense, over time every organization becomes a community of its members.

WHO "OWNS" AN ORGANIZATION?

Founders establish an organization, but over time the answer to the question of who owns the organization changes. Executives often think of the organization as top management only. According to this view, a limited group of executives define the essence of the organization, its purpose, and method of operation, structure, and culture. In other words, they own the organization, and the above characteristics have to reflect their best interest. True, executives and owners—including even impersonal shareholders—influence the characteristics of an organization in more ways than are apparent to the naked eye. Yet, as we will see, when top management is considered as the "owners" of the organization and, consequently, other employees as "instruments" of execution, a variety of ill-health symptoms begin to appear.

We define the second organizational health criterion by the existence of an organizational environment where all members encounter experiences leading to feeling that they also own the organization, what we call the feeling of belongingness. Having a sense of belongingness means that we do not primarily feel that we work for someone else, rather that we identify with our work. The feeling of belongingness comes from a combination of four distinct types of experiences:

- the feeling that we and our contribution matter,
- the feeling that we have a certain level of autonomy in our competency,
- the ability to identify with critical elements of the organization's culture, and
- the ability of having multiple layers of human relationships within the organization.

Before we discuss these four components in detail, we have to answer the questions, what is the difference between belongingness and ownership of an organization and why does it matter at all? Ownership means that by virtue of having provided financial resources for an organization we have the right to influence how the organization uses its resources. Owning the organization extends this right to executives by virtue of their position in the hierarchy. Ownership divides people between those who own and others who do not, such as employees. Belongingness, on the other hand, is a mutual relationship of an inclusive rather than an exclusive nature. If we belong to a family or to an organization, it also means that that family or organization belongs to us. It does not imply that we have invested financial resources into it or that by our position we call all the shots. The important point is that this difference leads to opposing behavior patterns. Where we belong, we invest ourselves. Where we do not belong, we transact.

Transacting indicates we evaluate the extent to which we need to give in order to gain what we would like in exchange. We then use a bargaining process to achieve these conditions. Our objective is to minimize our input for gaining maximum output. Investing ourselves indicates a very different approach, namely, that we put ourselves at the disposal of the organization and its objectives.

A good measure of having invested ourselves is the extent to which we stretch ourselves to obtain the objectives of the organization. When we do, we develop our competencies through the process. When we deliver as little as we judge is necessary to obtain the negotiated reward, our competence is underutilized and, over time, decreases instead of developing. This is the case even if we rise in the organizational hierarchy! It is not the extent of formal training, which is a crucial—although not sufficient—condition for individual development, but the feeling of belongingness, identification with our work, and the investment of ourselves into achieving the organizational goals. It is a positive spiral: the more we stretch ourselves and have a frequent feeling of developing the more we identify with our work, instead of feeling that we work for someone else, executing according to someone else's priorities. Missing the sense of individual development is one of the most frequently

Figure 4.1
The Feeling of Belongingness

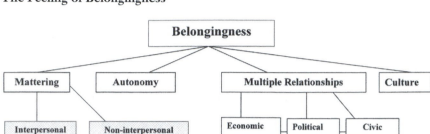

cited reasons for leaving an organization. It sounds benign, but taken in this context, it provides a deeper insight into the workings of the abandoned organization.

Furthermore, belongingness is not to be confused with loyalty. Being faithful in allegiance, otherwise known as being loyal, can arise from a single determinant component such as a sense of duty, or a sense of sharing values. Belongingness is the result of satisfying our individual objectives in joining the organization, reinforced frequently through our experiences of simply performing our work. Belongingness means that we are not strangers in the organization, we do not feel powerless in shaping the work and the organization, and we are challenged by our activities. It is true, however, that if we have a sense of belongingness toward our organization, we are also likely to feel loyal to it.

In Figure 4.1 we summarize the main factors that influence a person's feeling of belonging to an organization. In the following section we go through these factors systematically.

EVERY PERSON WANTS TO MATTER

What every person wants in life is a continuous experience of mattering. Every one of us wants to feel that we make a difference to any situation we may be experiencing. If we perceive that we do not make a difference, we do not feel aware of being alive. When we experience the opposite, we burst with life and energy. It is not our breathing and heartbeat that make us feel alive and energetic; it is how we interact with the world and affect it. Life as human beings, not just as organisms, lies in our making a difference. Mattering therefore is a very important concept, and we find it in every aspect of society. It has tremendous implications on interpersonal relations in any organization.

People do not tolerate the lack of mattering. When, for example, people feel that they do not matter in the family, they distance themselves and look for other sources of mattering experiences, such as spending time with friends. If they do not matter to their friends, they will spend more time at work in order to feel that they matter. Young people often spend their teenage years searching for the place where they matter. Parents who often have failed to provide the place for mattering are nonetheless surprised at this turn of events.

Erich Fromm, the famous psychologist, said that violence is the cry of the unheard. Children who feel they do not matter have more accidents. They figure, "When everything's fine, no one notices me; but when I have an accident, suddenly everybody is interested, my parents included." By this calculation, causing an accident to happen is a small price to pay. In the same way, old people who grumble and get hurt perceive that only through this process can they get noticed—punished, but noticed at the same time.

INDIVIDUALS DERIVE MATTERING FROM DIFFERENT SOURCES

There are two basic types of mattering sources, interpersonal and noninterpersonal. These categories are neither good nor bad; they just differ. For most people in most societies, the sense of mattering comes from other people. I matter if you smile at me, I matter if you respect me, and I matter if you are angry with me, because I am the cause of that love, respect, or anger. Other people are very important aspects of people's lives because they kindle the feeling of mattering for many. They substantiate the fact that someone makes a difference.

There are others whose sense of mattering comes not from people but from objects, ideas, and noninterpersonal sources. For example, an engineer, a research scientist, or an artist may experience mattering from the fact that they created a machine, an experiment, or a design. The machine does not smile at the inventor, but the inventor smiles at his creation. Creating a statue and working with the stone is a source of mattering. Ideas and discoveries are a source of mattering. In these cases, the sense of mattering is derived from the achievement, not from the reaction of other people or the value they attach to the achievement. Achievement is the aim itself for people like this. Money and prestige are subsidiary goals for an achievement-motivated person. They tend to view other people as the sum of their achievements, with fewer emotions and more as if they were objects.

We can further differentiate among people who get their sense of mattering through interpersonal relationships. Some get their sense of mattering through hierarchy. That is, we feel we matter if somebody respects us, obeys us, or is afraid of us because that elevates us. Others get the sense of mattering if they are loved, from experiencing affection, and togetherness. They feel that if other people need or miss them, they matter. In the former case, the source of the interpersonal mattering is power. In the case of the latter, the source of mattering is love and affiliation. We emphasize again that in spite of popular perception, there is no value attached to these differences. In itself, power as a source of mattering has no negative value attached to it; it is not undesirable per se, although it undeniably has a hierarchical quality to it. These three sources of mattering closely follow the motivational model of the three social needs of the late Harvard University professor David C. McClelland.

These differences originate from the differences in the ways we have been brought up. The tendency for deriving mattering from one source or another is substantially decided by early childhood experiences. In most families all around the world, obedience is inculcated very early. A good child is an obedient child. If the child grows up with this expectation, he or she very quickly learns that the world is hierarchically arranged. Father is more important than mother or the other way around. As children learn about their environment, they slowly develop their own life goals. They want to be high in the hierarchy in order to not have to be obedient but to be the ones obeyed. They learned how to be obedient; now they want to make other people to be so. If they derive mattering from interpersonal sources, their life goal is power, status, and prestige. How other people see them is an important concern.

Listen to the discussions of parents around you! There are many ways to describe what a good child is like. What kind of behavior would parents perceive as good? The most common answer would be that an obedient child is a good child. The second most common answer is that a good child is an affectionate, loving child. Only a few families would either explicitly say or imply that a good child is one who is independent.

Children who were brought up with the message of love, affection, and togetherness, and derive mattering from interpersonal sources, perceive life goals as to have a supportive family, meaningful relationships, and close friends with whom they can share their life experiences. In this family, people are horizontally arranged: the mother and the father relate to each other in a balanced way, neither dominant nor subordinate.

In the same way, achievement-oriented people often have a common characteristic in their background. In their childhood some circumstance occurred, which forced them to deal with certain issues on their own. This independence plants the seeds of deriving mattering from their achievements.

MATTERING DEFINES THE NATURE OF EACH INDIVIDUAL'S CONTRIBUTION TO A HIGH DEGREE

How does the source of mattering influence work? Individuals whose source of mattering is power learn to work for the boss and aim to be in a situation where people work for them, so that they can influence others. Individuals whose source of mattering is love and affiliation hold groups together and tend to like to work in a friendly atmosphere. Those individuals whose source of mattering is noninterpersonal work to produce results.

Who has not heard people in charge say, "I could have done it, if it was not for the people I had to do it with." However, if parents or bosses are conscious of this difference in sources of mattering, they have a better chance of making people feel that they matter. Organizations that want to create the feeling of belongingness must address this difference in members' sources of mattering. Individuals who look for power as their source of mattering need the feeling of the ability to influence. Without some opportunity to influence, they feel frustrated. Individuals who get their source of mattering through affiliation need opportunities in the organization to develop a supporting atmosphere around groups. Without some sense of "we are in this together," they feel unattached, "floating," in the organization. If an individual's source of mattering comes from achievement, he or she needs challenging work. When given routine work or tasks perceived as meaningless for achieving the final objectives, he cannot express himself and feels that he does not matter.

Self-awareness of our source of mattering is equally important. It is often the case that members of the organization who have numerous tasks will gravitate toward those who will provide them with their dominant source of mattering.

WHY MATTERING MATTERS

When we matter in legitimate ways, we are willing to take risks, our confidence increases, and we set and achieve higher and higher goals. When we do want to matter, but either do not have the skills to achieve our goals or are repeatedly frustrated in our efforts to derive mattering from our dominant source, fear and depression set in, leading to self-hate rather than achievement. Nonmattering originates in the perception that nobody notices me or in the perception that the work I did was meaningless and/or insignificant. When people experience nonmattering they turn to violence and become a nuisance or they become passive. Individuals who experience nonmattering at work fail to achieve their fundamental objective in joining the organization. Some people may not be explicit about this objective, or they may not even be conscious of the fact that they want to matter at work. It is a very real objective, nevertheless, and failing to achieve it has material consequences.

Soon after World War II, in my first job, I was working in the civil supplies department of the government in Bombay. Since it was my first job, I was devoted to it. The nation struggled with food shortages, and a rationing system was put into force for the limited quantity of basic food supplies. Shops sent us reports at the end of each week about how much was consumed. Our job was to total this up and submit a summary on Saturdays to facilitate the distribution of supplies for the next week. I thought that my work was very important. The food supply of Bombay and thus the life of many depended on it. I was concerned about the Saturday report and produced it with the utmost diligence. I had worked there for about six months when I had an unexpected visitor. One Thursday afternoon, a friend of mine came to the office and invited me to visit the town where I had studied. I said no, because the Saturday report was due. He was a very good friend of mine, very persistent, and eventually he persuaded me to accompany him. I left the office after lunch on Thursday without telling anybody. I felt guilty thinking about the Saturday report, but an inexplicable force pushed me to go in spite of my guilt. On Monday morning, I took the train back to Bombay and started to feel immensely uncomfortable again. From the train station I rushed directly to work. To my surprise, nobody had noticed my absence. My boss had not known that I was absent; neither had my colleagues sitting in the same hall known that I was away. I was absolutely shocked. Then I realized that I had left my jacket hanging on my chair. Seeing my jacket somebody said that I was somewhere around the office, and that settled it. Nobody missed me. What about the report? I discovered that the Saturday report, to which I attributed so much importance, was just a formality. The real decisions about the food supply were made on site using other considerations. I was so hurt by discovering how little my work mattered. I still feel the crunch in my stomach when I remember it.

Dissatisfaction and bitterness over nonmattering are not limited to lower ranks in the organization. As individuals rise in the corporate hierarchy, they often perceive that their salaries have changed, but their impact does not. Even the scope of the work may have enlarged, but still their sense of mattering does not change. They do not face new challenges or the types of challenges that would increase their sense of mattering. We have heard senior people who have worked for an organization for 30 years say, "The organization extracted all my energies, without providing me with the opportunity to really make a difference." This feeling is, of course, relative, but the level of bitterness reflects deep disappointment.

One of the most common causes for employees to leave organizations is the lack of the sense of mattering. Established organizations seem to us less likely to listen efficiently to these complaints. People often perceive a tangibly greater opportunity to influence a nebulous situation in a younger organization such as a start-up.

I PAY, YOU DO WHAT I SAY

We can conclude that some people invest themselves in their work, whereas most people distance themselves from organizations, and somebody has to extract work from them. This results in the widespread misconception of management, namely, that managers do exactly this—extract work from subordinates. "I motivate you," meaning that "I manipulate you," so "you do what I want." Our first conclusion from understanding individual behavior is that people invest themselves only when they experience the sense of mattering, not when they experience a sense of being managed.

When superiors in the hierarchy perceive individuals as conducting trans-actions for money only, they think, "I pay you, you do what I say." When the connection between the pay and the accomplishment is one-dimensionally linear like this, we experience a creeping feeling that we are being bought. Having sold our souls, now somebody has control over us. We look like puppets and not valued members, integral parts of the organization.

I joined a group of professors in the process of establishing the first business school in Hungary. We were very enthusiastic to build the institution and worked long hours to realize our vision. The school had appointed an American professor as dean, who had extensive experience in teaching in business schools. After a few months of working together, during a discussion he unexpectedly said to me, "Let's sit down to calculate how much time you spent on what, and we can decide on your compensation." I was taken aback and had mixed feelings about the way he approached me, and felt a strong resistance to just calculate my hours invested for the assessment of my contribution. I invested myself fully in the task of establishing the very first Hungarian Institution of the kind, working very long hours to develop the organization, the curriculum, and the executive courses. I did not consider it appropriate to use a linear calculation of time used to money earned and degrade my relationship to the school to being pri-marily transactional. Without at least the expression of our common achievement and advancing in the pursuit of our objective I started to feel alienated. He wanted to buy me, instead of working jointly as partners. He wanted to transfer my intrinsic motivation to an extrinsic one, perhaps because he felt that that is more easily control-lable by the boss.

Mattering influences the behavior of managers, not just their relationship with employees. When managers derive the feeling of mattering from having power, they want to perceive that they influence others in order to feel respected. Herein lies the paradox: one of the best ways of gaining respect is actually listening. If the manager knows how to listen to subordinates, subor-dinates are more likely to feel that they matter and in exchange provide the sense of mattering to the manager. Most bosses think that subordinates have to listen to them, but they do not have to listen to subordinates. They ignore the need to matter on both their own and the subordinates' accounts.

MATTERING AND AUTONOMY TOGETHER DEFINE OUR IDENTITY

In addition to mattering, individuals want to feel that they have autonomy, the freedom to make decisions. Autonomy exists in a context. In all groups a set of rules, norms, and values—not necessarily explicit—guide behavior. They define the things that can and cannot be done. If the code of conduct is so rigid that it limits self-expression, group members do not have sufficient autonomy to identify with their work. Identifying with work assumes that we have sufficient scope for questioning so that authority does not direct us all the time.

The difference between a machine and a human being is that the machine is built to have a certain utility, while a human being develops a purpose. A machine has limited capacity and objectives built into it by designers. Fulfilling a purpose is differentiated from performing a utility by the difference in the way to get there. To fulfill a purpose, individuals must have opportunities to express themselves, their judgments, feelings, and intellectual capacities. If the standards are too rigid, individuals feel that they are expected to behave as machines performing a limited prescribed range of functions to provide a utility. They cannot identify with that.

I have a set of very interesting though sad experiences from working with a multinational company. In this company, employees hired from different management schools spent their first year in a special program set up to familiarize them with the ways of the organization. These young men and women criticized the program, noting that during their one-year experience, nobody listened to them. They complained, "College professors used to listen to us, whether we had a question or an argument, but in this organization we are not allowed to ask questions or recommend anything." They concluded that they were supposed only to passively observe what is going on and perform simple instructions at the request of senior managers. That made them very unhappy. While we discussed this, I asked them to solve a simple puzzle. I thought that given their excellent academic records in those very prestigious schools, a simple puzzle of creating four triangles with six sticks would not be a challenge for them. None of them could solve my puzzle. We analyzed their approach. To solve the problem you had to think in three dimensions—they were thinking only in two. Coming up with the answer after much prompting, one of the young men said, "But, sir, you did not ask us to be creative. We assumed to stay in two dimensions because you did not tell us otherwise." They were on their way to learn during their first year in this organization to limit their thinking and problem solving to the parameters explicitly expressed to them. They did not identify with what they were doing, resorted to mechanical performing of tasks, and were very unhappy with the result.

It is mattering and autonomy together that provides us with identity. We are ourselves only if we have the experience of mattering and the autonomy to be ourselves. Otherwise, we feel like machines. The right to be wrong and the freedom to experiment is a basic autonomy. Experimenting means we can do things our way, as opposed to the right way, which is usually considered to be what is traditionally done—approved by authority. When we have the right to be wrong, we quickly develop the feeling of the duty to be right. We are not right, because we obeyed authority, but we have an internal reassurance that we believe we are right.

Giving someone the right to be wrong implies trust. Often it is the lack of trust in employees and/or other people in general that limits managers and executives getting out of the way of employees' autonomy.

CULTURE IS THE FRAMEWORK WITHIN WHICH WE EXERCISE AUTONOMY

Mattering and autonomy give us a sense of identity, but every one of us wants to be able to say "we," as well as "I." We want to be attached to some larger entity—a family, an organization, a society, a nation, the world. Unless we feel part of a larger entity, we do not get a sense of stability and continuity. In the absence of stability and continuity, in most cases, anxiety rises, creating a variety of psychological problems. On the one hand, individuals want autonomy while, on the other hand, they want a framework within which they can exercise autonomy. The third factor that is very important for an individual relating to an organization is his or her sense of the organization's culture. We think of culture in three different ways:

- the processes and standards by which we obtain results in the organization;
- the image of the organization, expressed in its rituals, traditions, and customs; and
- the underlying norms and values expressed in behavior.

Where there are no norms and values, there is no culture. Without norms and values, entropy reigns. Where there are only standards and rituals, and the underlying values are missing, people become cynical.

Interestingly, when talking about culture, people tend to look at the positive aspects, for example, "I am American, and this is a great country," or "I am very proud of my family," no matter how much they disagree with a particular political decision or the behavior of a certain family member. We create a mythology around the positive aspects of culture. Mythology creates pride. Where there is a strong culture, we are likely to experience a sense of pride. When an organization has an admired culture, it becomes a benchmark for society. Where such an organization is recognized for its impact, people feel proud to be members of the organization, and they experience mattering.

As much as culture can be a source of pride and strengthen the feeling of belongingness, it can also become restrictive, getting in the way of autonomy and learning. When culture turns into an expected assessment of the world and the events around us, it limits assertion and aversion from what is expected, independent of the changes occurring in the organization or the environment. If culture standardizes the way we view the world, it diminishes our reason for learning. People will fall back on standards as their guide in behavior. Standards often become rituals, further coming in the way of autonomy. If a ritual is connected to a goal, it may help curtail unnecessary costs. However, when people follow a ritual only because they have been doing it that way forever, the organization becomes rigid and irrelevant. On the other hand, where underlying values are explicit and reinforce culture, members are continuously concerned about the ways to apply those values. They evaluate situations and rather than blindly apply the rituals, they will reinforce the validity of the values. This process will increase pride and contribute to the sense of belongingness.

MULTIPLE RELATIONSHIPS ALSO INCREASE STABILITY AND CONTINUITY

As human beings, we tend to want to experience multiple relationships wherever we are. We nurture different kinds of relationships with people. Our relationship with an organization almost always begins as a purely economic type of relationship.

- An economic relationship is based on a transaction of receiving (fair or unfair) compensation for the invested effort. We become members of an organization so we can provide for ourselves by receiving compensation for the work we perform. To have an economic relationship on the most favorable terms we can obtain in the given environment is the primary driving force for becoming a member of an organization.

However, soon after joining an organization, we are naturally inclined to develop political and civic relationships, too.

- A political relationship is a relationship based on the sense of rights. In this context it means that the members of an organization can influence the way the organization operates as well as the way power mechanisms are used. It does not mean that everything members of the organization suggest will happen, but it means that members can speak up and their opinions and suggestions will be considered and respected. An organization has a "constitution" (rules of *modus vivendi*) describing members' rights and duties, and executives of the organization cannot disregard this and abuse power without consequence. If someone feels that he or she is not treated according to the rules, he or she can expect that the grievance will be addressed through a fair process.
- A civic relationship is based on the sense of duty and gratitude. A civic relationship is not a transactional relationship; we do not expect to receive anything in exchange for what we do; instead, we act because of our inner sense of duty. When, for example, we recognize that someone is in danger of suffering a personal injury, we feel a sense of duty toward our fellow human being and will try to avert the accident rather than checking out if that is included in our job description. Similarly, if we can avert environmental pollution, no matter what our role in the organization is, we will try to do so because of our sense of duty toward our environment.

People have a need for a variety of relationships. The wider variety of relationships the organization offers to its members, the more members will be loyal to the organization. Organizations where members have multiple relationships provide individuals with a variety of reasons for going there. This includes working and getting a salary at the end of the month, influencing how the organization works, exercising their inner sense of duty and, in addition, interacting with other people and having fun. Organizations that provide members with such a wide range of objectives for being there function like a community. The stronger the feeling of community, the healthier is the organization.

Having multiple relationships and being a member of a community contribute to our experience of stability and a sense of continuity. These relationships provide us with "roots." The more roots people have in an organization the better the chances for the organization to retain members. If the culture and operating policies of an organization do not allow us to develop multiple relationships, then our being there is reduced to fulfilling the economic transaction. In an extreme case, without multiple relationships, alienation sets in, commitment and morale become low, and performance suffers.

Developing multiple relationships is a natural tendency. If an organization does not put up barriers to block this effort (no small task in itself), multiple relationships develop spontaneously. Furthermore, organizations can encourage the development of multiple relationships in several ways, most importantly by organizing activities where the participants' relationships are neither hierarchical nor functional. These activities can be informal/recreational, such as sports or family events, or work related, such as participating in training together with employees from other units of the organization. The simplest way to encourage multiple relationships is to provide the physical space for occasions to form them, such as a cafeteria or health and exercise facilities. Interpersonal communication in general is a critical tool in developing multiple relationships. No relationship exists without interacting with others. If the organization explicitly restricts or prohibits communication, it limits interpersonal relationships and counteracts our natural desire to develop multiple relationships.

Members of organizations often find ways by their own initiatives to develop multiple relationships, without or even in spite of formal rules and incentives.

One of our clients had a senior executive whose educational background was in the performing arts, and consequently he had a strong interest in supporting cultural organizations. When the opportunity arose to spend some resources of the organization for supporting not-for-profit and charitable activities, he seized it by summoning a small team in a pro-bono project to advise a performing art company. This limited project had an unexpected impact on our client's organization. Employees from other cities and countries heard of the project through the grapevine and expressed their desire to contribute to it or if that was not possible, to be involved in similar projects. They proposed other projects to help the local not-for-profit organizations. Long after the project was finished the interest was still so high that a team was assigned to formalize the rules of under what circumstances and conditions employees could participate in such non-revenue-generating activities. Employees who could not participate directly were so disappointed with the limited opportunities for such activities that instead they spontaneously organized an interest group with a newsletter. They exchanged views on local initiatives for performing art companies, museums, zoos, schools, charities, and other not-for-profit organizations. They discussed their experiences in obtaining membership in the boards of these organizations. The group went as far as coordinating efforts to use employees' private resources in helping nonprofit organizations.

The role of management is very important in allowing multiple relationships to form. Encouraging multiple relationships implies that senior executives themselves find common aspects of interest with other members of the organization on an equal footing.

MATTERING + AUTONOMY + MULTIPLE RELATIONSHIPS + IDENTIFICATION WITH CULTURE = BELONGINGNESS

To summarize, every person, as part of an organization or any human system, requires the sense of mattering, autonomy, needing to identify with values underlying the organization's culture, and multiple relationships. Where you experience these four factors, that is where you belong. Where people belong, they contribute. Contribution means investing oneself and doing one's best. Where people do not belong, they transact. Transaction means investing the minimum effort necessary and trying to get the maximum gain possible. In organizations where people are involved in transactions, they do not grow. They hold back talent and do not put all their efforts at the disposal of the organization; after some time, their unused skills get rusty. Instead of growing, they slowly dry up. Belongingness is the soil in which people blossom and grow. Healthy organizations furnish an environment that provides these ingredients. Whatever the process, an organization benefits from an increased sense of belongingness. Where people invest themselves the organization becomes more successful in achieving its goals.

An organization is the context of individuals' development and growth. As we will see in Chapter 8, the level of its own growth and development also determines how accommodating it can be to individuals' personal and professional development and growth. Healthy organizations operate in a way that provides members at all levels of the hierarchy with potential opportunities for personal and professional development and growth through their daily performance of activities.

NEITHER ALIENATING NOR PAMPERING EMPLOYEES

As we discussed in Chapter 3, the prevailing belief of executives of an organization suffering from Alienation is that employees are the means to the end of the organization. Members of the organization, unable to satisfy their needs for growth and belongingness, become estranged. Their capacity to function beneficially for the organization and to add value decreases. Employees who have marketable skills leave. The feeling that they cannot afford to leave paralyzes others.

When organizations focus too much on the individual needs of their own members—either management or a broader segment of employees—and neglect other fundamental objectives of the organization, they suffer from the Pampering disease. At their most extreme, Pampering symptoms, like cancerous cells, feed on themselves, sapping energy and resources away from satisfying customers and the financial needs of the organization.

Where people belong and their fundamental human needs (as explained above) are satisfied, there is a good chance that—other conditions permitting—people will experience joy from their work. A healthy organization makes sure that concern for people's development and growth manifests itself in action. It does not treat employees as being of a given quality. This approach carries elements of critical thinking, a set of certain standards, clear objectives, and comparison of the accomplishment with those standards.

One of our clients introduced a program for workers. Employees, who normally worked on the shop floor, were given a chance to sign up for an evening college classes. If they were ready to take on the additional burden, the organization supported them through several initiatives. They could work reduced hours to enable class participation and attending exams. Their daily duties changed; they moved from the shop floor to the engineering department, as assistant engineers. This latter initiative supported learning especially well, keeping the motivation of employees during the study program high and enabling early success in the socialization process to the new profession. The program was well received, even among workers who did not take advantage of it. It communicated the message loud and clear that workers matter and have a future developing in this company.

Healthy organizations nurture rather than pamper their employees. Constructive confrontation and balanced resolution happens in the case of a conflict between the organizational needs and employee needs, not always in favor of either. There is an agreement, a clear psychological contract between the members of the organization and the organization itself—and this agreement is enforced. This is a difficult balance to find and maintain, but this balance has special importance among the criteria of organizational health. Where individuals contribute to the organization, the organization is better equipped to handle any issue that may arise and negatively impact organizational health. Where individuals transact, those issues are more likely to turn into acute problems and organizational diseases.

Disease: Organizational Paranoia

Lack of trust and fear characterize the organization.

Description

Organizational paranoia is a disease characterized by the widespread lack of trust in the organization, across the hierarchy, different teams, and among individuals.

Symptoms

- Lack of information is a significant symptom of organizational paranoia. People feel that they do not have enough information. They feel left out.

- Senior managers encourage promotion of their "own people"—people whom they expect to stay loyal to them, not to their new group—to different departments in order to gain more information.

- Management feels that it has to keep an eye on everything. Often there is a system of "spying" in these organizations.

- There is tight control in the organization.

- Rumors frequently circulate in this organization.

- Cliques, or "informal interest groups," are common. These groups perceive each other as rivals. Substantial internal politics take place among these groups.

- When people recognize that there is paranoia, anxiety, fear, and lack of trust, they try to cover themselves. People form cliques in the organization to try and protect themselves.

I was invited to work with one particular factory unit of a company, one of the largest industrial groups in India. The executive director explained the culture of the company. "Earlier it was, and still is, a culture of loyalty and fear." His father built the empire this way. He decided that the organizational culture needed to be changed. After this introduction I went to the factory. People already knew that the big boss had talked to me. I was identified as "his" man. The factory chief briefed people about what to say and what not to say to me. During the diagnostic work, I got the same answers from different people. The factory manager was convinced that I was the executive director's person, so he instructed everybody to be very careful. It took me a considerable time to make the workers and the manager's staff believe that I was nobody's man, I was their man. My first report was about fear in that organization.

- People try to ascertain who is whose man, who is closer to the boss.

- Management runs meetings behind closed doors. The executives discuss in detail the information they possess and what is to be shared with the rest of the organization.

- Many documents carry a "Confidential" sign on the cover page.

We were finishing a diagnosis for an organization and were discussing the results of feedback data with the executives. At the end of our discussion we decided to inform the rest of the organization about the result of the diagnosis. The question was how. Somebody from the team said, "I think that we could give the whole report to the people; they are adults they should know how to handle it." Another executive said, "No, I wish that they do not know about the written report, and we should be the only ones to discuss it." They followed the middle path and agreed that they would reveal some parts of the report to the employees. The discussion was about trust. They concluded that everybody should have access to the diagnosis, but not the quotes. The entire conclusion was published. In the corporate newsletter the summary of the results was published, and the article suggested that everybody could go and read the entire report. The first reaction came from one of the production managers. He said, "I am surprised, many diagnoses and assessments have been done before, but this is the first time that we have access to it. Now I begin to believe that this time they actually mean it, the company is really going to change."

- People are eager to close their cabinets and doors, clean their tables, and do not leave anything outside.

Causes

- Normally fear is behind the lack of trust and organizational paranoia. Managers cannot trust people and are afraid that employees will take advantage of any situation if they are not under tight control. This lack of trust is not limited to employees, but is apparent in the relationship of managers as well.

Origins

- The genetic origin is that the lack of trust typically starts from one key player who does not have the capacity to trust people, and thus this becomes part of the organizational culture. If some of the most powerful people in the organization have a tendency for paranoia, this can spread as a contagious disease, which is easy to get and hard to get rid of.
- The birth-related origin is that during the early life cycle of the organization, there was a major case when somebody abused some information, and the situation created some damage for the company. As a reaction, the management introduced strict measures, which might have lost their relevance since, but remained part of the organization's operation and the lack of trust remained as well.
- The environmental origin is that when the general sociopolitical system of a country is autocratic/dictatorial and it limits human rights, organizations are not exempt of this attitude either. Examples could be the communist or right-wing dictators spreading paranoia in different countries.

This disease often occurs together with Alienation, Bureaucracy, Self-Centered Leadership, Risk Avoidance, Aggressive Approach to the Environment, and Joyless Organization.

A structured list of causes and possible actions for improvements for this disease can be seen in Table 4.1

.

Table 4.1
Organizational Paranoia

Structure of Causes	Possible Causes	Possible Actions for Improvement
Personal, Leadership Related	1. Fear, apprehension, internal insecurities, and lack of self-confidence. 2. Negative perception of people and serious disappointment experiences. 3. Lack of trust in people. 4. Conflicting people-/leadership-related beliefs within the management team, which lead to clashes, distrust, and turf wars.	*Executive Coaching, Training Workshop, and/or Other:* • When relating to key individuals, coach about trust, self-confidence, and strengthen positive self-image. • Develop/strengthen trust among people in key positions. Confront them with the fact that if they distrust each other, it spirals down in the organization and has a detrimental effect on the performance of the whole organization. • Organize team-building and team-coaching programs where they will know each other better and develop mutual trust and respect. • Unify basic people-/leadership-related beliefs within the management team and, if necessary, remove managers who are not open to/capable of positive changes.

Structure of Causes	Possible Causes	Possible Actions for Improvement
Organizational, Operational	1. Fear of losing position, job, and power. 2. Prejudices, ingroup/out-group type of mental model and thinking; us against them is an inherent part of the organizational culture. 3. Due to a lack of trust I do not give information, due to the lack of information I do not trust others becomes a viscous circle. 4. Different parts of the organization are working in isolation having no relevant information about each other. 5. In the process and/or right after a merger or acquisition there are fights for limited position and resources; there are uncertainties concerning the future of different parts of the organization.	***Coaching, Training Workshop, and/or Other:*** • Provide common training for groups that have no trust toward each other. 　■ Know each other better; get closer to each other. 　■ Solve problems together; create bonds in the process (cross-functional projects). • Involve a third party (expert) in conflict resolution—"third-party consultation." • Employ large group interventions with real two-way communication and detailed analysis of the organization's situation, joint action planning, and implementation. • Increase transparency in topics that worry people. • Put the critical mass of people in one physical space from time to time to discuss issues of mutual interest. • Design and organize programs that will increase loyalty and trust:

Table 4.1 (continued)

Structure of Causes	Possible Causes	Possible Actions for Improvement
		■ Share important and basic information about the company in real time; do not let employees find out from outside sources. ■ Provide communication forums, for example, a one-hour question and answer session with the CEO regularly, and also one between the different departments. ■ Invest into employees in the form of training, outside experience, and opportunities for development. ■ Employ a transparent selection, promotion, evaluation, and compensation system. ■ Employ a fair and transparent approach to laying off and downsizing.
External, Market Related	1. Corrupt, unethical social/economical environment. 2. Owners considering selling the organization.	*Interventions:* ● Institute a professional organizational culture change program, which will take into consideration the outside environment, the organization's place in it, and the natural reaction of people. ● Share relevant information with employees and speed up the process as much as possible within the given circumstances.

CHAPTER 5

Balancing Professional and Private Life

Has a global norm developed that requires people who want to show interest in work to do so by spending long hours at the workplace? Why do we accept this demand? Who depends on whom? How does this demand relate to self-esteem? What are the signs that our lives are out of balance? How do individuals without this balance create an unhealthy organization?

REPLACEABLE OR NOT?

There is another aspect to the needs of the individual, one that has a profound impact on organizational health, and it is quite different from the degree to which people feel that they belong to an organization. In this chapter we examine the dynamics between the healthy and balanced life of an individual member and the health of the organization in which he or she works.

Considering organizations as living organisms has helped us to identify a set of concerns, which, if not addressed, prevent people from experiencing joy. The application of this analogy, as all analogies, has qualifying conditions. Even the fact that, in some aspects, organizations seem to violate the rules of operating as a living organism reveals something very significant about organizations.

What is the difference between a living organism and an organization? A living organism is not breakable into its parts without forsaking functioning. Parts of a specific living body cannot be replaced, except under special and rare circumstances. Nor can we remove most of them without dire consequences. Organizations around the world go about their operations seemingly defying this characteristic of living organisms. However, individual members of organizations, the lowest units of organization, are indisputably living organisms. They have a set of interests, relationships, and functions, which are not limited to the service of the organization. These connections are integral parts of their being, and human beings cannot be understood without taking the full set of these connections into consideration, and without forsaking their functioning in some manner.

PEOPLE FEEL INCREASINGLY OVERWHELMED

During the 1990s every year I traveled to Los Angeles to run courses at UCLA Anderson School of Management. While there, I talked regularly to colleagues, MBA students, consultants, and trainers and shared stories about their experiences in organizations. By taking snapshots of the "state of affairs" in American organizations regularly, I could perceive changes, even during a comparatively short period. Right from the beginning of the 1990s, my casual survey indicated that people in organizations felt increasingly overwhelmed, stressed, and even burned out by work. The hours they had to spend in organizations were far beyond what they felt were necessary, and the demand for more seemed to be growing. It appeared that most of these professionals liked their work and found it exciting, at least initially. Beyond a certain point, however, the same type of work, so enjoyable at the beginning, became a burden.

When asked what made them work so much in spite of the growing sense of being overwhelmed, people invariably referred to the organization in general, or to their bosses in particular: "The demand originates from the organization." This is a widespread phenomenon. Successful organizations are widely perceived as requiring the evidence of total commitment from their employees and rewarding workers who look like they are working extra hard. In the wake of multinational corporations, a global "standard" has developed: people who want to demonstrate their interest in work have to do so by spending long hours working. Another way of giving the impression of working extra hard, of course, is by coming to work early and leaving late. People may accomplish tasks beyond regular work hours, on holidays and weekends, but the amount of value that they add during this period is likely to be comparatively low. Sometimes they simply demonstrate pseudo-commitment and do not even pretend to perform tasks during the extended hours. They will emulate the same behavior, even using elaborate technology-based ruses as means to this end:

I know a director of a large telecom company well since we have worked closely in the past on a major cultural change project at the company. We became friends through our hard work, and I admired him for his intelligence. He was one of those children who are constantly bored at school, and the teachers could not keep up with giving him extra stuff to do. He is a talented and charismatic leader, too, instinctively understanding empowerment and using it well and effectively. He trusts people who work for him and lets them get on with their work. He does not micromanage them, and they in turn enjoyed working for him. His family is also very important for him; it has never been a problem to be home after normal work hours to be with his children and spouse. However, none of this could have been said about his colleagues and the CEO of the company. This man enjoyed his work, leading his team, and his boss was extremely satisfied with his results and performance; therefore, he did not want to leave. Yet he did not want to adopt the work culture either, so as a last resort came up with a technological scheme. "It is not acceptable to produce results without sweat and heroic efforts, so do you know what I do? I take my laptop home every night and at different hours, and I send the e-mail messages I had carefully written during the day. They are all very impressed with my level of determination and hard work..."

Naturally, on occasions when the bridge is washed out, the mail still must get through, and it is incumbent on a responsible team to rise to the occasion and do whatever must be done to accomplish the job. However, if an organization finds it is calling on its staff to be on emergency status as a rule rather than as an exception, this should be recognized as a symptom of a systemic problem.

One of our clients intended to cut costs by reducing the number of sales representatives. After the restructuring the typical work day of sales representatives lasted 12–14 hours, during which they drove around visiting customers. Representatives were caught speeding and violating traffic laws in increasing numbers. The issue seemed somewhat innocent at first but quickly became more serious. One representative explained, "After coming close to having an accident on the road, I asked myself why I push so hard to reach unrealistic targets. I have children and a family. How does it make sense to risk my life?" Representatives started to ask questions about how much commitment they were willing to give to an organization, which placed such unreasonable demands on them. Furthermore, being so stretched and rushed made it much more difficult to service customers politely. The restructuring backfired.

This systemic problem is widely recognized as "workaholism," and in the healthy organization framework we consider it to be an organizational disease, and a very serious one at that. Our research shows it to be the most widespread of all diseases listed in this book. Over the last three years we have been using this framework to diagnose organizations, and the accumulated results for more than 40 organizations show this disease to be the one most often and most seriously experienced by members. Figure 5.1 summarizes the most typical influencing factors of Workaholism.

PEOPLE CLAIM "HEROISM" THROUGH OVERWORK

Individuals who tend to accept this demand unconditionally tend to have low self-esteem. They do not have a strong identity of their own, so they have

Figure 5.1
Influencing Factors of Workaholism

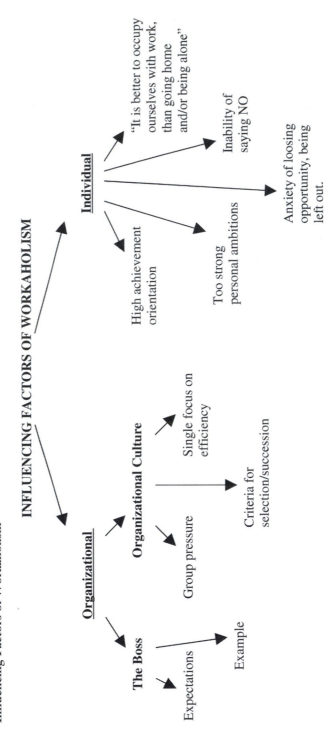

INFLUENCING FACTORS OF WORKAHOLISM

Organizational

The Boss

Expectations

Example

Organizational Culture

Group pressure

Criteria for selection/succession

Single focus on efficiency

Individual

High achievement orientation

Too strong personal ambitions

"It is better to occupy ourselves with work, than going home and/or being alone"

Inability of saying NO

Anxiety of loosing opportunity, being left out.

to attach themselves to the identity of a larger entity. These may be capable people, but capability by itself does not ensure self-esteem; it must be associated with earlier life experiences of success and recognition. If in early childhood they were encouraged to be obedient and look at others for recognition and if they were ridiculed and punished when they failed, their self-esteem was lowered. Merging their identity with that of the organizations compensates for their underlying feeling of inadequacy.

People who are encouraged to be independent, to experiment, and instead of punishment are taught to deal with failure feel capable and do not have a strong need of external recognition. They are confident and tend to have higher self-esteem. People who have a sense of uniqueness do not become organization "men"—people who have lost their special characteristics and/ or identities. They know instinctively that they contribute and that the organization depends on them, as much as they depend on it. Paradoxically, those who are likely to be of the greatest value to an organization are not the ones who show the most commitment, but those with independent minds. Such persons are more likely to put effort into the substance of their tasks, rather than the appearance, and are more likely to hold on to their values and sense of integrity than to take shortcuts. We know a number of people who rightly rose in the organization in spite of being initially ridiculed for not conforming to the widely established long working hours.

THE VICIOUS CIRCLE OF ADDICTION

Professionals work very hard in order to advance in their organization, to have a successful career, and to meet their high financial expectations. They feel they have to produce more and more to stand out. "If I work hard now, I will succeed, and later I can relax." They start out working hard and sooner or later get promoted. They progress in their careers and through this process, they become so involved in their work that slowly they give up the other aspects of their lives. A clear sign of this process being well under way is when dating becomes increasingly difficult for young professionals. They meet people only in a professional context, because these are the only circles they move in. The short time spent together puts at risk the development of any serious attachment.

In the case of addiction to a substance, for example, alcohol, the subject initially feels stimulated by a small amount, call it one glass. The amount required for generating the same level of stimulus quickly increases, but a stage comes when even a bottle of alcohol does not have the desired effect. However, when alcohol is withdrawn, destimulation sets in, and a variety of negative symptoms appear, in addition to a craving for alcohol. This same concept applies to workaholism. Initially work has a meaning, and working more appears increasingly pleasurable and meaningful, but a stage comes when we cannot stop working because without the structure work provides, we become anxious, uncertain, even disoriented. Being without work starts to hurt.

One of the only managers in a training program made a confession. "I work so much that I lost most of my skills to pursue common weekend activities." Not long before this training, I got a call to cancel a whole day of the weekend program. He explained, "I put the receiver down and I felt confused. I did not know what to do. I tried to argue rationally that this is a great opportunity. I could do many things, in fact, anything I choose. At the end, I didn't do anything. I floated around, neither passively nor actively relaxing. I felt embarrassment over my inability to do something with my time."

WORKAHOLISM HAS A NEGATIVE EFFECT ON HEALTH

Workaholism may originate in a personality or in an organization, but in either case, it has a negative effect on both the health of the organization and the individual. Workaholic people spend most of their time in the organization, they move in this environment comfortably, know their colleagues, and share languages and habits. At the same time, their other life skills get rusty, and their other senses become dull. Their relationship with the outer world becomes increasingly loose, and other aspects of their lives regress. Conflicts at home are also a good indicator that this process is advanced. Since they are less involved, their families become frustrated and amid complaints and such frustration, they have a hard time resolving conflicts. Since they let the problems accumulate, eventually they lose interest in going home altogether as a way of avoiding family confrontations, often using work as an excuse to be away from home. It becomes a vicious circle. There are companies where most executive managers are divorced. Workaholism, similar to other addictions, is escapism from other aspects of life.

A multinational company based in the United States had an alarming statistic. People who worked at this company and retired, died, on average, 18 months after retirement. While it is not possible to generalize, our research showed the perception that in this organization people worked very hard, with high overtime records as well. Employees' compensation was high compared to the local market. Their families were used to a comparatively high level of personal wealth, such as owning several cars, second homes, private schooling for children, and so forth. Our assessment highlighted that children of these families, who spent little time with one of their parents regarded that parent as a "source of income." Spouses, having gotten used to making decisions and living their lives on their own, also became alienated, if not divorced. Being so estranged, these ex-employees could not adjust to the new circumstances after retirement and died comparatively early.

People spend the major part of their lives—sometimes much more than they admit—performing perceived obligations. They feel they do not have enough time and opportunity to recharge their batteries and their lives go out of balance. Sometimes this has an immediate negative impact on productivity. When we are too tired, or burned out, our capacity to be innovative, creative, and to find joy in the work will be substantially lower.

Why are we doing it then? We may have reached a point where we are able to afford to say no and to have more control over our time. However, something does not let us do so. Initially, we were very ambitious and had all sorts of dreams. We dreamed about having a certain kind of company, a chance to lead hundreds of people, to be famous and give interviews, to lecture at well-known universities, to be members of prestigious clubs; we had a vision. Our efforts eventually bore fruit, and all of a sudden, we reached a comparatively high level. What we dreamed of is right here. Things we were striving for earlier in life are within our reach, and we are unable to manage them. We get addicted to the process of career progression, gradually losing our sense of achievement. We try to respond by better time management, attempting to be more efficient by using faster computers, cutting off meetings, being more focused, talking right to the point, but we still find ourselves continuously overwhelmed. In spite of our effort, new tasks fill up any gap appearing in our schedule.

Anxiety and fear may cause us to say yes to the overwhelming flow of business opportunities, invitations, and tasks. If we say no now, we fear being left out next time. Paradoxically, the more we say no, the more attractive we may become, acquiring the image that we are in demand. Nevertheless, saying no does not come easy.

Nowadays, "delayering" and "streamlining" projects follow each other with alarming frequency, claiming to remove whatever "fat" there was in the organization and forcing the remaining staff to work more. It is frequently the case that employees are afraid of raising their voices against such moves, fearing being next in line to be laid off.

When we first heard people who were self-employed admit to being equally overwhelmed, we paused. These individuals did not have a boss, and nobody told them how much or how long to work. Being very resourceful, they attributed the pressure to external factors—the competition, the clients, and the money they have to earn to grow the company or satisfy family needs —and so on. Almost nobody in our experience took the responsibility for the stage they were at. We can conclude that people who are perceived as successful are typically extremely busy by their self-created pressure.

We would like to explore this topic because we absolutely do not think that getting joy from work or being part of a joyful organization has anything to do with ownership or the lack of it. Ownership, in legal terms, means being self-employed or being an owner of assets and thus having the final say on how those assets will be used. However, self-employed people are as liable to experience continuous anxiety as employees of large organizations.

VICTIMS OF PAST OBJECTIVES

The first step in breaking this vicious cycle is to take responsibility and understand why we are so overwhelmed. To feed our ego, we give into temptations. Unless we reconsider ourselves, our situations, and objectives, we can easily run through life without getting the best out of it.

We brought together a few young people who were about to join a software company to discuss their views on careers. We facilitated a discussion of values, first in pairs, then in small groups. They questioned each other about careers. At the end of three days, they said, "This was the first time we looked at life in totality instead of thinking about careers in the sense of climbing a ladder. Rather than looking at ourselves only, we learned from what others had done." They decided among themselves that they would meet every six months to discuss again where they are in the process of building careers of self-fulfillment.

If we are unable to consider changes in the sources of our self-esteem, and of our opportunities and priorities, we are victims of past objectives. Reprogramming ourselves to the new circumstances does not take place. Organizations provide only a framework, a context in which to satisfy needs and interests in performing certain tasks. We are not saying it is necessary to satisfy all one's needs in a single organization, but we are saying one should not neglect the other aspects of life: family, friends, hobbies, physical needs, and a civil life.

I now live near a retired police officers' colony. Many police officers change the way they walk after retirement. While working, they walk as people in charge do—heads up, chest out, stomach in, the standard drill—but now they walk as if they had nothing to do. In our entire group of 40 families, there are only two retired officers who still walk straight, shoulders back with self-esteem. One of them was the chief police officer of a state. Even when he was a police officer he was well known about having a variety of interests. He was a very good writer; he had interest in music and the arts. In spite of all his other interests, his career never suffered. He rose because wherever he established himself, it was as someone who had something unique to contribute. Most other police officers become commodities in their rank, anxious, missing the feeling of unique contribution.

This question we pose again: is it a healthy organization that capitalizes on all the energy of an individual and leaves little room for other relationships and other activities? Overall, does the company get more out of these people or less? Our answer is negative. People who are tired beyond a certain point, do not have family support, and who do not have multiple relationships at their workplace may not be able to be creative enough or have the appropriate perspective to be flexible to adapt to changes. They most certainly are too inflexible and rushed to complete tasks well.

IS JOY A LOST CAUSE FOR YOU?

If people have already arrived at the conclusion that joy is a lost cause for them, they may have been too hasty. It is possible to train people to experience joy. Individuals are able to widen their perspective, to see things beyond their livelihood, and to have a sense of growth and ultimately joy. It is possible to help people to get over their anxiety, especially in the organizational context.

OBSERVABLE ATTRIBUTES OF A HEALTHY WORKLOAD

In a healthy organization, people work effectively but do not appear to be in a constant hurry. There is no continuous tension and nervousness in the organization. People go home at the end of the working day, although not necessarily exactly at the end of official working hours, since they focus on substance, not formalities. People use their vacation times and when they return, they are energized, recharged, and happy. Weekends are used for work only in exceptional cases, and in return, in exceptional cases working hours can be used for unavoidable private obligations. People's private times are respected by the organization. If work assignments conflict with private life, the solution is worked out by mutual agreement and a sense of mutual loyalty exists, without abuse on either side. The length of working hours is balanced throughout the hierarchy.

THE END OF LOYALTY TO THE WORKPLACE

Recent changes in the relationship between organizations and its members have given rise to the opinion that in the new economy, employees are free agents, and loyalty toward the workplace has disappeared for good. We think that organizations have not lost the need in getting committed, hard-working people who contribute to the well-being of the organization, if only temporarily. However, the former practice of optimizing employees' lives for the interests of the organization is not supportable any longer. Loyalty is now a two-way street. In order to have the commitment necessary to everyday operations, an organization has to be able to help people to develop multiple relationships and a rich life with many facets.

How can an organization play this balancing act? First, it can provide a broad variety of activities and access to facilities for its members, including sports, health care, and relaxation. Second, an organization can approach employees not only as members of the organization, but also as a part of other systems such as families, communities, and then go on to include members of these other systems in its activities. Third, to help balance professional and private lives, executives in particular can explicitly encourage employees to take all holidays. Fourth, the organization could encourage employees not to stay beyond working hours regularly, or in the case of private situations, encourage them to go for medical tests, school events, and take care of family members. In a climate of mutual trust, nobody exploits each other.

One of the most important ways of helping people to balance their professional and private lives is by showing model behavior and setting an example. No matter how hard the management emphasizes going home after regular working hours, if managment members themselves stay longer all the time, and take work home, this will impact on employees.

I worked with an organization that was acquired by a multinational company. On occasion, I found that a number of people from the organization were sitting after work in their respective offices, doing nothing. Most of them were just sitting there. I asked them, "Why are you sitting here—why don't you go home?" They answered, "The president is still in his office and if he is there, we have to be here, too." There was no value-adding activity, no working, not even pretense. They felt dependent on the organization, and the atmosphere was bitter with cynicism.

Disease: Workaholism

People work much beyond normal working hours.

Description

Workaholism is characterized by employees spending an inordinate amount of time working. It is a contagious behavior; the more people do it, the more pressure there is on everybody else to follow the example.

Symptoms
- The most obvious symptom is that employees spend long hours, in excess of the declared, official, working hours, in their offices.
- If you look at the office building, you see lights turned on during the night.
- People regularly take work home.
- Work-related programs are regularly scheduled for weekends.
- Employees receive phone calls regularly at home from the office.
- When people go on holidays, they are expected to provide access (phone numbers, e-mails, and so forth) so they can be reached. Sometimes they have to return from vacations early due to work issues.
- In workaholic organizations the higher the individual's place in the hierarchy, the more he or she is expected to work, though this expectation might not be explicit.
- Different signs of being burned out can be observed. People are tired and exhausted and consume a lot of caffeine.
- Employees' families complain about them working too much.
- Signs of stress appear, such as psychosomatic diseases or neurosis.
- In some organizations workaholism becomes an explicit or implicit requirement for moving up the hierarchy.

I've been working with a multinational company and worked closely with a senior member of the management team who openly resists the widespread organizational norm to stay in the office beyond 8–10 hours regularly, as well as working on weekends. She goes in around 8 in the morning and stays until 5 or 6 in the evening, works hard and efficiently. If there are no special circumstances, at the end of the day she goes home and lives her private life, enjoys her hobbies, spends time with her family. She looks happy. When I asked her whether she experiences pressure to stay longer, she said, "No, it is no problem, although it is clear that I could have advanced faster, but I have made a conscious choice to keep a balance in my life; it is more important to me than advancing faster in the hierarchy."

- Value addition is not proportionate to the amount of activity and work people are investing into performing a certain task.
- In workaholic organizations people do not use their vacation times. At the end of the year there are several weeks or days from the vacation time remaining unused. Some employees proudly declare in the disguise of a complaint that they are unable to take their vacation because of the tremendous workload.

Causes

- A typical cause is that the task of a particular person or a group cannot be performed by efficient work within normal working hours. In organizations streamlined beyond reasonable levels, fewer people attempt a large workload in the name of cost competitiveness.
- Another cause could be peer pressure. Colleagues put so much pressure on each other to stay after hours that it becomes a norm within the group or the organization. The priority is on the organizational needs, and they neglect their own individual needs. Peer pressure can become part of the organizational culture. Consulting firms, investment banks, and technology start-ups are likely candidates of facilitating extreme peer pressure.

Origins

- The genetic origin is that the founder or key executives of the organization are workaholics, insecure in some way about themselves, and gather the same type of people around them. Whoever enters later is faced with workaholism as a natural expectation.
- The birth-related origin is that a new organization is brought to life surrounded by excitement. Unexpected things are turning up at this stage, which puts substantial work pressure on the members for the sake of survival. Through this creation period, it is normal that people work much beyond the working hours. Once the organization is created—structures built and people trained—the workload should come down to a lower level. However, it is unlikely to happen, because of the work-addiction culture that has set in by that time.
- The environmental origin is that this has been typical since the 1990s. This virus probably originated in Japan where there is actually a word for working to death, *korashi*. Many people die because of the stress of their tremendous workload. Next to Japan, this is felt most in the United States, attributed to insecurity of individuals

Table 5.1
Workaholism

Structure of Causes	Possible Causes	Possible Actions for Improvements
Personal, Leadership Related	1. Fear of loosing employment. 2. Work dominates the lives of key executives and they extend that expectation to their environment. 3. Executives are too task and performance oriented; the human factor is ignored. 4. There is not enough time management. 5. Due to lack of delegation, executives are overworked.	*Executive Coaching, Training Workshop, and/or Other:* • Harmonize personal and organizational values, life coaching. • Increase self-knowledge, self-appreciation, and self-confidence. • Develop managers in skills related to time management, delegation, and empowerment. • Provide a framework where interested managers/employees can engage themselves in non-work-related activities (e.g., arts, sport, hobbies, and so forth). • Leaders should be role models for nonworkaholic behavior.
Organizational, Operational	1. There is no proper prioritization of objectives; all objectives are similarly important. 2. Distributing tasks and work is not efficient. Some tasks would actually be unnecessary; some are performed in parallel due to a lack of system thinking and inefficient process organization.	*Coaching, Training Workshop, and/or Other:* • Identify and communicate priorities of objectives. • Review resource allocation to resolve bottlenecks.

96

Structure of Causes	Possible Causes	Possible Actions for Improvements
	3. Old means are used to solve new problems, solutions that are not efficient enough in the increasingly competitive situation. There are no strategies for what should be done differently to meet the new challenges. 4. The organization is understaffed. 5. The organizational culture and the performance evaluation system put special value to the time spent at work. 6. Workaholism is regarded as the measure for loyalty and commitment. This can be a real or perceived expectation from management.	• Provide a proper performance evaluation and selection system, which rewards performance, not the time spent at work. • Review processes, roles, and tasks for simplification. Identify unnecessary parallel activities and doubled responsibilities. • Review and benchmark work and performance expectations where people show signs of overwork and burnout.
External, Market Related	1. Competition is pressuring the organization (price, hiring freeze, and profit expectations). 2. Due to the high unemployment rate people are willing to take on unrealistic burdens, and they are afraid of quitting. 3. There are cultural differences and different perceptions of what should be considered too much work. 4. A workaholic culture exists in society. It is chic to multitask and overwork; doing so is considered an indicator of one's high importance.	*Interventions* • Clarify differences in values; agree on common expectations, norms, and values. • Provide new strategies and paradigms for fulfilling organizational expectations under growing pressure, while avoiding being overworked and burned out (e.g., distance work—office work performed at home), which saves commuting time, stress, and so forth).

and the intense desire to "live the American dream." Multinational companies spread this virus almost everywhere. The perception is that if an organization wants to stay in business and remain globally competitive, it has to adopt it.

Privatization, buyouts, mergers, acquisitions, or just plain innovation put tremendous immediate pressure on employees to perform. During such transition periods, the complaints are very similar to those we have listed as the symptoms of workaholism. Sometimes these complaints cover only the dislike of the adjustment or transition.

This disease often occurs together with Money Mania.

A structured list of causes and possible actions for improvements for this disease can be seen in Table 5.1.

CHAPTER 6

Minimizing Entropy

Why do organizations have to produce the desired outcome with minimal resources? Why do organizations keep having to invest, even just to maintain efficiency, let alone to improve it? What is organizational entropy? What are the different layers of the impact—the double whammy—of organizational entropy? How do organizational diseases not only depress morale but also increase entropy? What are the most important tools of entropy reduction? Are rules entropy generators in disguise? How do the spreading of responsibilities and empowering people impact entropy? What is the role of feedback in shaping entropy? How can making long- or short-term decisions increase entropy? Why is entropy higher around executives? Change programs are supposed to improve efficiency, so why do they often increase entropy?

ORGANIZATIONAL HEALTH AND ENTROPY

One of the main ambitions of an organization is to organize itself in the most efficient way, hence use the least amount of resources for producing the desired output. There is a similarity between what happens to matter and what happens to organizations during transformation. In order to better describe the state of organizational operations that manage the process of turning resources into the outcome, we borrow the concept of entropy from physics.

Transforming things into a more desirable form requires the creation of order. However, the process of transformation always involves imperfect efficiency. The second law of thermodynamics describes this phenomenon in physics, stating that transformation of one form of energy into another in natural processes is accompanied by a loss because of increasing entropy.

Entropy is a spontaneous process, which—in closed systems—necessarily results in increased disorder, and it always involves wastefulness. The loss equals the amount of energy we have spent on creating the system. Entropy is unavoidable for closed systems. In open systems, such as economic organizations, however, entropy is avoidable by applying additional energy from outside the system. A higher level of organization can be obtained by applying more energy. In this context, efficiency is the optimization (minimization) of the necessary additional energy. Therefore a higher level of organization requires the application of more outside energy as well as more energy to sustain this elevated level of organization, thanks to the natural, unavoidable tendency to entropy. It also follows that if an organization operates very efficiently at the given complexity level, it requires less energy input from outside to sustain that level of efficiency.

When trying to construct machines for the transformation of heat into work, such as the steam engine, it was observed that as soon as the hot water moves into the cool air to produce the steam, their temperatures equalize. Unless the water is heated again, the engine cannot be used to make it move any more. In the language of physics, at the outset the system has a low level of entropy; the fast-moving water molecules are distinct from the slow-moving air molecules. As heat naturally flows into the cooler medium, the fast-moving molecules will spend themselves until all molecules are approximately at the same speed. At this point, entropy is at a maximum level, all the molecules milling about without any particular order. In order to keep the molecules moving fast—in other words, the only way to keep the engine working—one continually has to add energy.

The analogy for organizations implies that organizational entropy will increase, inevitably and spontaneously, without regular initiatives for improving efficiency. For an organization to operate efficiently, it is not sufficient to initially invest into developing effective systems and methods of operation. Maintaining the adequacy of the system requires continuous investment of resources, even when all other variables are held equal.

Furthermore, we can say that organizational diseases hinder the fulfillment of the economic objectives of an organization by increasing the level of disorder. This has the double negative effect of decreasing efficiency as well as increasing the amount of resources needed to return to a lower level of entropy. The goal is to create an organization that does not suffer from diseases, including inefficient operations. Instead, it maintains minimal entropy, where all the energies flow in the same direction, and there is alignment across the organization.

Using this analogy allows us to consider organizations as mechanisms attempting to make the most efficient use of resources at their disposal by increasing order and reducing organizational entropy. We continue to expand our definition of a healthy organization with the criterion that a healthy organization constantly attempts to reduce its level of entropy.

PROFITABILITY AND ENTROPY

Chief executives are ultimately held responsible for how efficiently the organization uses resources. They are also the ones who have the final authority on designing and shaping the organizational structure and culture in a way that makes every individual and subsystem of operations responsible for ensuring that the mission is realized with the least resources. Financial indicators measure different aspects of this effort. Profitability is the ultimate indicator of how an organization satisfies its economic needs because it combines measuring the efficiency of operations with measuring the demand for the product the organization produces.

LACK OF BALANCE AMONG FUNDAMENTAL OBJECTIVES AND ENTROPY

The importance of satisfying the economic needs of the organization renders the use of economic measures vulnerable to being under- or overemphasized. Healthy organizations are aware of the financial implications of their actions, without letting them solely dictate decisions. Finance is an expert consulting type of service for all organizational units. To ensure commitment to important resource allocation decisions, representatives of areas involved in a specific decision identify priorities together, while financial implications are worked out at relevant levels. There is no secrecy about financial matters. Budget variance issues are examined from time to time to avoid serious consequences later. Rather than trying to hide difficulties, departments or the organization openly addresses them and attempts to correct them in time. Thus, an observer of this organization would conclude that the financial department is an equal player in the organizational hierarchy, neither controlling other departments nor operating in isolation.

Interestingly, overemphasizing financial indicators—as we discussed in the last chapter—has the opposite effect intended. When these indicators single-handedly determine the outcome of organizational decision making, the organization as a whole will tend to have a higher level of entropy. An organization suffering from Money Mania focuses on the financial aspects of decision making at the expense of customer and/or employee needs. Its main objective is to operate with minimal cost resources, while maximizing short-term profit. Executives scrutinize operation processes with little or no attention paid to the value added for the customer or employee development and morale. There is no credible, shared vision of the organization beyond financial, economic, and profit targets.

The opposite of the above problem happens when an organization ignores the financial aspects of decision making. Sooner or later, efficiency declines and organizational entropy increases. This can accelerate quickly to such a level that the effort and energy required to turn this situation around will be too high to be worth doing. When organizations ignore the financial implications of their actions, they suffer from the disease of Negligence. People in the organization are just not interested and do not put enough emphasis on or pay enough attention to the financial consequences of their activities. Negligence leads to waste and inefficient allocation of resources that eventually put the financial stability of the organization at risk.

INFORMATION REDUCES ENTROPY

Once the basic business model of an organization is in place, assuming that the nature of demand does not change in a given period, the organization can effectively manage profitability by managing the efficiency side of the equation. We turn our attention to the transformation process, and, using the physics analogy, we identify the most important factors influencing the nature of this process.

Engineering aims to create machines that manage transformation with minimal energy loss. To this end, a machine often has sensors, which identify and continuously observe internal events as well as in the environment. In case an event is out of the range of preferred events, the sensors signal to the machine and a correction or shutdown procedure can take place. When a machine is able to adjust its operation to better match the situation, there is a substantial reduction of entropy and consequently less utilization of resources and energy during the transformation process.

SENSING IS A PRECONDITION OF SUCCESSFUL ADAPTATION

Successful adaptation assumes being cognizant of the state of internal systems as well as sensing changes in external systems, because only the comparison of these two will optimize the operation of the system. The efficiency of adaptation therefore determines the efficiency of operation.

In a healthy organization, individuals take part both in the value-creating process and in acting as sensors, rather than being rigidly assigned the role of either producers or sensors. Every individual and organizational unit operates as a subsystem of the whole, guided by the same objective but keeping in touch with its environment and adjusting to it as required. Nobody says, "Our job is limited to performing a role inside our department; don't ask for more." Unfortunately, this does not happen in most organizations. There was a time in the past when prototypical organizations described by Max Weber operated with roles and functions precisely determined. For example, at a car manufacturing company, the production department focused on creating the outcome, in this case, cars. There were other departments in the organization whose job was to sense what was happening in the environment. The marketing department studied the market to understand what customers needed. Development engineers researched technology, the newest materials, or innovations. Employees of the finance department provided information on economic and tax regulations, bank interest rates, and so on. Information received through all these sensors was used to determine how operations should proceed. This explicit work distribution model was seen around the turn of the century, operating under stable circumstances. Today, constant change in the environment renders these models less efficient. Sensing and interpreting the changes in the environment by every unit of the organization is crucial. The more every organization, department, and individual have the double function of performing their task and sensing the impact of environmental changes within their reach, the more they utilize this information for adjusting operations, the fewer the resources that will be wasted. Employees should not sit around waiting for the boss to tell them what to do, perhaps waiting till problems accumulate into a crisis, but should figure out what can be done to prevent trouble and initiate action. If people share an internalized vision and have the authority to make decisions within their realm, they are likely to initiate or execute the necessary intervention to correct an entropy-increasing situation.

A well-known company in India had imported an automatic machine to one of its production lines. Engineers from the manufacturer in the United States came and installed the machine. After the installation was finished, the machine started to work satisfactorily. About six months later it had a multitude of problems. Finally, the management got tired of organizing operations around the problems, shut the machine down in exasperation, and returned to the earlier ways of operation. There was a master mechanic in this factory who, though was not a qualified engineer, had substantial experience and a keen mind. He went from place to place and helped where help was needed. Naturally, he had observed how the troublesome machine was installed. Now he believed he could repair it. He went directly to the head of the plant and bravely said, "Sir, I would like to try and see what is wrong with the machine." The plant manager ridiculed him. "How dare you? This is an imported machine, far beyond your knowledge and experience." Not long after this, the plant manager was replaced. The mechanic went to the new manager, too, but he got the same answer. After two years, yet another manager came. He saw that this very expensive machine was lying idle, and could not but wonder why. When the master mechanic went to talk to him, too, he finally got a different answer. In about a month he made the machine work again—and he received a big award for this achievement. The style of the new manager, represented characteristically by this experience, shook up the culture of the organization. It encouraged people to come up with ideas for improvement, and which they then did with a vengeance.

An organization designed to achieve its purpose at minimum cost or with fewest resources develops procedures to facilitate sensing in real time or as close to it as possible. However effective sensors a system may have, delays in transferring information, and energy loss as a result, always occur.

Sensing is not just gathering information; it is also processing and interpreting this inside and outside information. Many organizations have good sensor systems, but adaptation to changes remains inadequate because management and employees do not take responsibility for acting upon the information and to adapt processes according to the changed conditions. When sensing is not efficient, organizations suffer from the disease of Insensitivity to Problems.

Disease: Insensitivity to Problems

Problems are neglected.

Description

Problems occur but sensing of the problems or acknowledging them at the appropriate level does not happen. Not being aware of issues naturally means that problems are not dealt with, not analyzed, and the necessary steps to solve them are not taken. Problems reoccur and stay for long periods of time, without appropriate action initiated at any level of the organization.

Symptoms

- There is a complete lack of awareness of problems. People do not feel or sense them. Only when a problem grows into a major crisis do they examine it to find that signs of the problem existed earlier, but were not noticed.

- If a unit of an organization raises an issue, other units or the management deny the existence of the problem.

- Even if a problem is raised and some promises have been made, action is not taken.

- There is a lack of regular departmental meetings to discuss problems. Even if there is a meeting, the agenda is not about problems and the individual who brings up a problem is considered as having a negative attitude.

- Management spends more time outside of the organization or in management meetings within its own circle. There is no management by walking around. Higher level executives rarely visit shop floors or offices.

- At lower levels people are suffering due to unsolved, reoccurring, permanent, smaller problems.

- Employees and managers at lower levels fight symptoms, and they are the ones who spend time on troubleshooting, focusing on eliminating the symptoms, rather than tackling the roots, while management observes this from an elegant distance, beyond the reach of lower levels of the organization.

- There is little interaction concerning problems among the functions and hierarchies of the organization.

- Customers and vendors complain of unresolved or recurring problems.

- Even when a problem is seen there is a tendency to deny the problem and the ownership of it, blaming each other rather than working collaboratively.

- The organization has a blind spot toward its own problems, and artificial optimism is the usual way of addressing problems.

- Higher and lower levels of the organization are isolated and lack interaction, and higher level management remains in its "ivory tower." Lower level people perceive

Table 6.1
Insensitivity to Problems

Structure of Causes	Possible Causes	Possible Actions for Improvements
Personal, Leadership Related	1. Leadership lives in the ivory tower, far away from everyday problems. 2. There is no sufficient operative management. 3. Laziness exists, and comfortable leaders do not want to get involved in small petty matters; they do not want their hands get dirty. 4. Managers rotate too quickly, and they do not have the time, the rewards, or the interest to tackle and to solve the roots of the problems. 5. A proactive attitude is lacking.	*Executive Coaching, Training Workshop, and/or Other:* • Introduce the concept and the PRACTICE (!) of management by walking around. Get executive members on the shop floor; make them engage in communication—listen to employees and follow up on the major issues with which they were confronted. • Increase sensitivity to problems; make involvement in problems conscious. • Assess the time spent on different issues in management meetings; reconsider it by giving more time to the operational issues that are major concerns of the organization in lower levels. Follow up on actions decided, and communicate the results to the rest of the organization. • Stabilize management by letting people spend a reasonable time in their positions, and expect them to solve the roots of the problems, so they will not reoccur time and time again.

Table 6.1 (continued)

Structure of Causes	Possible Causes	Possible Actions for Improvements
		• Include hands-on pragmatic managers in the executive team, and give the necessary weight to their positions so they can influence the management team.

Operational Organizational	• There are no forums or platforms where middle- and lower-level managers can candidly share their everyday challenges and problems with people of higher rank.
	
	• Crisis management takes up all the work hours; no time and resources remain to tackle the roots of the problems preventing reoccurrence.
	
	• In an action-oriented culture, a low tolerance and a lack of skills exist for systematic problem solving, root-cause analyses, and preventive methods.
	
	• Acknowledging and/or raising problematic issues creates a negative image of the person/manager as being incompetent, a trouble maker, or having a negative attitude; hence people have learned to stay quiet.
	
	• If somebody raises a problem, it tends to end up on his or her plate to solve, so people choose to remain silent.
		Coaching, Training Workshop, and/or Other:
		
		• Implement a culture change program focusing on the following:
		
		  – bringing closer different levels of the hierarchy,
		
		  – creating a climate of candid, open communication,
		
		  – introducing practical tools for problem solving,
		
		• Create forums or platforms where middle- and lower-level managers can candidly share everyday challenges and problems with people of higher rank. Follow up these meetings regularly with specific actions.

Structure of Causes	Possible Causes	Possible Actions for Improvements
		• Empower people in lower levels so they can effectively tackle problems and meet every-day challenges. • Make calculations/case studies of how much resources and money are vested for reoccurring, unsolved problems. Invest part of this in solving them, adding necessary resources if needed.
External, Market Related	• There is a shortage of higher-level executives who are equipped with the necessary leadership and managerial skills and practices.	*Intervention:* • Consider hiring from outside the industry or even the country and/or identify and train high potential successors for the necessary leadership and managerial skills.

management members as not being interested in problems, which eventually makes people apathetic about those problems and they become careless as well. In these organizations people do not think much of their management. They have the feeling that top management does not want to get its hands dirty.

- Feedback mechanisms are not appropriate, resulting in poor interaction and communication between organizational layers.

Causes

- The management approach is different for the different "classes" of employees. Once you get into the higher circles you get privileges and prestige and your self-concept changes. This is not empowerment, but negligence and avoidance of problems.
- Organizations that are beyond their maturity phase may develop insensitivity to everyday problems, either coming from outside or inside. They show apathy toward those problems and get tired of tackling them. There may be older people waiting for retirement who do not want to be bothered with deeper underlying issues.
- Individuals might be moving very fast, either horizontally or vertically, in a young, fast-growing organization. By the time they understand the job, the issues, and the problems, they get promoted or moved to another position. A new person comes in and the whole circle starts again, with acute, recurring problems never being solved.

Origins

- The genetic origin is that the founder has an exclusive, "aristocratic" style while creating the organization's structures and culture. Individuals who have this style are isolated from everyday problems and show interest only in one area. They provide a role model for followers and together they create a culture where sensitivity to the problems is not typical.
- The birth-related origin is that an organization that was in a monopolistic situation at the early stage of its existence and its top management was appointed through personal contacts rather than expertise could develop an insensitivity to problems.
- The environmental origin is that this can be similar to the birth-related origin in that there is a small "elite" group of people circulating around in the top managerial positions of different organizations. If they fail in one organization they may be moved to another in a similarly high position, probably with similar results.

This disease often occurs together with Alienation, Bureaucracy, and Longsightedness.

A structured list of causes and possible actions for improvements for this disease can be seen in Table 6.1.

INSULATION REDUCES DISTURBANCES FROM OUTSIDE THE ORGANIZATION

Input from the environment may prove detrimental for the organization. As an open system, organizations are subject to inputs having both positive and negative impacts on the organization. One aspect of health is the ability to cope with and cure or adapt to the effect of unhealthy inputs, before they increase the level of internal entropy. Coping is a continuous process in any organization and living organism. It entails recognizing an input as a problem and treating and solving it in the short term. No living system is totally insulated against the environment.

However, entropy is reduced by insulation from disturbances negatively influencing the organization. Insulation requires deciding what information is relevant. One of the most effective means of insulating the organization is training people and disseminating organizational culture. To illustrate this effect, consider the following example:

One of our clients, a multinational company invested in a significant green field development in an emerging market. The headquarters are located in a country where the culture can be characterized by trust, where safety is considered a value, and people tend to show regard for each other and for private property. This, however, cannot be said about the culture of the emerging market where the company chose the location of its new investment. Not informing themselves properly about the specific circumstances and their consequences on operations, it has not occurred to members of management that a different kind of information and control system may be needed for running operations in a different culture. Furthermore, the product could fit into a person's hand or pocket and was readily available and sellable on the black market. The information system—unprepared as it was for noticing stealing, confused management for a while, signaling instead administrative mistakes and quality problems. Even when it started to become clear that products were disappearing, it was unclear how the crime happened. Was it just individuals taking a few products home or was it organized? However, the problem started to endanger the process of running up to full capacity operation of the new factory, and headquarters started to have second thoughts about widening the product range to produce more expensive items. It was harder to discover the real problem and create preemptive measures since the information system was not built to handle situations like this. Under new management a new and more effective information system was introduced and local management was trained in business and ethics. The most effective measure, however, was that with the broad involvement of employees a vision building and culture change program had been launched. This had the effect of increased engagement and loyalty, and employees did not turn their backs when they saw something out of the ordinary. The number of individual crimes has dropped exponentially; however, the organized crime remained a longer-term challenge.

If the insulation is so "thick" that it prevents sensing important environmental changes, the organization is dysfunctional. We describe how organizations decide whether the environmental input is harmful or not in Chapter 9 about the organization's relationship with its environment. Here, it suffices to say that insulation is necessary in specific cases to avoid a negative impact, but continuous sensing is necessary, too.

RULES, REGULATIONS, AND POLICIES: EFFICIENCY SHORTCUTS OR ENTROPY GENERATORS?

Typically, organizations start with everybody enthusiastically being involved in everything. As the organization grows, this operation reflects confusion, because routines have not yet developed. Even repetitive tasks have to be reinvented from time to time. For instance, if employees were left to themselves, nobody would know where to find contracts or the history of a particular account, or how to train new employees. In certain stages of development, every organization reaches a point when it has to introduce new rules and procedures. Naturally this is met by resistance, because people are concerned about losing flexibility: They struggle to remain flexible, while attempting to become more professional in the sense that they do not have to focus on routine tasks. Bureaucracy and difficulty start when the amount of regulation supposed to reduce entropy coming from reinventing routine tasks at every turn exceeds a certain level. There is no set of standards for where that level is; organizations have to ask themselves whether these new rules help to reduce entropy or whether they become a straitjacket to be accommodated without apparent reason. In an organization where adding value and minimizing entropy become part of the culture, a very good chance exists to minimize bureaucracy.

Disease: Bureaucracy

Document and authorize. If you need fast action, ask for favors.

Description

We call it bureaucracy when the defining character of organizational culture is the attitude of overriding compliance to hierarchy, which leads employees to want every action documented and authorized by higher levels. This trait then defines a chain of additional behavior patterns and cultural characteristics, which together form the symptoms of this organizational disease.

Symptoms

- Processes, rules, and regulations are more important than results. Differing from the procedure is punished.
- Employees want to defend themselves rather than take risks. They follow the required process of doing things, even when circumstances would require otherwise. "I can't do it because the policy states otherwise." Employees follow strict rules and regulations in order to avoid tasks and pressure rather than help each other to achieve their common objective.
- Attention focuses on the way to do and record things. As a result, bureaucratic organizations are past driven rather than future pulled.

- Customers, both external and internal, are at the mercy of the bureaucracy.
- A corrupt way to solve problems is often the only way. Only through special contacts and an informal exchange of favors can things be arranged quickly, for example, where two departments are mutually dependent and an employee from one department asks his or her counterpart in the other for help, bypassing the rules for a quick solution to a problem and offering to return the favor when required. People are doing favors in order to perform the task, rather than acting professionally.
- Individuals who are responsible for developing procedures through regulations have undue power.
- Decision making and taking responsibility are clearly ruled and regulated. Diversion is not tolerated.

Causes

- Traditions and predictability have a higher value in the organization's culture than creativity, flexibility, and result orientation.
- These organizations or departments are often in a monopolistic situation. They put the main emphasis on procedures and policies, not on results. Government institutions or companies in monopolistic situations are likely to be bureaucratic organizations, struggling when environmental changes make those regulations out of date.
- Even if a problem is raised and some promises have been made, action is not taken. Because it is convenient, people point out that they have no time for playing anything other than their limited roles. They do not realize that they may already have other competencies. Many executives think that past experiences define the core competencies of departments and the organization. Often they overlook other developing competencies, which then over time sink into irrelevance. These organizations do not develop, and their choices may decrease. Strict following of the core competency framework may often be the cause of becoming rigid and bureaucratic.

Origins

- The genetic origin is that the founders believe in processes, rules, and regulations more than in initiative and result orientation.
- The birth-related origin is that the organization has been founded in stable and secure circumstances when speed or flexibility is not of great value.
- The environmental origin is that the environment requires the organization to perform tedious reporting and administration. This is the case when the regulatory environment is very strict and has controlling power over the organization.

This disease often occurs together with Decision Paralysis, Risk Avoidance, Insensitivity to Problems, and Organizational Paranoia.

A structured list of causes and possible actions for improvements for this disease can be seen in Table 6.2.

Table 6.2
Bureaucracy

Structure of Causes	Description of Causes	Possible Actions for Improvements
Personal/Leadership Related	1. Leaders believe that efficiency assumes minutely detailed regulations and strictly following them. 2. Management believes that thinking is primarily its task, while employees should execute only according to rules and regulations. 3. There is lack of trust in individuals. Trust is replaced by rules and strong control, which are considered the only means of sustaining order. 4. People in all levels of the organization do not accept responsibility; they prefer to shift it to others.	*Executive Coaching, Training Workshop, and/or Other:* • Implement programs to improve achievement, motivation, and result orientation versus being stuck too much with following rigid rules and regulations. • Expose key players of the organization to different organizational cultures and operation to experience and learn more flexible ways of managing. • Encourage, reward, and rapidly publicize independent actions.
Organizational, Operational	1. The life cycle of the organization is over the summit and has started to decline; members are more concerned about their private agendas; they prefer a safe, comfortable life in the organization. 2. High-value complex technology and high-volume production do not allow individual initiative; deviation from the rules may cause expensive problems.	*Coaching, Training Workshop, and/or Other:* • Revise organizational processes and procedures according to the value addition point of view and streamline them as much as possible. • Strengthen the "internal customer" concept by clarifying needs and expectations toward

Structure of Causes	Description of Causes	Possible Actions for Improvements
	3. Roles and responsibilities are too isolated. Lack of system thinking and system approach exist in running the organization. 4. There is one organizational norm: if you perform according to the rules, you can avoid getting into trouble. 5. Performance evaluation rewards seniority and predictability more than ambitious, outstanding performance, so people who prefer the latter leave the organization.	each other in order to streamline and speed up processes. • Implement a culture change program: from role culture to task-performing culture. • Renew performance evaluation, selection, and promotion systems by giving higher priority for initiation, speed, result orientation, and simplicity.
External, Market Related	1. There are expectations from outside regulatory and other agencies (such as the Sarbanes-Oxley Act of 2002 or European Union regulations). 2. Customers need detailed quality control certifications. 3. Customers are eager to have increasing insight into how the supplier is solving its problems. The organization has to over-document every step it takes.	*Interventions:* • Develop a common understanding and acceptance of reporting and certifying. • Involve outside stakeholders, including customers in the simplification of processes.

DISSEMINATING INFORMATION

The level of entropy decreases when relevant communication happens within an organization, without distortion, on a real-time basis. With sophisticated information technology being widely available, organizations have more tools for smooth information flow, but in a healthy organization information is exploited, although not necessarily by the latest technology. More important is the approach to handling information: trust in employees and openness about this information. Further, lack of rigid boundaries among employees facilitates free communication. There are plenty of organizations that have the latest information technology available, but are unable to utilize it.

Insufficient or incorrect information delays or even prevents efficient performance of the task and thus increases the level of organizational entropy. Information can also be superfluous for the efficient performance of the job. A flood of irrelevant information overwhelms employees with incongruous data, causing them to lose their understanding of the big picture and the context of their tasks.

Minimal distances among different layers of the organization may decrease the opportunities of distorting information by hierarchical layers. When a decision turns out to be wrong, minimal distances among layers may also localize the possible negative effects. In such organizations, decision making is organic: everyone is appreciated as an important contributor to the final product and to the fulfillment of the organization's vision. One way to apply this approach is to eliminate the status symbols that distance people even further than their different roles do. Another is to show respect for all employees by regular interaction, knowing people and understanding the work they do. Listening alone is not enough. If a problem develops, executives who follow up with addressing that concern are both effectively improving operations and sending a symbolic message. Follow-up shows respect for the work and for the people who performed that work. It is helpful for an executive at any level to better understand the everyday experiences of employees in order to balance aspects of decision making. It is also an excellent opportunity to obtain valuable information from informal conversations.

A chief executive used to invite me to technical meetings with vendors of foreign technology. At first, I was surprised; after all, I'm not a technologist. He explained that he needed someone who was ignorant but curious. "Your job is to ask the kind of questions technologists don't think of," he instructed me. Thus, while getting to know people in this organization, I found that some held the belief that workers are not supposed to think. One day I made a proposal: since they considered the workers' trade union representatives ignorant, I suggested that they may be curious, too, so why not utilize their ignorance and curiosity. The challenge was accepted, and workers were invited to ask questions before and during those meetings. Their questions received answers promptly. In a short time it became not only all right, but also expected to ask questions. Later, referring to this new and popular attitude, they began to call the human resource department the I.R. Department, short for Intelligence Resource Department.

EMPOWERING PEOPLE RESULTS IN INFORMATION WITH LESS DISTORTION

Empowered organizations give their employees more independence, decision-making authority, and responsibility than their traditional counterparts. These organizations rely on self-directed work teams, empowered—within certain limits—to make decisions that managers reserve for themselves in traditional organizations. Empowered organizations have at least two significant advantages:

1. At all organizational levels, more connected employees use their creative powers more efficiently. In contrast, most of this creativity lies fallow in traditional organizations, where bosses make most of the decisions and subordinates are expected only to support and implement them. Empowered employees generate cost-saving and quality-improvement ideas, likely putting the organization into a better competitive position.

2. In addition to being cheaper to run, empowered organizations are also much nimbler. Empowered organizations have flatter organizational hierarchies. This follows from the reduced need to escalate decision making up the hierarchy. When the front line makes decisions, the need for mid layers shrinks. Empowered organizations focus their employees' attention on solving problems. In addition, these employees enjoy a fairly high degree of autonomy regardless of their job titles and have better opportunities to grow. On the other hand, highly structured, bureaucratic organizations spawn individuals and teams that are often busy proving their importance, competing with each other, and seeking the boss's favor.

Empowered organizations are made, not born. Granting immediate autonomy without investing and developing the conditions of such an operation will only increase entropy. Developing the conditions of successful empowerment requires discipline. Only when teams go through the process of developing and committing to a set of goals, defining and accepting boundaries, clarifying roles, identifying a common set of norms/values, and internalizing discipline (meaning that all team members commit to follow these agreements) will the conditions then facilitate successful operation. See Figure 6.1.

1. The development process of effective empowered teams starts with the members agreeing with, accepting, and committing to a set of common goals. Unless the group accepts and commits to basic goals, it cannot be expected to pull in the desired direction. Such a lack of alignment will create problems down the line, provoking managers to seize direct control and start micromanaging the team. In order to have team members agree on goals, they must be involved in their

Figure 6.1
Empowerment: The Development of Effective Self-Directed Teams

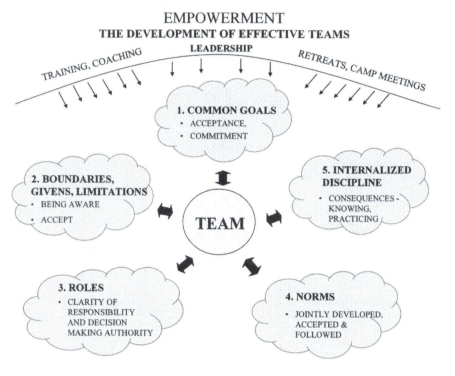

selection, definitions, and eventual modifications. The strength of the team's commitment is directly proportional to its involvement in all these steps.

2. The team must be aware of and accept its boundaries, givens, and limitations. Many autonomous work teams get into trouble when the teams' all-embracing democracy blinds them to the boundaries their environment imposes on them. Such nonnegotiable conditions may include environmental regulations, safety rules, and budgets. A number of conditions must be accepted as givens for a particular time frame. Teams can waste a lot of energy trying to negotiate or complain about them.

3. Once the team has understood and accepted external givens and limitations, it has to identify internal roles, responsibilities, decision-making authorities, and members' mutual expectations from each other. Everybody must clearly see how he or she contributes to reaching the team's common goals. On the one hand, roles and responsibilities must be clearly understood. On the other hand, they must be kept flexible to prevent the erection of walls along functional boundaries and to enable team members to help each other when needed.

4. The team must develop a common set of norms and values. These represent the team's day-to-day code of conduct that everybody must agree with, accept, and

follow. The process of developing these norms and values is at least as important as the final result. It is through discussions, encounters, debates, and common thinking that team members internalize these values. Simply issuing the team with a ready-made list of norms and values in writing is counterproductive and futile. Team members will neither own nor have the motivation to observe and apply norms and values they have not helped to shape and develop.

5. Finally, the team needs internalized discipline for its successful operation. Team members commit themselves to follow all those points they have agreed upon. Interestingly, advocates of people-focused management practices tend to shun this word. They feel discipline is an attribute of authoritarian or traditional management styles. In reality, however, discipline is at least as important for empowered teams as it is for traditional organizations. The difference is that traditional managers impose and enforce, while empowered teams willingly assume and internalize discipline. Positive consequences for keeping and negative consequences for violating agreements are necessary in an empowered team, because the lack of these easily demolishes the team, leading to skepticism about empowerment.

USING INFORMATION IN DECISION MAKING AND PROBLEM SOLVING

One of the most typical managerial dilemmas is which decisions the manager should individually make, which ones a wider circle of employees should participate in, and how this wider circle of employees is to be identified. In a healthy organization, decisions are made at the level where the most adequate information is available. Frequently, this information does not reside in one person, department, or subsystem of the organization. In a healthy organization, people think about the whole system and consider the potential consequences of their decisions on other parts of the organization with the help of cross-functional teams. Due to the characteristics of work distribution, it is quite natural that people working on different aspects of the organization's vision have different views. Where people see differences as a source of better decisions rather than controversies, diversity contributes to those decisions. The involvement of people with different views may be considered a waste of time, creating a higher level of entropy, but it can also be looked at as an investment and a time-saving device in the long term. Investment in finding the best possible decision can save much entropy later. Experts who have the most pertinent information participate in teams at all levels of the organization. Together they can make the most efficient decisions. These cross-functional teams may also help people to understand the interdependencies across the organization. It facilitates system thinking, because people will see the impact of an action as a chain reaction. Team members start to perceive themselves not only as being bound to a certain role or function, but as a part of the whole system, and consequently part of the solution. As soon as they see themselves as part of the solution, they start to take responsibility for solving problems with the best possible results for the organization as a whole. Through this process, an organization starts to learn about itself, and that learning spreads across the organization.

WHAT DO YOU MAKE OF BAD DECISIONS?

Whatever level decisions are taken at, they are supported in a healthy organization. The evaluation may later reveal that the decision was not right, but when the decision is taken, it is supported. Everybody is empowered to take the decisions that pertain to that level. When all decisions turn out to be "right," the organization probably has spent too much time on making them or is performing well below its potential; it is avoiding taking risk and missing opportunities. We illustrate this point by the example of the high jumper who never drops the bar. We can immediately be sure of one thing: the jumper performs lower than his or her potential. We can also assume that the jumper stopped developing, because for development to take place a high jumper needs to face challenges and expand limits. While doing so may lead to failure from time to time, it is also the only way to learn, develop, and reach higher and higher standards.

If some decisions turn out to be wrong, it is a sign that risk taking is encouraged in the organization. The main question is that, after a decision turned out to be wrong, is the organization ready to stop and analyze and learn from the mistake and disseminate this learning across the organization, thus modifying decision-making mechanisms? If employees are given responsibility as if they were the owners of a department or function, and the right to be wrong, they are aware of the risks involved in their decisions. When they are implementing the decision, they do it with planning and awareness, and if corrective action is to be taken, they do it immediately.

Autonomy essentially means that people can decide about their immediate work. If they feel that hierarchy does not block them, they do not have to wait around for somebody else to decide; they sense that they are free to make decisions related to their work, and they have the right amount of information to make those decisions. They identify the major stakeholders of the particular decision and consider their interests.

There are three stages of decision making: collecting data, turning it into information by developing a consensus about the meaning of the data, and making the decision. Frequently, substantial time is lost in information collection itself. Where people have the skills of working in teams, the consensus-building mechanism operates in a timely manner, too.

Even if substantial time is spent on information collection, the process leading up to decision making is often not adequate. Interestingly, in a healthy organization, the greater emphasis is on results, not on procedures. Result orientation and present or future orientation is a sign of health. Procedure orientation can lead to the disease we call Decision Paralysis.

Disease: Decision Paralysis

If in doubt, discuss.

Description

Decision paralysis means it takes too long to make decisions. By the time the decision is made, reality may well have shifted again. The decision, necessary in a particular context, is taken after the context has changed. When the organization does not have mechanisms for providing a timely response to the challenges of the environment, it operates with higher entropy.

Symptoms

• Work is withheld by the lack of timely decisions from the authorities who have the right to make the decision.

• Committees do not take deadlines seriously and when they conclude their work, they usually do so with a proposal rather then a decision.

• Proposals are pushed upward for finalizing, and through this process, information collection is repeatedly required. This introduces another source of delay.

• Upper level managers keep most of the decisions to themselves and do not delegate decision-making authority.

• Though people have adequate information, they pass the decisions upward to avoid responsibility.

In a car manufacturing company, during a period of increased competition and cost cutting pressure, a housing and rent allowance decision had to be reconsidered. A strong trade union was advocating that workers should continue to be given housing and rent allowances. A committee was established to work out the formula of how to calculate the allowance. The committee did a lot of work and studied other organizations' practices. It took three months to prepare a recommendation to the management. Everybody expected that it would take two or three days for the president to sign the recommendation. Instead, the president asked for more data, going into such detail as to how many people rent part of their houses to others. It took another two months to collect the new data. After collecting all the facts and figures, the proposal waited on his desk for six months, and then the decision was made—to accept the original proposal submitted by the committee.

• Business opportunities are lost due to indecision.

• Decision-making authorities are not defined clearly; people are not sure who should make what decision.

• Politicking happens. People pull the rug out from under each other in devious ways. There are various aspects of this behavior: gossiping, talking behind people's backs, and saying one thing and doing something else. Politicking very often happens in an organization that is motivated by power. People are concerned about position, not performance.

- "The head leaves behind the body" syndrome exists. Management is living in the future. There is no real, lively, genuine communication between the top and the rest of the organization. Executives have meetings among themselves, discussing issues that are related to the rest of the organization; but they are detached from the rest of the organization, so they speculate. They lose touch with reality.

Causes

- There is hierarchical thinking, a lack of trust in lower levels of the hierarchy, or in others in general, and as a result, overall a lack of empowerment in the organization.
- The cause could be uncertainty about roles. In any given situation, it is often unknown who is supposed to make the decision; along with this, there is no clear perspective, direction, or strategy.
- Decision Paralysis could be the result of a lack of coordination in activities. Because the coordination is not adequate, information flow is not correct, and decision making is too slow.

Origins

- The genetic origin is defined by the character or temperament of the founder. If the founder is uncertain, his anxiety, fear, and need to be sure of everything prompt repeated requests for data collection. For cautious leadership, it takes much time to come to a decision, and this becomes part of the organizational culture.
- The birth-related cause takes place when at an early stage, the organization made an "almost fatal" bad decision. Since then, the decision-making culture has become overly cautious, and people try to avoid responsibility for decisions.
- The environmental origin could be when major changes involving the stakeholders of the organization result in uncertainty. When privatization is taking place, mergers or acquisitions are expected; at that time decision paralysis is typical in the organization.

Other causes of Decision Paralysis could be the uncertainty manifested in the thinking of the executives, the organizational structure, or the environment. If the organization is uncertain as to what is going to happen, for example, a merger, an acquisition, or privatization is expected to take place, it is very hard to make decisions impacting the future of the organization. Employees do not know the resources they may command or lose, they do not know the future structure, and sometimes they are not even sure about the profile of the organization, the product, and/or service the organization will keep or cancel. Consequently, they are unable to make decisions. The organization itself could get paralyzed.

Decision Paralysis often occurs together with Risk Avoidance and Bureaucracy.

A structured list of causes and possible actions for improvements for this disease can be seen in Table 6.3.

Table 6.3
Decision Paralysis

Structure of Causes	Possible Causes	Possible Actions for Improvements
Personal/Leadership	• Top executives want to control everything and trust only their own decisions; there-fore, they are overworked and decisions get delayed. • In previous experiences bad decisions were catastrophic for the decision maker, so managers do not dare to delegate. • Fear of taking responsibility, being self-reliant, and a lack of self-confidence abound. • Lack of competence abounds. • The belief of top executives is that if they let other people make decisions further down in the hierarchy, they may appear weak or out of control.	*Executive Coaching, Training Workshop, and/or Other:* • Clarify expectations to executives. • Clarify the personal approach and the ability of decision making. • Help leaders to coach their people to be able to make decisions. • Increase self-confidence and success orientation. • Provide problem-solving training. • Use delegation and empowerment. • Provide decision-making training. • Provide meeting-management training. • Provide time-management training. • Provide trust-building and team-building workshops.

Table 6.3 (continued)

Structure of Causes	Possible Causes	Possible Actions for Improvements
Organizational, Operational	• Too many levels exist in the organizational hierarchy, and there are too strict regulations on how processes should work. • Thoroughness and security are valued instead of speed. • There are not enough data for secure decision making and educated risk taking. There is a lack of a sufficient information system. • Unclear tasks, responsibilities, and authorities lead to uncertainty and delays in decision making. • The culture is too democratic; people are constantly searching for a consensus.	*Coaching, Training Workshop, and/or Other:* • Clarify roles, responsibilities, decision-making authority, and delegation. • Introduce competence models, with special emphasis on decision making and delegation. • Change systems, information channels, and performance-evaluation systems based on decision-making competence and ability. • Analyze and show consequences of unmade or delayed decisions. • Introduce a self-directing work group model. • Delayer the organization.
Environmental Market Related	1. What is true today will change tomorrow. It is a turbulent, fast-changing environment. 2. Good market position exists, and there is tolerance in the market for less prompt decisions. 3. An uncertainness exists related to ownership. Possible changes are expected (e.g., merger or acquisition).	*Interventions:* • Map and share unutilized opportunities due to the lack of decisions. • Develop strategy, identify priorities, and follow execution steps closely. • Owners or investors should reinforce the position of management.

SYSTEMIC FEEDBACK REDUCES ENTROPY

In a healthy organization, systemic feedback mechanisms are established. Feedback comes through the internal processes and is required in order to take the necessary corrective actions. Feedback is also the vehicle for continuous improvement, development, and growth. There are three types of feedback: recognition of what is happening, positive reinforcement, and negative feedback.

One of the most frequent problems subordinates at all levels complain about is that they receive only negative feedback from their superiors. As a consequence, they become defensive about feedback in general and are less inclined to take it seriously. If positive feedback is also given, people tend to appreciate receiving feedback. Some organizations—although not many— face the opposite problem, namely, that negative feedback is hardly ever given, in fear of the consequent discomfort and conflict. If this "people pleasing" is the case, positive feedback loses credibility and becomes meaningless. An individual's need for improvement and development decreases. Both extremes are unhealthy. A healthy organization is characterized by a balance between positive feedback and feedback given for improvement.

Feedback for improvement occurs when something does not function well. In a healthy organization, people listen to feedback openly rather than defensively, because the feedback is not accusing. Improvement based on feedback and openness go together. The objective of feedback is to positively reinforce and to give help for improvement. Organizational health does not mean absence of pain, fear, sorrow, or other negative feelings. For instance, in the absence of fear, we will do things that cause calamity. If fears are specific, they are very useful because they make us plan and thus be prepared. When negative feelings are utilized as feedback for taking corrective action, they indicate health. On the other hand, when negative feelings become the only way of gaining sympathy, they become dysfunctional.

When employees are clear about their internal and external customers and the value they add to them, they require feedback about how they perform their tasks, whether they meet the standards and expectations, and whether their customers are satisfied. Feedback is the means of staying on track, but also of making the necessary modifications before bigger problems arise. That is why the dissemination of feedback is one of the most important mechanisms of minimizing entropy in an organization. A healthy organization should build a systematic appraisal system, one that is developmental, focusing on the growth of individuals and groups. The following three factors determine the feedback mechanism:

1. The vision of the organization is vital, including its organizational culture elements. Feedback should reflect vision and values. In a healthy organization, selection, promotion, and training take into consideration a contribution to the vision and values of the organization.

2. The feedback mechanism should be derived from the more specific departmental vision, objectives, action plans, and milestones. This way the feedback has measurable elements. When employees meet their objectives it gives a feeling of success and fulfillment. It also provides a specific basis for evaluation of what has and has not been accomplished.

3. The feedback should reflect the expectations of the internal and/or external customers.

It is useful for executives to look at themselves not only as leaders of groups, but also as people in service of the organization and its people. They should look at their employees as their internal customers. Facilitating the development of their employees is one way executives add value, and it is worthwhile to get feedback from those to whom we attempt to add value. Feedback in this case flows in all directions, horizontally and vertically. Healthy organizations design opportunities for employees to voice opinions frequently about the way the organization operates, and about how their managers and executives lead it.

The "Messages" exercise is one of the most popular ones from the range of exercises we use in executive workshops. Every participant in the given group writes a message to everybody else, in which they attempt to answer the following two questions:

• What are your characteristics that I appreciate because they are very useful for me and the team?

• What are your characteristics which, if they could be changed, would be better and more useful for me and for the team?

In the first part of the exercise participants write their messages to each other, in the second they distribute their messages and collect and read the ones written for them, in the third they meet the writer one-on-one, for five to ten minutes to thank each other for writing (not argue about it, but to accept the perception of the other person), to ask questions if they have anything to clarify, and to commit to it if they can do it. Although this is a very simple exercise, it is very interesting to observe how unusual it is for executives and how valuable they consider afterwards to find out in greater detail how their colleagues see them, given that these are the exact people they spend a lot of time together with at work.

We were conducting a workshop for the Hungarian subsidiary of a French multinational company, and we wanted to conclude the last half day of the two-and-a-half-day program with this exercise. We were surprised by the intensity of the reaction from the executives. Some executives (from both nationalities) suggested that if we carry on with the exercise and they tell what they think about each other honestly, they will only achieve a conflict and a further deterioration of the relationship. At first we argued about the objectives of the exercise, but then seeing the resistance we were ready to not force the issue any further, when the other side started to speak up arguing of the negative effect of not doing the exercise now, because it may lead to decreased trust among them. From eight thirty in the morning till eleven they were going back and forth about it, bringing up never explicitly mentioned beliefs about teamwork and their team. Finally, they decided to go through with it, and at four in the afternoon, when they finished, they declared in unison that this was the best thing that happened to them since they were working as a team.

It is crucial that the feedback should focus on developmental purposes, not on finding faults or blaming. People will participate voluntarily in the appraisal process only if they feel that this mechanism is serving their personal growth and development as much as it serves the organization and the internal clients of the employee. It is also important to discuss the whole process leading to the results: Development consists of improving those processes, not just the results.

After receiving feedback, it is necessary to take corrective action. It is important that organizations have effective mechanisms for corrective action, analyzing root causes, coming up with alternative solutions, prioritizing, implementing, and measuring results.

COORDINATION OF WORK AND COMMUNICATION

How efficiently work is done is a measure of health in an organization. In spite of this idea being relatively simple, our experience is that to some degree, all organizations face the problem of lack of coordination and communication among various parts of the organization. Shifting the burden from one part of the system to another, creating more trouble over there as an "entropy generator," applies to groups as well as individuals who want to exploit the whole system for their own convenience. Operating as if they were the center of the organizational universe, they expect other units or individuals to adapt to their needs. Suboptimization is a common phenomenon. Instead of collaborating for common goals, departments overfocus on their particular objectives and forget the fact that they are part of a larger system, which is the reason for their very existence in the first place. Incentives, when designed exclusively to reward individual performance, result in competitive, not cooperative, work practices, where winning over, rather than working with, others dominates. The following quotation from one of our organizational diagnoses would be a very typical characterization of some other organizations as well:

Everyone finds the relationship of different units within the organization problematic. Units and their leaders focus too much on their own areas and do not pay attention to the interest of other departments and thus the whole of the organization. There is suboptimization, which does not allow for attaining the optimum with regard to the entire plant. A lack of concord and mutual acceptance among top managers also constitutes a problem that escalates further down the organization. At the same time, it is still the role of top management to motivate its managers and colleagues to increase cooperation with other departments, to support and assist each other, and to adopt the "internal customer" concept. Of course, in order to do just that, it first would have to organize its own ranks, form an atmosphere of trust and cooperation, and accept common goals....

In a healthy organization, people serve a common goal and understand others' concerns with an attitude of "what can I do for you" rather than "what should you do for me." The shared vision and the attitude of having internal customers legitimize all departments and are perceived as adding value to the final product. Therefore, every subsystem helps others, resulting in a coordinated work process. Incentives extend to the success of the whole group. It is natural that departments develop functional identities, but friction among departmental identities is not a necessary by-product. One of the most common causes of entropy in an organization is that energy is wasted in cross-departmental and cross-functional conflicts. Working together is a necessary skill to counteract this tendency to ensure that conflicts do not lead to an unnecessary waste of energy. Different forums can ensure smoother cooperation, coordination of work across the organization providing information sharing, and more efficient joint decision making. Cross-functional teams can effectively utilize these forums. Nevertheless, most organizations suffer from some level of Suboptimizing disease.

Disease: Suboptimizing

Our department is the center of our universe; every other department has to serve us.

Description

This widespread disease occurs when different parts of the organization lose sight of the whole and optimize the operation to their particular objectives. There is inadequate cooperation and communication among the various parts of the organization, leading to suboptimizing and entropy from the perspective of the whole system. Suboptimization can be compared to its opposite, "internal customer" driven operations by the different units of the organization.

Symptoms

- Departments work in isolation. They focus on their individual activities. They organize process flows around themselves to serve their own purposes, rather than serving others.
- Cross-functional teams are rare. If they exist, they are plagued with interdepartmental fights.
- Interdepartmental conflicts are frequent. Senior managers have to interfere to solve these conflicts. Blaming other departments and finger-pointing are common.
- Employees do not rotate or move between departments because of the mutual disliking between departments and suspicion toward employees of other departments. Instead, hiring from the outside is common.

- Employees of a suboptimizing organization do not share a strong common vision. If there is any vision or strategy in the organization, it is probably held by a few persons at the top.

One of our clients, an American food company, became multinational by expanding in Western and Eastern Europe and Australia by acquiring several previously independent brands. By the mid nineties it had a strong market presence in every continent of the world, supported by production in North America, Europe, and Australia. Some products were sold globally, while some only regionally. Some country operations were focused on production of a limited number of brands, while others were mainly importing products produced in other countries. In the headquarters it created an export department to coordinate sales, and its original request was to increase efficiency of this department. Our investigation revealed a multilayered suboptimization in operations, logistics, marketing, and sales across the different units. The level of integration remained low after the acquisitions, and the corporate structure of geographic management in addition to the functional management created an environment that was conducive to pursuing narrow, local interest whether it was based on brand or geography, production or sales department. Fulfilling sales orders became a complex exercise not supported by the infrastructure. The honest effort from an export administration department could by no means overcome the deep layers of inefficiencies inherent in corporate operations.

- Employees fulfill their roles within their own "boxes," not seeing the interrelatedness of their actions. Job descriptions focus on technical aspects of tasks, not on the role of the function within the system.
- The lack of cooperation is even truer higher in the hierarchy, in the boardroom, among the vice-presidents and heads of different departments. If something goes wrong, the first question asked is whose fault it is, rather than how to solve the problem or what can be learned from it. This approach sets the tone for the rest of the organization.
- Blaming is the word to describe the language of the suboptimizing organizations. There is no willingness to take responsibility for failure.

Causes

- Very often the cause of suboptimization is that some departments have greater importance than others. In these core departments, obtaining resources is easier and the rewards are higher than in the rest of the organization. A tremendous amount of envy might occur, leading to low levels of cooperation. A common reaction of other departments is to try to ensure that the core departments will fail somehow.

Origins

- The genetic origin is that founders or key executives believe more in competition— "divide and rule" principles—than in cooperation. Their management style commonly includes giving favors.

Table 6.4
Suboptimizing

Structure of Causes	Possible Causes	Possible Actions for Improvements

Personal, Leadership Related	1. The value system of several key executives emphasizes winning over other people and rivalry, which results in rivalry among departments.
	
	2. A lack of system thinking exists.
	
	3. Executives deal with the different departments separately.
	
	4. Certain people or departments get preferential treatment.
	
	5. Managers are mostly concerned about pursuing their own careers by focusing solely on their own areas, and they try to get all the possible resources that help them to succeed.
		Executive Coaching, Training Workshop, and/or Other:
		
		• Make assessment/diagnoses regarding co-operation and teamwork in the organization and feed the data back to the management team members. Make them see how their leadership style and practices may contribute to the problems. Agree on necessary steps to take together including, but not limited to, developmental programs in the following areas:
		
		   – system thinking,
		   – cooperation,
		   – teamwork,
		   – conflict management, and so forth.
		
		• Implement executive team-building training, clarifying common goals, shared responsibility, and interdependencies.

Structure of Causes	Possible Causes	Possible Actions for Improvements
		• Increase awareness of each other's values and the added value each area is providing to the success of the organization.
		• Revise bonus systems and closely tie them to joint results.
		• In promotion put special emphasis on co-operative, team-oriented results.
Organizational, Operational	1. People are unaware of the common objectives and of the cooperative efforts needed to achieve them.	***Coaching, Training Workshop, and/or Other:***
	2. Organizational units do not understand well the value added by other departments.	• Introduce the internal customer concept and practice and strengthen system thinking. Clarify expectations among different organizational units.
	3. The incentive system focuses solely on departmental objectives and ignores common goals.	• Redesign the performance-evaluation and incentive systems to put more emphasis on common organizational goals in addition to functional objectives.
	4. Some departments are treated as more important than others.	• Start cross-functional projects based on the common objectives.
	5. In the case of multinational corporations that operate with a matrix structure, fulfilling the expectations of the functional boss(e.g., in the regional headquarters) is more important than cooperating with	• Create forums, where different parts of the organization can get together to discuss

Table 6.4 (continued)

Structure of Causes	Possible Causes	Possible Actions for Improvements
	other departments in the local organization. 6. Operations are overly decentralized, and departments work in isolation; there are no forums for communicating, sharing issues of common interest, joint problem solving, and no cross-functional work.	issues of common interest, can solve problems together, and can learn to appreciate each other. • Emphasize cooperation and teamwork among the organizational values. • Implement job rotation. • In the case of multinational corporations that operate in a matrix structure, reconsider the meaning of the different reporting lines and empower the local CEO to be able to make his or her direct reporting units cooperate closely with each other. • Analyze the reason why some departments are perceived as "more important" while others are perceived less so, and develop actions to make all departments feel important for the sake of the organization.
External, Market Related	1. The general culture within the society is very competitive and individualistic, and this is reflected in organizational cultures.	*Interventions:* • Create experiential situations that represent the power of cooperation and teamwork and help to build this value into the everyday work culture.

- The birth-related origin is that several small units or co-founders have joined together to fund the organization and they cannot quite harmonize their interests. Separation following self-interest at the expense of others remains part of the culture. Equally, if the organization is born by combining several already existing organizations, pursuing self-interest at the expense of the interest of the whole organization is likely.
- The environmental origin is that the broader culture of society is more individualistic and competitive and this self-centered behavior is more prevalent in the organizations' culture. People are pushing their own personal agendas and career objectives.

Subsidiaries of multinational companies operating in a matrix structure—where the functional lines are strong—are, in particular, vulnerable to suboptimization. Local, functional managers tend to be keener to satisfy their functional bosses sitting at headquarters than to cooperate with their peers or to make compromises in the interest of their local organization as a whole.

We have been working with the local subsidiary of one of the world's best known high-tech companies, with the objective of increasing cooperation among the executives and divisions. The company just went through with a significant merger. We have been successfully addressing the cooperation among the individuals, but the dynamics of operating in a regional matrix and separate divisions turned out to be a harder nut to crack. This subsidiary consisted of four divisions and the country manager was one of the division heads, who has been instructed by her boss to spend only max 10 percent of her time on the organization and 90 percent on the division. Divisions also reported to the regional division; therefore, they clearly followed expectations coming from there. While it was obvious that there were synergies in cross-selling the products of the different divisions to the customers, the interest of the regional division mostly overrode the initiative. By the time the division leaders within the subsidiary came to an agreement about coordinating selling, bringing their people together in one office, one of the regional division leaders intervened and stopped coordination, insisting on the interest of his division. This approach led to high demoralization in the local subsidiary and made employees feel that while they are expected to always consider the interest of the full company and work as a team, the regional executives benefit from applying a double standard and chasing only their regional divisional interest.

This disease often occurs together with Pampering, Negligence of Financial Matters, and Tunnel Vision.

A structured list of causes and possible actions for improvements for this disease can be seen in Table 6.4.

SYNERGY AMONG PEOPLE REDUCES ENTROPY

All of us have experienced relationships or moments in relationships where we sensed synergy, easy creativity, or the merging of energies. In this situation, there is a low level of entropy and a feeling of being and flowing completely together. This may be either an intellectual or a physical experience. In the organizational setting it manifests when we have a good meeting, for example. We feel energized, finding ourselves full of energy at the end of the meeting. We gain this energy from each other, from the process, and from the results. Consequently, we experience mattering and the strong feeling of being potent.

Everyone has surely experienced the opposite situation as well, when the time spent working with another person feels like a complete waste. We feel the other person does not hear, or understand, us, and he or she likely feels the same way, evident in the fact that the focus is on his or her individual agenda. The situation is one of interference and high levels of entropy.

When more than one individual is involved, a common goal is central to the successful reduction of entropy, as well as an implicit agreement on how to work together. Cooperation is synergistic. Synergy creates a new quality by enhancing the impact of the individual components. The opposite of synergy is explosion, in the sense of wasting away the qualities of each agent in a process of destruction. Once in a while, we all take part in the pastime of dragging issues in meetings. Yet, when participants leave a meeting exhausted, with a feeling that the meeting went nowhere, the situation ends up much worse than it was before, with a lot of wasted energy.

Why does this happen? In most interpersonal relationships, personal agendas tend to force the issue of "who is right" rather than "what is right." The who-is-right conflict tends to produce a higher level of entropy, in contrast to the what-is-right orientation. When we have to prove ourselves continuously as a person, our actions waste energy from the point of view of fulfilling the common purpose. We do not focus on a common vision; we focus on our personal agenda. We have a hard time listening to and understanding others, probably provoking similar behavior from them.

The what-is-right, "win-win" orientation is the driving force of empowerment, as a result of which every employee feels valued. When employees feel valued, they do not have to fight, prove themselves, and impose their ideas all the time. They have the luxury of being good listeners. Listening is risky for an insecure person; if we listen to someone, we may have to change and thus feel defeated. The obvious way to avoid this is to close our eyes and ears. A secure person is willing to change, rather than feel defeated.

An organization can easily go either way by virtue of its structure and culture. It can create an environment in which people feel insecure and anxious, so they are likely to avoid risks. In these organizations, there may be great concern about short-term entropy. With perspective, this appears penny-wise and pound-foolish. In an organization where people are trusted, they are also allowed to fail; failing is part of the regular operations. In this climate of acceptance people learn from risk taking and failure rather than feel insecure because of possible punishments. Employees then feel more relaxed and ready to focus on the job at hand and the larger vision, rather than on constantly defending themselves. The economic needs of the organization and the employee's needs converge in this important characteristic of decision making. As we discussed in detail in the chapter about the needs of individuals (Chapter 4), to build confidence, individuals must be given autonomy, including the basic autonomy of the right to be wrong. If employees have the right to differ from authority, they inevitably will make mistakes, but this process results in long-term reduction of entropy through better results and long-term commitment.

ENTROPY AROUND INDIVIDUALS

In addition to the organization and team level, entropy can also be interpreted in the individual context. The skills you show in tackling certain tasks can create a feeling of being immersed in performing tasks and which, in turn, result in efficiency. Conversely, the lack of those skills increases entropy.

We extend our discussion of entropy at the individual level to examine executives because of their significant impact on an organization. Executives may have individual weaknesses that create a chain reaction of problems for people around them since they are routinely involved in numerous activities and play important roles in various associations, organizations, and boards. One typical example of a weakness executives possess is that they notoriously underestimate the time needed for meetings and consequently arrive late for later appointments, with the obvious result that others waste their time waiting. This has a domino effect, creating a higher level of entropy in their environment. The concept of "shifting the burden," in which one subsystem has problems but other subsystems suffer the consequences describes this chain reaction well. Our executive runs from one meeting to another, utilizing his or her time "optimally," while others are idle, paying the price for the lack of discipline and the inability to accurately plan his or her agenda.

When we look at individual efficiency and reliability, it is worthwhile to look at the individual and their interactions as part of a system. To evaluate an individual's ability to work collaboratively, we can examine entropy around him or her. The above executive's work mode of shifting the burden increases entropy.

The lack of efficient self-esteem also increases entropy. If executives have ego problems originating in a lack of sufficient self-esteem, they need to prove themselves right in every situation almost under any condition. Their fighting every point, rather than participating constructively, is likely to lead to inefficient meetings, destructive confrontations, and win-lose-type situations, which absorb energy and create entropy. Self-awareness gained through self-understanding along with social, managerial, and technical skills plays an important role in minimizing entropy around them (we will discuss the role of leaders in building a joyful organization in Chapter 10). The validity of this principle increases exponentially with every step up in the hierarchy.

Disease: Self-Centered Leadership

Pursue your private agenda using the means of the organization.

Description

Occasionally, leaders who are supposed to have a vision and be concerned about the organization take personal advantage of their positions. They promote themselves. They use the organization and their positions to increase their self-esteem, feed their egos, build their careers, and enhance their own wealth and prestige rather than adding as much value to the organization as possible. When employees perceive this kind of attitude in their managers, they become skeptical about fancy mission and values statements and tend to focus on their own needs.

Symptoms

• The leader continuously promotes himself or herself to such an extent that he or she does not even think of promoting or developing others, including successors.

• Lack of loyalty is more prevalent than pride, or even the sense of belongingness. If there is any loyalty, it is ridden by the concept of dependency and fear. For example, people in the lunchroom talk fearfully about the organization and about the leadership rather than with a sense of respect.

• People tend to have low self-esteem. Their view of themselves slowly goes awry. They are there because there is nowhere else to go.

During a training program I was conducting, participants complained bitterly about the ways of the organization and especially about the chief executive. I asked them with curiosity, "Why are you still here if you are so unhappy?" They replied, "We are here because we are tied with golden chains. We are slaves in this organization, but we earn good money here." "What does this statement say about you?" I asked. We left the topic to return to the training, but the question lingered. After some months, a participant called me with the news that he had resigned from the organization and moved to another firm. This time he made sure that the content of his job, the relationship with the chief executive, and his own decision-making power was wider and deeper. He negotiated autonomy upfront.

• There are unreasonably high salaries, bonuses, other benefits, and perks for people in high positions.

• There is a limited amount of trust among the people. Typically, the self-centered manager has a problem trusting others. A self-centered manager once explained to me: "If I don't keep a tight control, then I'm not sure what will happen. I have to carry the weight and the responsibility of the whole organization. I'm the only one who understands the vision; I'm the only one who knows how to run this organization, to reach this vision. I have to do everything. I keep an eye on everything, because otherwise it would not work." This lack of trust will be typical all across such organizations. The whole organization tends to be person centered, rather then vision centered.

- When succession is not planned properly or there is no systematic procedure for identifying and positioning a successor, there is usually political infighting among the potential successors. Their primary aspiration is to get into the position, not to fulfill the vision, but to fulfill their own personal agendas.
- The leader is the person who makes most of the decisions. The leadership function is identified with a person. Every decision has to come up to the leader's level.
- The vision in the organization is attributed to the leader rather than to the organization. People do not have a sense of owning the vision, which is identified with the person of the leader, and there is a tendency to avoid responsibility by pushing it up to the leader.
- In debates, the boss is always right, so people do not raise their voices.
- People are cautious and try to avoid contradicting their bosses.
- People talk negatively about their bosses if they feel they will not be caught.

Causes

- There is a belief that a leader should be strong and cannot be questioned or confronted. One of the reasons of the phenomenon "power corrupts" is that top managers, who cannot be questioned, confronted, or given honest feedback, lose sight of the reality of their self-image. Based on mostly positive and the lack of negative feedback, they start to think of themselves in unrealistically high terms, which may result in the series of behaviors and attitudes mentioned above.

Origins

- The genetic origin lies in the personality of the leader itself, which can be the result of anxiety arising from the unconscious lack of trust in himself or his strong narcissist tendencies. The founder sees the organization only as a means of satisfying her different needs: "I'm here to get money or fame out of my position in the organization." Where the entrepreneur is self-centered, the leaders of the organization also become self-centered because they follow this model. The leadership function is not visualized, but the leader is.
- The birth-related origin is that self-centered leadership develops out of centralization needed in a crisis at an early stage of the organization's life cycle. There are varieties of crises: financial, production, or high turnover related. For example, in the case of a substantial financial problem, it is necessary that the organization has a finance-oriented leader. If this leader is successful at the critical time, there is a tendency to credit and promote that person, and if he or she is not connected with the organization's goals, he or she can become self-centered. This individual is experienced in running the organization with a strong hand in a crisis. Little time is spent on decision making. If this situation lasts too long, employees tend to reject responsibility at lower levels and develop a variety of internal insecurities. People with internal insecurities tend to use the organization for their private agendas.
- The environmental origin is that, depending on the historic moment and the culture of the country, a certain kind of person-centered leadership is seen as the relevant one, reinforced by media. All over the world we find so-called "successful

Table 6.5
Self-Centered Leadership

Structure of Courses	Possible Courses	Possible Actions for Improvement
Personal/Leadership Related	1. A big-ego personality holds the top position. 2. Top executives consider the organization as their personal property and exploit it as such. 3. Managers believe that on the top you are always right and you have all the right to do whatever you want. 4. Their individual careers and financial advancement is the main focus of managers in key positions.	*Executive Coaching, Training Workshop, and/or Other:* • Use a strong external coach who can help to make the person at the top face the consequences of his or her leadership style and practices and take corrective steps. Help to be able to receive, even obtain critical feedback. • Develop real listening skills. • Help to be able to get satisfaction out of coaching and developing others and enjoying their successes. • Make an organizational diagnosis, including the dominant leadership styles and practices, and facilitate a reflective data feedback workshop. • Implement team coaching to create a safe environment for facing the situation; restructure the information and decision-making processes of the organization. • Remove the (self-centered) leader from the key position.

Structure of Courses	Possible Courses	Possible Actions for Improvement
Organizational, Operational	1. The organizational structure and procedures ensure that the top person has all the information and all the decision-making authority. The checks and balances for top positions are lacking.	*Coaching, Training Workshop, and/or Other:*
	2. Critical comments or negative feedback toward managers on the top is unacceptable, unprecedented, or rare, and, due to the lack of it, top managers tend to develop an unrealistic positive self-image.	• Restructure the current information and decision-making processes, delegating more to lower levels.
	3. In the prevailing culture, there is no practice of the following:	• Reconsider organizational structure and procedures to build in stronger checks and balances of managers in high positions.
	• upward feedback,	• Assess the current culture against the desired culture and the difference between the two. Create space where management and employees have a chance to reflect, conclude, and start to change.
	• asking questions, and	• Implement strong impact training for giving and receiving feedback, both positive and developmental, for all directions.
	• challenging or arguing with people in higher positions.	• Employ 360-degree feedback (ensuring anonymity) for top managers followed by personal coaching.
	4. The organization looks to the top leader as the savior of the company, but who eventually loses touch with reality. There is no channel for honest confrontation.	• Develop appropriate selection and promotion systems: a systematic assessment of potential appointees to a higher position, in particular, emphasis on their personalities. Select strong managers to key positions who have a participatory, open, challenging style.
	5. There is a lack of an appropriate selection and promotion system; the organization tends to select and promote "yes men."	

Table 6.5 (continued)

Structure of Courses	Possible Courses	Possible Actions for Improvement
External, Market Related	1. The culture favors and promotes celebrities and individual heroes. 2. Nepotism, an "old boys club" mentality, is common in the society. 3. By the nature of the given economy and corporate regulations people in the top position have almost unlimited power and influence with little or weak checking/control systems and regulations. 4. The local culture is predominantly authoritarian (with big power distance).	*Interventions:* • Create a structure and a culture that promotes teamwork, which recognizes team performance rather than just individuals. • Choose, promote, and empower (including providing a necessary power base) people who are not part of the old boys club.

organizations" that, upon inspection, show a high degree of corruption, where the top person turns out to be the main beneficiary.

This disease often occurs together with Organizational Paranoia and Joyless Organization.

A structured list of causes and possible actions for improvements for this disease can be seen in Table 6.5.

ORGANIZATIONS, LIKE MACHINES, NEED REGULAR MAINTENANCE

We began the discussion with borrowing the concept of entropy from physics in order to observe that organizational entropy will spontaneously increase without regular initiatives for improving efficiency. It is common knowledge that a machine needs periodic maintenance, in which you stop its operation, take it apart, and examine it closely to fix existing and prevent expected problems. It is not so widely accepted that groups need the same regular maintenance. Any group, including a management team, should stop periodically and remove itself from the daily operation to have a distant view of everyday problems in order to come up with more efficient ways of addressing them. The objective of this exercise is to take a broader and deeper look at how the organization tackles problems, as well as the way people actually work together, utilizing resources and their talents. This does not mean that improvements cannot occur during everyday operations. However, any important modification should take place in the context of the whole system. If we adjust something in one subsystem, that may create problems in others. If we do not consider the all-important aspects, we may fix something at one point, but create larger damage somewhere else. Developing a distant view is best done in a calm, settled atmosphere, away from the physical surroundings of everyday work. "Camp meetings" originate in the native American way of life. Native Americans had two ways of doing things. One was the running of everyday life, where they had their functions. The other was gathering around the campfire in a circle, listening to the others. This was the place where they decided about strategic issues: moving or staying, starting a war, etc. These camp meetings were good opportunities to reflect on the way they were operating, to arrive at new conclusions, and to apply them to everyday use.

Of course, suspending operations for this type of maintenance activity, because production is halted, looks like entropy in the short term. However, the investment made in reviewing processes, interactions, and relationships will clearly be beneficial and should contribute to smooth operation in the future, reducing overall organizational entropy. When different parts of the organization operate in a dysfunctional way, and crucial issues are neglected, consequences spread all over the organization, and more and more complex and expensive interventions are needed because the organization now has a higher level of entropy.

CHANGE MANAGEMENT AND ORGANIZATIONAL ENTROPY

Change programs by definition are supposed to improve efficiency by presumably making organizations better adapted to the environment, better able to meet challenges, and provide superior products for less. However, change processes absorb energy and increase entropy in the short term. Resistance against change is a source of additional entropy. That does not mean that resistance to change is unhealthy. If human beings did not resist change automatically, we would continuously modify ourselves for little or no reason, without ever reaching any stability. Resistance to change can be interpreted as a measure of expected benefits from the change, that is, time and resources invested into overcoming resistance compared to the expected efficiency gain from the investment. It is important to design the change process in such a way as to minimize resistance. While this book is not about managing change, we want to emphasize the crucial importance of professionally managing the change process. Changes shake the organization up, absorb a tremendous amount of energy, time, money, and eventually, as is often the case, fail to produce the expected long-term reduction of entropy.

When external changes take place at a faster pace, it becomes less and less possible to see a change process as a linear move from a starting point to a destination. A healthy organization absorbs the necessary information about changes from its environment, filters the information through the organization as fast as possible, and continuously adapts its operations based on the interpretation of the information. This way change is not a time-to-time linear process, but the nature of operation itself. When an organization is able to adopt this flexible culture, change will not be perceived anymore as a threat, either to the organization or the people of it, but as a natural way of life.

Centralization and decentralization represent two of the most typical reorganization processes. These seem to follow worldwide patterns; in the 1980s there was a decentralization cycle, then the 1990s were characterized by centralization. We have found that these periodic changes often had more to do with internal power struggles in the organization than efficiency improvement. Headquarters promote centralization, which strengthens their power position and command of resources. Once centralization has taken place, its weaknesses become obvious and then decentralization processes are initiated. In turn, the shortcomings of too much decentralization manifest themselves and the organization comes full circle. When employees do not share a vision, internal power struggles result in periodic reorganizations. This consumes a disproportionately large amount of energy and results in a higher level of entropy.

SIMULTANEOUSLY DEALING WITH LONG-TERM AND SHORT-TERM ISSUES

A healthy organization is concerned with minimizing entropy in the long term, not with increasing efficiency in the short term. It is necessary to expand energy on, for example, research and development, training or learning to improve processes, to raise competencies, and to reduce entropy in the long term.

Any system can fail and accidents happen all the time. You need a backup mechanism, so in case of a breakdown, operation can continue and losses can be limited. Backup mechanisms do not contribute directly to production; thus they may be viewed as entropy generators. Do not be fooled though: Devices that initially may seem to be creating entropy may reduce it in the long run, if they are sufficient for the purpose.

A modern chemical factory was built, with the latest technology and highly computerized systems. During a visit to the computer center, my host proudly announced that processes were so entirely automated that one person could continuously observe what was happening anywhere in the factory. To my surprise, the person controlling the indicators was dozing. Indeed, it was a tedious and seemingly monotonous task and difficult to expect one person to monitor the screens for eight hours without any interruption. One would have expected more diligent control over this dangerous process since somewhere something might go wrong when the person is dozing and too tired to observe the featureless process. These breaks in the observation did not show up in the log books though, the entries there always looked normal. "There is no need for an additional person there, with such a high level of automation," was my host's comment. About three years after my visit an explosion shook the factory. Part of it had to shut down for more than a year. I was invited back to participate in the investigation of the accident. The official examination concluded that it was due to the negligence of the person who was at the control. The decision of not wanting to add one more person to the controls appeared in a different light with hindsight.

A healthy person can keep both short-term and long-term issues in focus at the same time. We are concerned about not sacrificing today, but if we focus only on today, what we can do and how we feel tomorrow may be at risk. If we do not study, develop, and learn new skills, we may have fun today, but tomorrow we will not be able to do the things we wish to do. Keeping a healthy balance between long- and short-term objectives is equally important for any organization that would like to stay around for some time.

Even though this also seems to be a simple principle, we find that few organizations are able to maintain this balance. Some organizations are too concerned about the here and now; meeting the budget is their most important issue. They do not see that, for example, cutting too much from the marketing expenses costs future customers and thus market share. Some organizations are even ascetic trying to optimize daily operations, watching the smallest expenditure. They experience continuous suffering for the sake of the future.

The other way around is equally tricky. If we continuously look at the future, we see only mountains to climb. We do not let ourselves pause to enjoy the journey to the top. Once we reach the top, we find another hill. We continuously focus on the long-term future without letting ourselves enjoy the here and now. Although such an organization works with monumental ideas, it is unable to manage daily operations, secure resources, and work the process to reach them. These organizations tend to be dominated by "visionary personalities," and often a manager with a long-term focus has a hard time tolerating others who have a more pragmatic, operational view, and vice versa.

A healthy organization simultaneously considers and manages long- and short-range perspectives, neither overemphasizing the pragmatism and short-term issues, nor the vision and strategy and other long-term issues. People appreciate differences in perspective, and they capitalize on them, though they are aware of conflict among members with present and with future orientations. Instead of oppressing those who think differently, they cooperate to build on each other's strengths in order to bring added value to the organization.

The importance of long-term and short-term focus is different at different stages of the organization's life cycle. In the early stages of organizational life, the short-term focus of addressing immediate survival issues is very important. The practicalities in this stage are much more important than down the road, when the organization is larger and more stable. A young organization has to immediately solve financial issues, develop a system to hire and pay people, develop a system to supply products, and so forth. Once the organization is established, the special importance of practical tasks decreases.

Disease: Shortsightedness

Only the going itself is important, not the direction.

Description

Shortsightedness means that the organization has a short-term focus, similar to persons walking while looking in front of their feet and not realizing that they are walking toward the cliff edge. Organizations that suffer from shortsightedness say they are short of time, when ironically it is fire fighting that takes up most of their time. This is due to insufficient analysis of the situation, lack of learning from mistakes, and indecisiveness on the direction of the solution. They could have saved time and effort if they had a long-range focus as well, involving the right people at the right time in the decision-making process.

Symptoms
• Dealing with "everyday" issues takes up most of the energy of the organization.

- Top management spends most of its time identifying, checking, and controlling specific and detailed objectives.
- Little, if any, consideration of long-term effects is detectable.
- The organization fails to assess long-term trends in the market and/or new opportunities originating from changes in the environment. Shortsighted organizations do not have long-range plans; they do not use strategic planning. They hire consultants to develop strategy, and then they put their recommendations on the shelf.
- The organization tends to repeat mistakes time and time again because employees fail to see the underlying structure or pattern and they treat each problem as a separate problem to be tackled individually.
- Executives do not have a vision for the organization. Formally, because they had to, they may have a mission statement that they submitted to the board, but they do not refer to the vision. If you ask rank-and-file employees, they may not even know that a vision has been articulated.
- Lots of fire fighting goes on in a shortsighted organization, and there is a constant sense of crisis. All problems seem to be of the same magnitude.
- Shortsighted organizations typically do not invest in people's development. They may provide some pragmatic microtechnical training, but they do not tend to send their people to MBA courses or make any major investment in a consistent, well-designed training system. They are antilearning and antideveloping because they do not see the immediate impact or benefit for the organization.
- They favor practical departments that clearly add short-term value, such as operations, sales, finance, and do not respect marketing or strategic planning.
- Typical symptomatic language and sentences are "practical," "down to earth," "let's be realistic," "no nonsense," "this is a workplace," "focus only on your job," and "keep your heads down."
- Employees have a feeling that what they do is meaningless. They do not see the long-term reason for why they are there or what they are going to accomplish, taking a microview of things, of life, and of organizations.
- These organizations manage working capital well, but cannot handle longer-term money management or capital investment issues.

Causes

- Strong external pressure on the organization exists (which may come from the headquarters in the case of a multinational company or from the investors of venture capital companies and hedge funds) for immediate results. Rewards and punishments are tied to short-term results.
- There is a lack of stability or continuity in the life of the organization and in its management.
- People and managers move around too quickly in the organization, so their incentives are tied to short-term results and quick fixes.

Origins

- The genetic origin is that the executive management or the founder of the organization has a pragmatic, practical, "realistic" approach to life. They are typically

Table 6.6
Shortsightedness

Structure of Causes	Possible Causes	Possible Actions for Improvement
Personal, Leadership Related	1. The key executive team is made up of personalities who like to pay attention to details and short-term operational issues rather than strategic thinking. 2. Employees have short-term plans to stay with the company just to attain good references or learn practical skills. 3. There are more "manager-" than "leader-"type executives in the ranks. 4. Executives are rewarded for quickly achieved short-term results. 5. In subsidiaries of multinational companies expatriate members of the management team are stationed only for a short term in the given country, so they focus on short-term results.	*Executive Coaching, Training Workshop, and/or Other:* • Clarify manager and leadership roles within the organization and strengthen the leader-type behavior/skills. • Bring leaders to the management team who have long-range strategic thinking and ensure the necessary power base for them. • Ensure a reward system that recognizes both short- and long-term results. • Hire people for key positions who can be expected to stay with the company for a reasonable period of time; adjust the bonus system accordingly.
Organizational, Operational	1. There is high turnover; people spend only a short time with the organization, and they are interested only in fast solutions. 2. The performance evaluation system takes into consideration only the short-term measurable results.	*Coaching, Training Workshop, and/or Other:* • Develop an attractive vision, based on analyzing the changes in the environment and market trends. Involve a broad range of key employees to gain their longer-term commitment for the organization.

Structure of Causes	Possible Causes	Possible Actions for Improvement
	3. The ownership situation is in flux; it is not possible to plan ahead.	• Decrease high turnover by carrier development and changes in the performance evaluation system that will reward long-term results.
	4. There are too many changes too quickly; people do not trust the future.	
	5. Strategic planning and marketing are either not strong enough, or they do not exist.	• Change the training and education support system so that it includes long-term training support for employees.
	6. Immediate problems absorb all the energy of the organization; there is little time left for dealing with longer-term issues.	• Strengthen marketing and strategic planning by hiring new, competent people, adding resources, and communicating and positioning them better.
External, Market Related	1. The competitive pressure is so strong that it does not allow a focus on long-term issues.	*Interventions*
	2. Demand for the existing products is high.	• Assess potentially changing market trends; develop longer-term strategy by adding necessary resources if necessary.
	3. Owners are interested in a very fast return on their investment.	• Demonstrate the potential short-term benefits of long-term thinking.

"doers." Management does not believe that a medium- or longer-range shared vision is important to guide the organization and its people. They tend to appreciate people who are like them, speak their language, understand their issues, and tackle the type of problems they consider important. This way they promote a one-sided organization culture.

• The birth-related origin is that in an early, unstable, uncertain stage of the organizational life cycle, the organization employed a group of "doer"-type managers who took over and salvaged the company. They have become the heroes and role models in the organization even when different methods would have worked as well.

• The environmental origin is that during unstable social/economical circumstances, organizations tend to focus more on short-term success and survival, because they feel they cannot control or predict the long-term future of the organization.

This disease often occurs together with Customer Exploitation, Money Mania, and Insufficient Interaction with the Environment.

A structured list of causes and possible actions for improvements for this disease can be seen in Table 6.6.

Disease: Longsightedness

Thinking big is great, but following up is boring.

Description

A longsighted organization focuses on the future, ignoring everyday operations–related issues. It loves to deal with strategies, and visions, but fails to give adequate attention to frequently occurring problems. Detailed planning, pragmatic execution, and follow-up are rather weak in this organization.

Symptoms

• Significant resources are allocated to long-range planning, developing gigantic ideas, and strategic plans. Employees spend a lot of time in workshops and meetings related to strategy. They observe trends and build plans without adequately connecting these plans to the present and without developing action plans. They also do not address issues of how they can put these plans into practice or what they should do today and tomorrow to reach their vision five years from now. Ideas do not have roots in current reality.

• They let existing problems accumulate to a point where these problems become too large, too acute, and too costly to be solved.

• New projects are launched, but the organization loses interest and these remain incomplete. Instead, new ideas are developed, and resources are redirected.

• Longsighted organizations favor departments like strategic planning or marketing—departments that are related to their long-term vision. They neglect more

Table 6.7
Longsightedness

Structure of Causes	Possible Causes	Possible Actions for Improvement
Personal, Leadership Related	1. Many executives and employees are attracted to distant "revolutionary" objectives and are less interested in everyday activities. These executives appreciate a similar type thinking and promote people with a similar approach to management. 2. Discussing specific problems and short-term operational issues irritates impatient executives; they either ignore or avoid these discussions. 3. The nature of the organization's activity attracts visionary, innovative, future-oriented people (e.g., a mission-driven, not-for-profit organization). 4. There is no outside pressure on executives to produce short-term results.	*Executive Coaching, Training Workshop, and/or Other:* • Clarify manager and leadership roles within the organization and strengthen the pragmatic-/manager-type behavior/skills. • Bring leaders to the management team who have pragmatic, down-to-earth thinking, and ensure the necessary power bases for them. • Ensure a reward system that recognizes both short- and long-term results. • Break down longer-term goals of the executives into short-term milestones and check/reward the fulfillment of these.
Organizational, Operational	1. Resources are available and are used to develop long-term plans. 2. Half yearly or yearly performance review/ evaluation is lacking and there is no consequence of not meeting those.	*Coaching, Training Workshop, and/or Other:* • Use the existing vision to analyze the present internal and external situations and define concrete steps to be taken for achieving the

Table 6.7 (continued)

Structure of Causes	Possible Causes	Possible Actions for Improvement
	3. Introduce a general approach that favors long-term planning and visionary work. 4. Comparatively low compensation makes it easier to attract mission-driven individuals rather than real professionals with hands-on experiences.	objectives. Develop mechanisms for closely monitoring and supporting execution. • Regroup available resources so that organizational groups actually executing the vision also have proper rewards. • Analyze losses and costs of ignoring problems in execution on a daily basis, understand the consequences, and act on them. • Train in pragmatic day-to-day management skills, problem solving, and decision making. • Introduce a performance-evaluation system that includes both long-term and short-term goals and incentives.
External, Market Related	1. A good supply of investment capital or foundation money exists. 2. All players in the market segment are building a revolutionary, attractive, high-returns future.	*Interventions* • Emphasize a more realistic approach to the future, assess possible less beneficial impacts underlining the importance of execution on a daily basis. • Use more detailed feasibility studies before commitment to projects or investment.

practical, everyday operations, frontline people, sales, and so forth. People who work in these departments are treated as secondary citizens of the organization.

- Typical language in these organizations would be "do not get lost in details," "do not let yourself be bound to reality," and "use your imagination."
- Longsighted organizations can easily suffer from a cash crunch—they may have problems with short-term money management, liquidity, and cash flow.

Causes

- Substantial resources are available for the organization to develop and execute gigantic plans. There are charismatic, convincing visionary personalities in key positions who are able to attract big resources for the organization (for example, in the case of some foundations, organizations that have socially attractive missions).
- Departments and/or managers are not held accountable for measurable, tangible results.

Origins

- The origin of these causes is typically genetic. The founders, and most likely the selected successors, also have a long-term view and like to deal with long-term issues. They tend to appreciate people who have the same kind of attitude and skills and are partners in long-range planning, building visions, and gigantic plans. Most of the time they disregard people who are practical, pragmatic, realistic, and down to earth.
- The origin is birth-related if the organization was started with a substantial fund sufficient to mask the inefficiency of the operations.
- The environmental origin is that there is plenty of capital looking for an investment opportunity in the market. Investors are too eager and get too easily attracted to fancy, well-presented ideas without looking thoroughly to the details of the plan, execution circumstances, and feasibility studies.

This disease often occurs together with Insensitivity to Problems and Insufficient Value for Customers.

A structured list of causes and possible actions for improvements for this disease can be seen in Table 6.7.

PRACTICING ORGANIZATIONAL LEARNING

Every living organism consistently receives and processes information from the environment and goes through a learning process in order to adapt to change. Sufficient learning ensures adaptation, growth, and survival in changing circumstances.

It is important for an individual and for an organization to try out new things and to develop by learning from these experiments. Learning is becoming aware of what is happening. Healthy, stable individuals can afford to experiment and fail because they are not afraid that their self-esteem will collapse if they are seen making a mistake. The precondition of experimenting is being allowed to fail. A learning organization takes risks willingly and the lack of risk taking is a sign of ill-health. If individuals are punished, they naturally conclude that failing is bad and then they perform only within the safe zone, not venturing to extend their skills and potential.

The chief executive of a large multinational company was famous nationwide, and widely considered the dynamo behind the success of the organization. During a workshop for the executive management of this company, he dominated the discussions constantly. It was a formidable performance. He showed good judgment, intelligence, keenness, and energy. He kept coming up with new ideas. Other executives found it hard to throw in a word edgewise. When they tried, he ridiculed and humiliated them. After one of these letdowns I asked him, "It is wonderful that you have all these ideas. Why do you need these bright people? Everybody is highly intelligent here, yet every idea is coming from you. You waste a lot of resources, even second- or third-class people would be able to carry out your ideas." This caused considerable shock and disbelief, so we conducted a role-playing game of an actual executive meeting. During the role-play the others opened up and admitted to being afraid of risk taking in his presence. Based on this learning, the group created a risk clearing house to encourage everybody to take a certain amount of risk specified in financial terms, independent of the chief executive. A new culture started to spread around the organization and junior employees felt better as a result.

   While learning is essential for survival, the fear of failure makes experimenting look like deviance, prompting a vicious circle of self-protection and incidentally prevents learning. The real question, however, is not whether we succeed or fail in certain situations, but what we do with the success or failure. If you stop, reflect, draw a conclusion, and build this learning into your future way of operation, even failure can be very fruitful. Success is also more productive if you analyze why you succeeded in given circumstances.
   Change means danger—it gives rise to fear. Fear is a double-edged sword. It is helpful in that it makes us plan and be careful; our very survival depends on fear. On the other hand, if our fear is so strong that we do not want to even experiment, we will not grow. Willingness to take risks is a sign of health.
   Still, comparatively few people like to take risks and learn. When we talk about creating a learning organization we are not talking about creating chaos by promoting a learning atmosphere. Those who like to take risks also grab opportunities. Their learning needs to be disseminated to the relevant parts of the system in order to create a learning organization.
   Belief systems need to be shaken from time to time for learning to take place. Instead of achieving learning by training, sometimes you can create an atmosphere promoting learning. Training means we know what to teach, and the program is evaluated in terms of objectives, such as increase in the desired skill. Creating learning means facilitating the environment in which learning can take place.

For one of our clients we created little incubators for learning. We selected reading materials and encouraged participants to consider and question whatever they had read. This became increasingly stimulating when the reading did not agree with participants' experiences. It forced them to analyze their experiences, treating reading materials only as a trigger for thoughts. What they had to trust increasingly was their own experience and ability to interpret it. From time to time, participants of this training still come together to confront experiences with readings.

As we discussed in Chapter 4 about the needs of the individual, in order to ensure continuous development, regardless of age, you have to put yourself in situations that you have never experienced before, and for which you do not have a ready set of behavior patterns. You have to work it out. Working out how to handle a new situation brings development and growth, and a healthy organization encourages its members to enter new situations. For example, rotating people among departments and positions may promote learning and growth.

Learning is not just experimenting and coming to conclusions. For example, if we learn to swim, it does not just mean we can float in water. A stage must come when swimming is automatic. That means we have mastered the various strokes enough to make it routine. In an organization, learning is not only developing conclusions, but creating opportunities for developing adequate skills, which lead to the sense of joy. One test of whether learning has taken place is if the new activity has already become the source of joy or not. Without experiencing joy from what you learn, this process becomes boring and, consequently, much less attractive.

Consultants advise that organizations should stick to their core competencies. From an early age, a child's aptitude is tested in various ways, after which it is categorized accordingly to fields of study. As a result, we become adults without being aware of the multifaceted aptitudes we possess. We do not put ourselves into new situations; we do not learn. In our view, focusing on organizational core competency has similar dangers. Core competencies are based on belief systems in corporations, and, from time to time, it is necessary to reexamine if the competency is still relevant or if something new is needed. The organization may not learn about the new competency unless this is consciously performed. Core competency is necessary, but putting oneself into a box of competency is similar to wearing blinders; an organization that wears blinders has no opportunity to develop. We will define the concept of development later, but to summarize here, development is having multiple exercisable choices rather than one alternative defined by any authority, be it mother, father, psychologist, or boss.

Learning is also learning about self, as we discussed in the section about feedback. In a fear-ridden organization, you are afraid to give feedback because you may get feedback in return that you may not want to hear. Where there is fear, there is no consideration of feedback and that is where learning about the self stops. In an organization where there is openness, learning takes place.

Information-sharing systems, cross-functional forums, and idea marketplaces facilitate capitalizing on useful learning. If there is a geographical barrier between different parts of the organization, organized trips could take place. We would like to emphasize that these forums are not just for executives, but for representatives of all groups to develop relationships and to break down walls between departments and organizational subsystems that limit learning.

Employees usually attend various training programs. When they come back, they share their experiences with other people who did not have the opportunity to go. It is worthwhile to call employees from different parts of the organization to attend training together. In addition to developing skills, they have a secondary benefit of knowing each other as individuals, learning from each other's experiences over a beer or during breaks. Developing informal relationships, which they can use during their work, helps to develop empathy that results in a willingness to assist when the need arises. In a healthy organization, people have a chance to share experiences with other people in the organization.

Disease: Risk Avoidance

Risk Avoidance is the fear of failure, avoiding taking on new challenges and experimenting with new things.

Description

In this kind of organization, people are unwilling to experiment and take risks because they are afraid that they will fail and then be punished for failure. Fear of failure leads to avoiding challenges and experimenting. If you stop trying out new things, you freeze your potential of learning and growth. This is why we consider Risk Avoidance a disease. A risk-avoiding culture can be best recognized by the limited decision-making autonomy given to individuals.

Symptoms
- Over a substantial period of time very few things are initiated: no new processes, policies, research, exploration of market opportunities, or innovation.
- Research and development (R&D) is concerned with fine-tuning previous models rather than coming up with new, creative ideas.
- Experimentation is exclusively a task of R&D and the rest of the organization is not allowed to try out new things.
- If an unknown task is given, people tend to do very thorough planning, analysis, and information gathering, so there will be no problems with the execution of the task. For this period of preparation an unreasonable amount of time is spent.

- If people have a chance to prove that the new task is not a good idea they will certainly do so.
- Decisions on any issue that is perceived as risky—like investments—are delayed or postponed.
- There is ongoing bargaining about the targets; the employees responsible to meet those numbers are trying to minimize the risk of not meeting them.
- There is a culture of resistance to trying out anything new or different than what is usual to people and the organization. "Never leave the old path for a new, undiscovered one" is the philosophy. The immediate reaction to change is denial.
- In risk-avoiding organizations weaknesses are emphasized rather than strengths. In other words, employees are more aware of their weaknesses than their opportunities, resources, or strengths. Targets are typically met, but expectations are only mediocre.
- People try to avoid responsibilities by hiding behind committees or authorities, getting as many signatures as possible, in order to cover themselves in case something goes wrong.

Causes

- The most typical cause of all these symptoms is that more emphasis is laid on problems and negative feedback than on strengths and positive feedback. People receive a yearly evaluation instead of spending time regularly on what they have done right, accomplishments, or special tasks performed. During the feedback session they hear about the unperformed tasks and things that went wrong. If something went wrong it is likely that managers use a language of blaming. Those who are held responsible go through an emotional trauma, are sometimes removed from their positions, or are informally stigmatized. After seeing this happen to other employees of the organization, people are careful not to take up risky tasks, wanting to avoid similar punishment or even the feeling of insecurity. One way to secure their jobs is to avoid being held responsible for any problems. They lower their ambitions and targets to ensure the accomplishment.
- Another potential cause could be that top management focuses on managing the daily business rather than on being entrepreneurial. Being interested in the growth and development of the organization would imply discovering new areas, new business opportunities, and accepting risks and possible losses along the way. Management is more concerned about potential losses than the potential profit and gains it might get by entering unknown waters.

Origins

- The genetic origin is that starting an organization itself holds a certain amount of risk. If founders fear that things may not work out, they want to take no unnecessary risks. This will result in planting the seed of a risk-avoidance culture. Even after the founder has gone, this behavior still characterizes the organization.
- The birth-related origin is that at an early age this organization has bet incorrectly in a risky situation, a decision that has fundamentally weakened the organization. As a result, it has barely survived, and the event has had crucial negative consequences.

Table 6.8
Risk Avoidance

Structure of Causes	Possible Causes	Possible Actions for Improvements
Personal Leadership Related	1. In the case of success, there is no reward; in the case of mistake or failure, there is blame. A critical, not positive, leadership style exists. 2. Failure while trying out a new thing is not tolerated; there are negative consequences. 3. There is not enough autonomy. 4. Fear of losing face exists. Lack of success equals shame. 5. Previously there was a strong "no leeway for even the slightest failure" attitude, and this impacts the present culture. 6. Whenever trying anything new, executives look for guarantees such as overinsurance.	*Executive Coaching, Training Workshop, and/or Other:* • Reflect on personal leadership style, its consequences on others, and take steps for improvement. • Implement leadership development, delegation training, and empowerment areas. • Train on achievement motivation and intelligent risk taking. • Hire and promote executives who can be role models for performance orientation, an entrepreneurial attitude, positive thinking, creativity, or educated risk taking. • Identify and implement ways for generating and using new ideas (e.g., brainstorming sessions, idea collection boxes, and so forth).
Organizational, Operational	1. A fear exists that the cost of "mistakes" is not affordable. 2. Innovation acceptance requires immediate or very short-term returns.	*Coaching, Training Workshop, and/or Other:* • Assess the scenario of not taking any risks at all; if the expected value of the outcome is

154

Structure of Causes	Possible Causes	Possible Actions for Improvements
	3. The performance-evaluation system does not encourage risk taking. 4. Some failures in the past were glossed over.	less than taking the risk, then create the financial conditions for risk taking. • Revisit the real practiced values in the every-day operation and make intelligent risk taking part of it. • Include risk-related objectives in the performance-management system so they can be treated as a learning situation. • Create an internal risk fund that is awarded based on internal applications. • Implement an "Innovation of the Year" award in different categories, such as in sales, technology, operations, and so forth. • Implement the "Mistake of the Year" award, which identifies the ones from which the most was learned and is also based on ones that cause the biggest changes.
External, Market Related	1. There is a lack of competitive situations and environmental challenges. 2. The broader culture does not appreciate outstanding achievements and is very critical of failures. Loosing face is to be avoided at all costs.	*Interventions* ♦ Demonstrate the forthcoming danger of increasing competition, changes, and development in the industry. Create a sense of urgency.

This has become an imprint in the memory of the organization and explains why the organization avoids risks.

• The environmental origin is that when the broader society or culture is typically risk avoiding or does not appreciate people with different skills, who perhaps outperform others, it creates a culture where people try to avoid being different. This was the norm in the socialist societies, where similarities among individuals, their skills, and circumstances were emphasized and differences were not welcomed. These cultures promoted mediocrity rather than outstanding personal accomplishments.

A certain type of envy can also contribute to this kind of organizational culture. If people suffer negative consequences, discrimination, and social punishment due to being envied by others, then risk taking and higher accomplishments stop being attractive options. People do not feel motivated and encouraged to make an extra effort to achieve higher accomplishments and do not take risks. In a society where people are ridiculed for failures, people will want to avoid risk. When the socialization process, through education and the school system, is focused on correcting shortcomings and weaknesses of children, rather than searching for strengths, risk-avoiding behavior will probably be more prevalent. Where the uniqueness of the individual is encouraged and teachers are trained to find the strengths of children, they learn to stand out and each success will be celebrated. Even if they have failed, they are appreciated because they take risks. In this type of culture, people openly speak about the numerous failed attempts in starting an enterprise before they finally succeed.

This disease often occurs together with Decision Paralysis, Organization Paranoia, Bureaucracy, Stagnation, and Tunnel Vision.

A structured list of causes and possible actions for improvements for this disease can be seen in Table 6.8.

CHAPTER 7

Satisfied Customers

What do customers give to any organization? How do customers of a healthy organization feel and what generates that feeling? What is the role of customer feedback in improving quality, lowering costs, and providing even better value? How does the culture of extracting value from being members of an organization relate to adding value to the customer? Is this a conflict systematically built into any organization?

AN ORGANIZATION EITHER HAS EXTERNAL CUSTOMERS OR IT DOES NOT EXIST

Customers play a special role in the life of an organization. Through the act of buying or obtaining the product they legitimize the existence of the organization and provide the resources necessary to meet the other two fundamental objectives—the economical needs of the organization and employees' needs—on an ongoing basis. If there are no customers, resources eventually dry up, or, in the case of not-for-profit organizations, sponsors reevaluate the cause as not worth funding. It is the customers' want of a product or service that makes an organization valuable, whether business or not for profit.

A healthy organization therefore is continuously concerned about providing value to its customers. This happens, as we saw in the previous chapter, neither at any price nor by requiring unreasonable efforts from employees, but by balancing all three fundamental considerations.

CUSTOMERS ARE OUR PARTNERS

In order to provide great customer value, a healthy organization treats customers as stakeholders, soliciting their feedback and applying it to the development, production, and delivery processes. We know organizations where customers regularly participate in meetings to express their views, and their competence and knowledge are tapped regularly in the value creation process. Direct contact with customers not only results in a better understanding of the customer's needs, but also improves morale. In a healthy organization, communication to customers—publicity and advertising—is not seen as a process of seduction, but as providing information and initiating dialogue. Guarantees are seen not only as being legally binding, but as a moral obligation.

We bought a refrigerator. When it was delivered and installed, the representatives of the distributor and service provider encouraged us to keep in touch with them. "Consult us about the refrigerator whenever you feel the need to, not just as a last resort. We will gladly replace the unit at any time." As it happens we have never needed any help with the refrigerator, but we already have purchased several more appliances from the same distributor.

By involving the customer, transactions are likely to become the foundation of a win-win relationship; customers develop an attachment to the organization and return to it repeatedly. To summarize, our second criterion for organizational health is as follows: A healthy organization provides an excellent product at a competitive price and a great value to its customers.

Since satisfying customers is one of the fundamental objectives, it is necessary that organizations constantly strive to make the value of their product attractive to customers. They can do so in many ways, by improving quality, lowering costs, and, of course, by treating the customer with respect. When customers are treated with respect, they feel that they matter and perceive that they receive a customized product or service.

Some years ago, a pharmaceutical company commissioned us to develop training programs for medical representatives. We started with assessing how they performed their functions and what they learnt in training programs. We found that the existing programs taught representatives to behave exactly the same way with every client. They received instructions down to how to hold the brochure, how to talk, and how to get out of the doctor's office in ten minutes. When I asked the training officer why the training concentrated on specific behavior instead of skills, he said, "Doctors have little time, representatives have little time, and doctors don't like spending time with representatives, because the patients are waiting outside." Contrarily, research as well as our instincts indicated that doctors actually prefer medical representatives who understand the requirements of the doctors and personalize their approach accordingly. Statistics also showed that doctors prescribe medications more often produced by companies whose representatives personalize their approach. Try as I might, the training officer was not convinced. Not long after this, we agreed to introduce a new training program for the representatives of a different pharmaceutical company. This program included a session on how to build a relationship with a potential customer. After the training, representatives developed their own individual approaches to each of their customers. A few years later, reviewing results at both training centers, we found that sales targets in the second company were significantly higher than in the first. Curious about such a gap between the two groups, we interviewed the representatives and the doctors. The representatives overwhelmingly felt better about providing personalized service. "I can relate to my job as a person. I experience less stress during work." Doctors reported that "no matter how good their technical skills were, if I felt that a sales representative behaved in a preprogrammed way, I suspected I was being manipulated. If the product was substitutable, I preferred to purchase it somewhere else."

Services provided by doctors, consultants, and architects, for example, are more conducive to a considerable time investment into specifying client requirements than others. Occasionally this effort leads even to convincing the customer that he or she does not need the particular service. These professionals learned through the faster feedback loop that treating customers as partners gives them the feeling that they matter, and the professionals can satisfy their customers only by managing their expectations.

Defining the scope of a consulting project is notoriously undermined by tensions between perceived interests. Organizations suffering, for example, from a conflict-ridden climate, often invite training firms to run a conflict management program. There are two ways to reply to this request. A servile organization may answer: "Sure we are delighted to undertake the assignment, we have significant experience in designing such a program, and it will be successful." However, to address the root causes of the problem requires more than satisfying the immediate apparent need of developing conflict management skills. If the prospective client's objective is to address the problems, the consultant would do better to discuss the structural aspects of those conflicts such as contradicting bonus structures or lack of role clarification. Training could be a useful tool in helping the organization to manage conflicts constructively, but by itself, it won't solve problems. If the consulting firm is healthy, it would investigate the origin of the problem and provide a solution accordingly, regardless of the size of the contract.

What do we mean when we say that customers like to receive personalized service? In general, personalized service is simply behaving as a human being and considering the customer as a human being. Let us explain through an example: When traveling by plane, we may choose to fly economy or business class. We pay a higher price for the latter than for the former, and, depending on which one we chose, we expect different levels of service and personal attention. However, different expectations for the service level do not mean passengers expect less care and a different attitude from the attendants and crew in economy class than in business. It should not mean that economy-class passengers get substandard service at the level for which they paid. Personalized service naturally manifests in different ways in different markets.

I was teaching at UCLA, when one day I noticed that my colleague was in a really bad mood. "This is just not my day," he said gloomily. To cheer him up, I suggested that we go out for dinner. At the restaurant, a very pleasant waiter was serving us. It was not that he spent more time with us than with other guests, or more than other waiters would have, it was the way he talked and listened to us, which made us feel important as guests. That was just what we needed, to lighten up. We chatted with him with pleasure, and eventually I mentioned in the conversation that I taught a course on leadership. He was very interested in the topic. As it turned out, he was a part-time student in the school. He ended up asking whether he could join the class, right there in the restaurant, between serving our main course and dessert. The class was over-crowded as it was, but I made sure he was included. He went beyond the "should" type of behavior as our waiter, and he received similar attention from me.

ADDING VALUE BY RECEIVING VALUE

Let us examine the process of adding value in order to understand the con-sequences of customer interaction dynamics on the employees of the organi-zation. Value is created or added whenever a product or service provides greater utility, becomes more attractive by quality and price, than it originally was before it was "worked on" by the organization.

For most people, the main purpose of joining an organization is not to add value but exactly the opposite, to receive value. Employees focus on how to extract the most value from the organization, a value derived from fulfilling their own needs. It is everybody's subjective judgment what values they are seeking. Most people want to get monetary compensation because with money they can buy value to satisfy their needs. People desire other values as well. They may like to be part of a good cohesive team because they value people's company. If power has value for them, being influential and having an impact on others is what they want. In this case, they will get value from being in a position where they can exercise influence. They may like to be in a position where they can unleash their creativity and make their achieve-ments valuable for the organization. Paradoxically, basic problems in organi-zations originate from people focusing on the value they want to get rather than what they can add. If this culture prevails in the organization, it becomes exploitative. All the members exploit the organization and its resources in order to get the maximum value for themselves.

Contrast this with the win-win situation of getting value through adding value. We have said that when employees try to overcome organizational dis-eases and share the vision of the organization, they get satisfaction from con-tributing to the creation of a product or service by using their best talents. When they feel that their contribution made a difference, they feel that they matter. Feeling appreciated, they get value in the form of increased self-worth by adding value. They do not see it as two separate actions. They do not perceive that they have to sacrifice their freedom for adding value, and they still get their paychecks, too. Adding value becomes the natural way of life. It is great for customers, and, of course, when this actually happens, employees are closer to experiencing joy from work.

When we talk about the principle of value addition, we apply it to all customers, not just external ones, but internal ones, too. If employees are aware of the value they add to their internal customers, the organization operates more efficiently. Value-chain meetings help to clarify how a product goes through the organization and how the different work stages add, or do not add, value.

TAKING RESPONSIBILITY FOR CUSTOMERS' PROBLEMS

A typical sign of being aware of customer needs is when employees attribute importance to what they do and take pride in the product. They are happy when they get positive feedback from the customers, sorry when the feedback is negative, and work hard to correct problems leading to customer dissatisfaction. These employees take the responsibility for customer problems, understand what the customer needs, and go beyond the call of duty to clarify the need, solve the problem, and ensure that it does not happen again. This behavior should not be confused with the attitude expressed by the servile organization, where customer complaints are compensated without understanding the need and considering other related aspects of this action.

Pride originates in the mind-set of key players. If they would like the organization to be identified as an excellent provider of the product or service, it is likely that they will initiate a self-fulfilling prophecy.

An entrepreneur started a boiler manufacturing company. He had a partner who was very quality conscious, who supervised all technical issues, while the entrepreneur focused on the business aspects of the enterprise. Their company sold most of its boilers to large hospitals. It was a highly cyclical business: The government's financial year is from April to March; consequently most of the boiler sales happened in March to utilize the remaining current year budgets. In February, the partner of the founder suddenly had to travel abroad to fulfill a personal obligation. While he was away, the company delivered a large number of boilers, as it did every year. In about a month or so after returning to India, the partner started to receive phone calls from distressed hospital officials: "Our new boiler leaks steam." He was shocked. He personally supervised quality, and until then boilers delivered by the company had operated faultlessly. He decided to visit the hospitals where the calls came from and examine the boilers one by one. He found the culprit in a small hole on the body of each boiler from which the steam was leaking. The holes were painted on, so as not to be seen by the customers! He was outraged. Before more complaints poured in, he ordered his staff to visit all the recent customers. He took back the boilers at great expense—he had to open an additional line of credit with the bank to finance this recall. He fought with the founder, who disagreed with the measure. He believed very firmly that what the company delivers to customers has to be flawless quality. The founder, on the other hand, had a strong belief about how the company should spend money, or rather, how it should economize and not spend too much. On this occasion these values inevitably and irreconcilably clashed. Their partnership was terminated.

Competition in a buyers' market stimulates organizations to serve the customer better. For a healthy organization, competition is not a hurdle but an opportunity to focus on customer value. When the customer is demanding quality, timely delivery, and competitive price, it has a similar effect that exercising has on people—it makes them healthier. In a competitive market, organizations are forced to keep their focus on the customer value and so become healthier by reducing costs and better matching the customer's needs. In a monopolistic market, the focus shifts to the various needs of the organization and its members.

Increasingly, healthy organizations rely not only on market events to extrapolate underlying customer preferences, but customize their products and services by understanding the individual customer's needs and preferences before purchasing takes place. Using one-to-one marketing methods is a good example. Technology makes individual customer data readily available and enables the organization to tailor a product to the individual customer. Understanding customer data requires an initial investment and possibly increases the cost of operation, but over time costs decrease by improved processes and lower marketing expenses, for example, and revenues increase as more customers walk in through the organization's door.

A healthy organization extends this approach to the purchasing-supplying relationships. Vendors and buyers mutually respect each other. Both parties consider transactions mutually beneficial. A perception by the purchaser that "what I get is worthwhile buying, *and* it is exactly what I need," and one by the vendor that "what I provide is worthwhile receiving, and I receive a reasonable compensation for it" provide a much sought-after stability to such relationships. The objective of the purchasing process is not operating purchasing transactions, but interactively developing these perceptions.

Accumulating customer complaints or a lower-than-expected sales volume indicates the existence of acute organizational diseases, although not always necessarily limited to customer-related ones.

A high-profile e-tailer started operations during the fall of 1999. The founders and their story was a favorite with the media, making the name of the company well known before it spent a cent on advertising. The enterprise had the support of prestigious venture capital firms. Expectations about the future were high the day the Web site was launched but dropped rapidly. The first week's number of visitors was lower than expected, and so were the second, third, and fourth weeks' numbers. The executives were engaged in endless rounds of discussions about why this happened and how could it be changed. They extended the targeted range of customers, added new products to the site, then changed the target group completely and then finally changed the definition of product. The software team could barely keep up with the changing tasks and priorities. Customer service followed a close second, struggling for the attention of management to solve and report complaints and issues. Sales stayed low, and customers kept complaining that the site was too difficult to use. Morale started to tangibly sink: Employees went from the euphoric identification with the vision to the daily struggle with crisis. Several critical months had passed before executives started to question the business model and the value the company actually provided to customers. By that time, however, the market's increasingly cynical view of e-tailers did not allow even a few months for identifying and providing the right value for customers.

As we discussed in Chapter 3 about balance, when an organization ignores customer interests by putting unwarranted emphasis on financial and/or employee needs or overemphasizes them in its operation at the expense of financial or employee needs, it suffers to some degree from the Customer Exploitation or Customer Servility Diseases. In an organization suffering from Customer Exploitation, members perceive customers primarily as an income source, a means to an end. This attitude results in an abusive approach to working relationships, serving only the overall goal of getting rich quick. When this culture predominates, it is likely that the exploitative approach is not limited to customers, but extended to other stakeholders as well. Let us summarize the philosophy of the organization suffering from customer exploitation as follows: "It is the customers' responsibility to fight for the value they need. Let us gain the most, while we give the least we can get by with." The opposite disease of Customer Exploitation is Servility, focusing on customer needs at the expense of the organization's financial needs and/or the employees' needs. The extreme philosophy of such a slavish organization can be summarized as follows: "Never confront a customer, never turn down any business, no matter what it takes."

Customers are traditionally fussy. They will come only if they perceive that they get value through the consumption of the product or service. Since finding the right combination of utility and price in order to provide great value is always a trial-and-error process, in time, most organizations are likely to suffer from some degree of Insufficient Value for Customers disease.

Disease: Insufficient Value for Customers

If only customers understood that they need our product badly.

Description

An organization suffering from this disease has few customers. This disease can appear temporarily in the start-up phase, when the organization is still experimenting with the product design. It could also prevail after the introduction of a revolutionary product, for which the demand is still latent. It could take place anytime when customer requirements or technology changes sufficiently. The process of matching product features, quality, price, and experience to meet customer requirements, while satisfying other fundamental objectives of the organization, is, as was pointed out earlier, a trial-and-error process. Insufficient Value for Customers can also characterize any organization that has an effective monopoly and thus lacks any incentive to go through this trial-and-error process.

Symptoms

- An insignificant number of customers purchase the product or service. The number of customers is not sufficient to bring in enough revenue to maintain the going concern; adaptation is not growing at the expected rate. In the case of a monopoly, customers are forced to purchase the product and have no alternative supply from which to buy.
- The marketing expenditure is comparatively lower than the industry average.
- The return on marketing and advertising is not measured, and information on customer acquisition is not utilized.
- The organization does not actively utilize customer feedback in its processes. Operations is unaware of, or ignores, user issues. Similarly, instead of addressing user issues, operations personalize every sale, altering the product in such a way that it changes the business model.
- If the product is revolutionary, there is not sufficient customer testing involved during the development.
- Product development focuses on the idea or technology, and so forth, rather than on understanding demand first.
- Customers' comments are regarded as expressions of ignorance or lack of information on their part rather than as tools useful in serving them better.
- Departments fight for legitimizing their efforts and gaining recognition of their specialized expertise, but a lack of customers decreases their ability to achieve either.
- The technical, creative, and research and development (R&D) departments have higher prestige, bigger budgets, and more decision-making power than other departments in the organization. At the same time, information about their work may be withheld or kept completely secret.
- During executive meetings, substantial time is spent on "playing with the product" and its technical details, and less time on the expressed need of the customer, the business model, or management issues.

Causes

- There is simply no demand for the product or service. Customers do not perceive any value and are unwilling to pay for it.
- There is no demand for the product or service in its existing format. The value equation has to be significantly altered to meet the existing demand.
- There is only latent demand for the product and customers need to be educated to perceive its value. Unfortunately, it is only with hindsight that the cause can be ascertained, at which point intervention may very well be too late.
- Employees and executives are convinced that they know better than the customer. This conviction is different from understanding customer needs in that it is not a

Table 7.1
Insufficient Value for Customers

Structure of Causes	Possible Causes	Possible Actions for Improvement
Personal Leadership Related	1. Key members of the management are predominantly technical/product oriented and have little interest in marketing and customer needs. 2. Some dominant members of the management team have a vested interest in pursuing the introduction of certain product to the market, regardless whether there is sufficient market information. 3. Lack of sufficient knowledge or deep suspicion for marketing research exists among the management; hence product development works without a good understanding of the market.	*Executive Coaching, Training Workshop, and/or Other:* • Provide training to make management understand the importance of different marketing tools in the pursuit of company strategy and in the process of product development. • For the same reason, organize a study tour and attend conferences, which provide opportunities to learn the best practices. • Bring fresh blood into the management team, which would bring a healthier balance and respect among the different functions. • Implement job rotation within the management team to provide new perspectives on the market and the product.
Organizational, Operational	1. Research and product development are working in isolation in an ivory tower without knowing what the market really needs or is ready to pay for. 2. Both market research and promotion are weak in the organization, so they do not know what the market needs and they do	*Coaching, Training Workshop, and/or Other:* • Provide "Marketing for non-Marketing Managers" training (in particular, for R&D)—this helps them to understand its role and its vital importance to company success.

Table 7.1 (continued)

Structure of Causes	Possible Causes	Possible Actions for Improvement
	not promote their products well enough either.	• Implement programs in customer orientation that will develop respect and understanding toward customer needs.
	3. There is low respect for customers. Members of the organization consider themselves experts and look down on customers who "do not even understand what they need to buy." The attributed importance of product development and technology is out of proportion, while information from users/customers and the market is ignored.	• Provide cross-functional programs for R&D and marketing in order to ■ Improve the understanding of the importance of each others' functions, ■ Institutionalize effective information flow among the respective departments, and ■ Identify joint responsibilities and processes to make them work in everyday life.
	4. In the case of multinationals, product development is done or controlled from abroad; therefore, marketing conforms to the international standard and disregards local demand.	• Organize meetings with a selected group of customers to get firsthand feedback.
	5. Operations is optimized for the organization, not for consideration of the needs of the customer.	• Develop a joint incentives system for marketing and R&D.
	6. A customer-feedback process is not established or integrated into other processes in the organization and such information is lost.	• Implement job rotation between marketing and R&D.
	7. The different areas of the organization are working separately with minimal	• Bring in experts and professionals from headquarters to assess and experience local market conditions.

Structure of Causes	Possible Causes	Possible Actions for Improvement
	interaction. There is no culture of listening to other departments.	
External, Market Related	1. There is some sort of monopolistic situation in the market, so the customers reluctantly have to buy the product or services even if this is not what they really want. 2. There is plenty of free capital in the market for investment, and certain industries are seen as having great prospects without well-grounded reasons.	*Interventions:* • Project the arrival of competition and market liberalization and capital shortage. Help the organization to become more customer oriented, improve product development, and improve marketing activity.

dynamic effort to understand customer needs, but a static conviction of the existing product's utility.

- There is too much internal and technical focus in the organization ("introverted organization").

Origins

- The genetic origin is that in the case of a start-up founders are stuck with the original idea, or the product is based on their personal taste and personality, so they are unable to modify it based on customer feedback. Key people are convinced of the product fulfilling the needs of the customer, and they commit personally to fulfill the need they perceive. They enjoy the role of dispersing their personal taste and values, or the celebrity role they play as founders. They focus on identifying the need and the product and in time stop paying attention to the actual realization of the product and business model (or do not have the skills to do so), emphasizing instead their achievement in developing the organization, obtaining the funding, the scientific discovery, or style statement behind the product.

- The birth-related origin is that developing the product captured such a significant portion of the resources available at the founding of the organization that the functional expertise which could have evaluated customer concerns and needs was never developed.

- The environmental origin is that it is very easy to obtain the basic resources for the kind of activity the organization is pursuing, and the environment is tolerant of the organization not meeting expectations. This could be the microenvironment inside a bigger organization, or a segment of the market in general. In the case of a monopoly, regulation and/or the limited nature of resources makes the organization a distributor with no incentive to observe customer needs.

This disease often occurs together with Longsightedness, Insufficient Interaction with the Environment, Self-Centered Leader, and Stagnation.

A structured list of causes and possible actions for improvements for this disease can be seen in Table 7.1.

CHAPTER 8

Growth and Development

What is the difference between growth and development? Why are both stagnation and unsustainable growth the sign of ill-health? What is the most sensitive indicator of growth and development in an organization? What happens when founders or key executives cannot keep up with the demand to grow?

AMBITION TO GROW AND DEVELOP IS NECESSARY FOR HEALTH

Growth means that an organization's resources are increasing; thus, it is able to apply more resources toward its purpose and impact a larger environment. Growth is usually measured by the change of revenue, or market share. Development, on the other hand, requires changes in the organization's perception of its environment. When the perspective enlarges, a variety of alternatives appear and development means that an organization can handle these increasingly complex situations. Development comprises three phases: becoming aware of new choices, acquiring the resources or skills to make those choices exercisable, and having the freedom to exercise them. In this sense, development is a way of operation, allowing innovation to pop up everywhere in the organization and treating it in a systematic way so the right ones become usable. Development is usually indicated by signs such as widening the product range or the customer base and investment into new areas and innovations.

Growth and development have an asymmetrical relationship. Development prepares an organization to face changes. If development is successful, it inevitably leads to growth, perhaps in a different direction. Whether or not growth leads to development depends on the stability of the environment. An organization may experience growth without development in a relatively stable environment. Organizations that only grow but do not develop decline when the market or another segment of the surrounding environment changes.

Development and growth constitute a criterion of health in a changing environment. In any living system, the ambition to grow and develop is a sign of health. If an individual does not want to grow, develop, learn, or try out new things and aims only to stay alive and maintain the status quo, this person is already dying. If an organization lacks ambition to find improvements or new choices, it will stagnate and eventually disintegrate. Therefore, the fifth criterion of organizational health is growth and development over time.

Growth and development health in a new organization is different from that of a mature one. At the birth stage, creating existence is the focus, finding the first successful model of operation, one that can form the basis of later development. Until this first business model is established, the organization only has a "lease of life."

I was attending a conference with one of my colleagues. We were chatting after a session, when suddenly he turned to me with an idea: "Why don't we buy a company?" At the time, in the early 1990s, privatization was in full swing in Eastern Europe. The government compensated individuals for property lost during the socialist regime with coupons, using which one could lease a company without significant cash investment. We both had a decade of organizational development experience as consultants under our belts. Buying a company and running it on our own appeared to be a feasible and challenging proposition for us. We spent all the following week investigating our options and concluded that the available companies might not be the best targets for us. Therefore, instead of buying one, we decided to build one from scratch.

We went for an "off-site" and developed the idea for our company. First, we identified the market we wanted to enter based on not yet satisfied existing demand, on our reputation and skills, and the resources available to us. We came up with "project management" as the profile. We discussed the kind of company needed for the type of services we wanted to provide. We envisioned how we would like to see our organization five years down the road: the characteristics, clients, employees, climate, and leadership. We also identified the number of people we could start with, office space, equipment, furniture, hardware, and software.

We had many reasons for establishing this organization. We wanted to test our managerial and leadership skills, to create an organization beyond ourselves, to accumulate wealth. It was a wonderful, exciting experience to see how a whole organization developed out of our idea. One day it was still an idea, the next it became a living entity, five years later it was a respected player in its domain. However, since we were not dependent on the new company financially, we didn't focus on it enough. As a result the growth of the organization was not as fast, nor were its operations as efficient as they could have been had we focused our full attention on it. The incentive, motivation, and skill of the founders all seem to impact the growth of the organization directly.

If an organization has been around for years and yet still aims at survival, this is an indication of ill-health. The lack of growth over time results in stagnation or decline. Ignoring complexities of the environment or new challenges results in "Tunnel Vision," prohibiting development.

Disease: Stagnation

We are fine the way we are.

Description

In their visions organizations define the organizations they want to become. Growth and development can be expressed in size, market share, or in quality terms such as diversity of products and new technology. Stagnation is the lack of such development over time. If the organization does not want to grow further, does not want to learn or try out new things, aims only to maintain existence, it has already started to decline. The lack of ambition for growth and development of any living system is a sign of ill-health.

Symptoms

- Routine, repetitive activities make up all the operations.
- Things are done in exactly the same way for long periods of time; few innovations take place.
- The organization has a few predictable customers and rarely acquires new ones.
- Typically, the resistance to change and new ideas is substantially higher than in similar organizations. People seem antichange, and there is a climate of perceived stability. Employees let go several opportunities of which the organization could have taken advantage. They think that taking those opportunities would not have been worth the problems. Let it go!
- There is a general dullness and lack of ambition in this organization.
- There are lots of visibly low-energy, burned-out people. They are tired of what they are doing. They have little excitement in their work. Their personal appearance may reflect their lack of interest in work.
- The risk-taking ability of employees declines.
- Old values, rank, and the importance of doing things in accustomed ways is overemphasized. Sentimentalism toward what has been or an imagined past colors present-day operations.

Causes

- Fear exists that growth is not manageable. For example, executives may feel that they can manage the present stage, but cannot go beyond that.
- Attitudes such as "don't rock the boat—we may lose what we have" and "if it isn't broke, don't fix it" appear to mask the insecurities of the founder or executives about the future.

Table 8.1
Stagnation

Structure of Causes	Possible Causes	Possible Actions for Improvement
Personal/Leadership	1. Executives and employees lack energy and ambition. 2. Personal development is not an objective. 3. Personal skills have reached their limits. 4. The present and the future of the organization or its strategy are not important enough for the key executives. 5. There are no new, ambitious executives in key positions, or if there are any, they do not have enough influence to make a difference. 6. A key executive is getting ready to retire and is too tired to take on new challenges.	*Executive Coaching, Training Workshop, and/or Other:* • Analyze the nature of growth/development versus stagnation with the key executives; help them to understand the negative consequences of stagnation and find energizing new development paths. • Start energizing, vision building, and future search programs, first for the executive team, then involving the whole organization. • Involve dynamic, ambitious, energized employees in management and key positions; if necessary, hire from outside. • Introduce new aspects in performance evaluations, such as personal and professional growth-related objectives, with new challenging tasks.

172

Structure of Causes	Possible Causes	Possible Actions for Improvement
		• Provide life coaching, and/or outplacement for executives who have lost interest and energy in this organization.
Organizational, Operational	1. Low-energy executives negatively influence the culture and operations of the organization and limit the possible influence of more ambitious employees. 2. Old organizational structure and/or technology outlives itself and becomes a constraint to development. 3. Past successes become constraints to development. 4. Sustaining the status quo is the most important objective. 5. There are not enough recently arrived employees from the outside who can bring new ideas and new perspectives, and/or the old-timers do not let them make a difference.	*Coaching, Training Workshop, and/or Other:* • Reach closure on the past and increase explicit awareness of new challenges. • Develop an attractive new vision, and consequently change the organization's culture and structure. Develop a new strategy with challenging objectives. • Seek "new blood"; hire new, creative, ambitious people who can also manage change. • Base product development on new market demand and customer satisfaction analysis by new development teams.

Table 8.1 (continued)

Structure of Causes	Possible Causes	Possible Actions for Improvement
	6. The organization cannot, or does not, know how to get resources to fund developmental activities.	• Get outside support to explore opportunities to get external funds for developmental activities. • Create lively, energizing programs inside and outside the organization to rekindle the manager's/employee's energies. • Provide outplacement or early retirement programs for those who are too tired to renew themselves within.
External, Market Related	• The organization is not pressured by the market to change because of its monopolistic position. • The owners do not require a return on their investment. • There is a shortage of financial resources for further development. • The demand is changing so fast that the organization gives up with keeping up.	*Interventions:* • Help the organization to prepare itself to meet the challenge of potential competition or other outside pressures. • Help the owners to reconsider their roles and the expectations toward the organization, and identify the necessary steps to take for this change. • Hire management members who are up to meeting the challenges the organization is facing.

Origins

- The genetic origin is that the founder's ambition is limited, or the founder has a laid-back style and does not want too many problems.
- The birth-related origin is that the immediate growth after being established caused a trauma for the organization, so stability has become an overriding value.
- The environmental origin is that the demand for the product or service is continuous and competition is not too strong.

This disease can be paired with Risk Avoidance, Shortsightedness, Insufficient Value for Customers, and Tunnel Vision.

A structured list of causes and possible actions for improvements for this disease can be seen in Table 8.1.

Disease: Tunnel Vision

Focus on existing competencies.

Description

We use tunnel vision to describe the organizational disease of not seeing what happens on the periphery of the field of vision. The focus is on one or very few aspects of business, while neglecting the rest. This focus could be just on the product/services or even just a narrow segment within it, or on a functional area such as finance or marketing. Organizations with tunnel vision wear blinders and organizations that wear such blinders may move but do not develop. Because such an organization is capable of seeing only a certain part of its operations, when it is forced to turn, it leaves the previous parts behind, forgetting and neglecting traditions. This shift is neither organic nor gradual, but drastic.

Symptoms

- The organization is repeatedly surprised by events that—in its interpretation—happen suddenly.
- A typical aspect of wearing blinders is favoring only certain stakeholders, the ones who are perceived to be in charge, for example, focusing on the government in order to attract government orders because the government allocates important resources like licenses or bandwidth.
- Some or several stakeholders feel neglected. Since they feel neglected, they tend to escalate action, such as going to court or going on strike.
- A few areas or departments are privileged when resources are distributed while others are unreasonably neglected.
- The organization is not looking at the whole value chain or the global competitive situation.

Table 8.2
Tunnel Vision

Structure of Causes	Possible Causes	Possible Actions for Improvement

Personal and Leadership Related	• The competence and interest of key executives is limited to a certain area of their business:
	
	   • a market segment such as government projects or a geographic region, and so forth and
	
	   • an organizational function such as research and development, marketing, controlling, and so forth.
	
	• Only employees with a certain type of education have credibility, for example, only engineers or people with finance and accounting degrees. These employees fill all key positions; therefore, management lacks diversity. Employees with other types of degrees or background are ignored and looked down on, not considered partners to discussions.
	
	• People in management are older, in the last phase of their careers before retirement, and are uninterested in new areas or
		Executive Coaching, Training Workshop, and/or Other:
		
		• For the key executives organize business and conference trips to widen their perspectives and present them with alternatives.
		
		• Organize a series of trainings for key executives, which pairs interesting, exciting field trips, to widen their horizons in thinking about the future of their organization.
		
		• Provide personal coaching for the key executives to increase awareness of Tunnel Vision and its impact.
		
		• Bring in new blood; involve new people in management who have wider perspectives and skill sets.

Structure of Causes	Possible Causes	Possible Actions for Improvement
	possibilities that lie outside their existing competencies.	
Organizational, Operational	1. Some functions dominate the way the organization operates; other functions do not have influence. 2. There is no forum for floating new ideas, or new ideas are disregarded. 3. The organization is closed, turned inside, employees have limited connections to the outside environment, and the existing connections are limited in scope and strictly related to the profession. 4. The selection and promotion system is inflexible, favoring candidates with the exact same backgrounds. 5. Low tolerance is frequently expressed toward other than the usually expected attitude, competence, or argument.	***Coaching, Training Workshop, and/or Other:*** • Present diversity and difference as a key resource for the success of the organization; help to develop an open-minded attitude toward noncustomary approaches. • Provide cross-functional workshops, where the task can be solved only by listening to different perspectives and cooperation among the departments. • Reorganize decision-making authorities, resource allocation, and information channels in such a way that different expert areas have similar weight. • Ensure that a broad range of necessary competencies is included in performance evaluation systems, promotions, and hiring criteria.

Table 8.2 (continued)

Structure of Causes	Possible Causes	Possible Actions for Improvement
		• Establish forums and open communication channels where new ideas—even unusual ones—can surface and where these can be discussed and considered.
External Market Related	1. A high level of specialization and perhaps traditions developed over long periods in the past characterize the economic sector and business thinking. 2. Stable government contracts, limited competition, conglomerates, and associations dominate the economic sector.	*Interventions:* • Gain international experience; provide training abroad for key people in the organization. • Promote managers who have experience from abroad. • Open new market segments in addition to the existing, traditional ones.

- Thanks to its blinders, the organization changes direction and focus too rapidly and suddenly.

Causes

- Giving and wearing blinders are ways of controlling or gaining the illusion of being in charge. Blinders seem to reduce fear of new things coming into the field of vision, increasing the perception of control and comfort. Anxious people and managers tend to promote this kind of behavior. Tunnel Vision is a form of self-protection against risks and having to undertake too many tasks.

Origins

- The genetic origin is that founders were worried about their ability to manage all opportunities in a defined environment. That is why they limit perspective, focus on just a few things that they personally prefer, and then expect others to align with these. The founders could also fear that in other areas their expertise would be less valued, causing them to lose prestige or control.

- The birth-related origin is that in the early stage, a specific area played a dominant role in the success of the organization. It has kept its position within the organization, and the others have become used to being subordinated to it.

- The environmental origin is that the broader culture emphasizes specialization. From early childhood children are taught to be focused on a single profession, "you will be a doctor, an engineer, a poet." Taking interest in too many things is discouraged. Specialization becomes the very definition of success, and experimenting and trying out different aspects of life is forgotten.

This disease often occurs together with Suboptimizing, Risk Avoidance, and Stagnation.

A structured list of causes and possible actions for improvements for this disease can be seen in Table 8.2.

EMPLOYEES SENSE QUICKLY IF AN ORGANIZATION STOPS GROWING AND DEVELOPING

As we have discussed, people usually join organizations for employment and the immediate benefit of compensation. However, after joining, their other objectives come to the fore. Employees want to grow in various ways.

One of our clients specialized in providing contract labor for developing banking and financing software. This company had a 22 percent turnover, one of the highest in the industry. In the exit interviews employees frequently named higher salary as a reason for leaving. One of the interviewees expanded on this. "I do routine work, way below my qualification and interest. I have no opportunity to break out from the role I am forced into. I cannot identify with any purpose in this reduced role." We persuaded the executives to reexamine their perspective. Eventually, they established an R&D department and redefined how employees could influence the work they were doing. After this the retention rate showed a significant increase. Turnover dropped to less than half of the previous high, to 8 percent.

If an organization does not grow, its members cannot grow. Some employees have an intrinsic motivation to develop, to improve their skills, and apply them in increasingly complex situations. They want the organization to provide the soil for development. If an organization does not develop, members who have an interest in developing cannot do so. They become frustrated and will sooner or later leave the organization.

I was invited to the "All Hands" meeting of the New York office of a medium-sized, well-established consulting company. The program started with a motivational speaker and continued with the executives' report of the state of the business. Although the report sounded positive enough to me, I observed the faces of a group of consultants around me expressing doubt. Finally, the question and answer session started, and a consultant asked for the microphone and posed a very straightforward question about the breakup of revenue by type of engagement. To my surprise, I heard people sigh around me. Still, I expected a similarly straightforward reply. Instead, one of the executives stood up on the podium and made the following speech: "We are well aware that many of you consider our most frequent type engagement boring routine work and that several of the consultants made cynical comments about working on such engagements and even tried to maneuver out of them. Look at two of our consultants (and he named them) who were just promoted to managers. They have done an excellent job on consecutive engagements of exactly the same type and not complained that the engagements were not interesting or challenging. I warmly recommend everybody follow their examples instead of criticizing the type of engagements we undertake." A few months later the company announced that it missed the revenue forecast by a wide margin, and has to "refocus on its core competency" manifesting in a 25 percent combined layoff and turnover.

HOW DO ENTREPRENEURS MANAGE GROWTH WHEN IT TURNS INTO PRESSURE?

Some young organizations grow initially, but for a variety of reasons stop after awhile. One likely cause of this is that family members have demands on the founder and limit involvement with the organization. After the organization has reached a certain size, it is also often the case that the risk-taking ability of the founders does not keep pace. They become inhibited. Early in the growth phase their organization succeeds in overcoming challenges. Later, when problems prove too difficult, the founders question growth, and the accompanying stress. They find excuses: "We are happy as we are. Why should we grow?"

This reaction tends to be the sign of ignoring an environmental challenge, or the lack of personal or professional expertise and skills to manage growth. Entrepreneurs or organizations have a variety of abilities and competencies. One competency is proper management and acquisition of material resources, another is management of people, and a third is daily management of operations. Often founders are, for example, good technologists, creating an organization focusing on an invention. However, once an organization has been established, it has to run every day, and entrepreneurs have to manage the complex puzzle of people, money, and environmental impacts all at once, which they may find difficult to do. Unfortunately, if the competency of the founder stops growing at a certain level the competencies of people in the organization do not grow any further either. Those who have more ambition leave the organization. Founders who recognize their personal limitations in handling challenges either radically redesign the role they play in the management of the organization or step back altogether. Widespread understanding of the limitations of founders as individuals in handling the demands of running a growing organization has led to new roles such as serial entrepreneurs, who take their ideas only to the established level and then leave the organization they created to do the same with another idea. Lately the "virtual CEO" has also come into existence, one who is active in amassing the assets necessary to build the organization around somebody else's idea, but after the organization reaches a critical size and "normality of operations" leaves.

CHAPTER 9

Living in Harmony with the Environment

How do organizations interact with their environment? Do organizations adapt to environmental changes? How do organizations exploit and pollute their environment? How does a healthy organization cope with the environmental stresses and difficulties? What are the common forms of shifting the burden to stakeholders? Is it really a jungle out there?

ORGANIZATIONS EXIST WITHIN THE CONTEXT OF THEIR ENVIRONMENT

In order to understand how organizations relate to their surroundings, it is important to view them as open and living systems. An open system continuously interacts with the environment, taking inputs from it and releasing outputs. Through this exchange, the environment determines certain qualities of the open system, and the system influences its environment. Organizations as social systems are determined to a large degree by the society surrounding them. Socialization of behavior has a direct impact on how organizations work. For example, keeping strong family ties and respecting age are widely held social values in China. This has a direct impact on the culture and structure of Chinese organizations, regardless of the type of business, or the character of the individuals who work there. This organization would differ from a similar organization in, let us say, the United States, even if both provided exactly the same services or products. The environment influences organizations through three types of inputs:

1. The first type of input is directly used by organizational operations: employees, with their skills, education levels, and work ethics; materials, goods, and services the organization purchases, including the availability of supplies; and facilities the organization may use, such as existing transportation and communication infrastructures.

The managing partner of one of the established accounting and consulting firms—an expatriate himself—turned to us for assistance in easing the tension between Hungarian and expatriate employees. In the course of a few months, the firm won several clients and expanded to employing 30 professionals, a great achievement by any measure. At the same time, internal conflicts reached a disturbing level, destroying morale. This puzzled him exceedingly. "Supposedly we are doing well, yet Hungarian employees complain bitterly of being delegated to the position of 'slaves' and that they feel exploited. Why? How can they complain and not participate in firm building initiatives at the same time? Why do they feel confronted when they are trained in our standard operational practices? Expatriates, me included, are frustrated, having to fight constantly to apply their knowledge and skills in this hostile environment. The smallest provocation, for example, a joke, fuels arguments out of proportion. Not that I understand their jokes, mind you. What is going on here?"

2. The second type of input is the regulations, laws, and political and economic systems, all of which shape the relevant environment of a number of organizations.
3. The third type of input is a set of output requirements expected from the organization by present and future customers.

In Eastern Europe 15 years ago, we were pleased if we were let in a restaurant. If this statement surprises you, let us explain why. Restaurants were the antithesis of customer service. Rundown furnishing, rude waiters, cold meals, the proverbial fly in your soup. We were happy if eventually we got something to eat at all. Of course, not every single restaurant exhibited all the above characteristics, but in general, a restaurant had no external incentive, material or otherwise, to please customers. Customers on the other hand, based on previous experiences, expected to stand in line and be abused by anyone who had authority over distributing goods or services. Not every purchasing or consuming occasion supported this expectation either, but suspicion on the customer side and no incentive on the restaurant side turned this situation quickly into a self-fulfilling prophecy. Years later, people not only demand food, and good food at that, but value, a comforting or interesting atmosphere, quick and polite service, on occasion, entertainment, and a clean toilet. Customers are still less demanding of smoke-free air, or healthier cooking, for example, but it is coming.

Organizations also influence society, so its not just one way. If an organization does not just meet, but actually shapes, customer needs, perhaps by offering revolutionary products or setting a fashion trend, it actually impacts consumers and nonconsumers of their products alike. Interestingly, sometimes when an organization shapes commonly accepted norms, the actual impact turns out to be unintended or unforeseen.

ADAPT OR ELSE

In their interactions with the surroundings, organizations also exhibit characteristics of living systems. One of the most important, and sometimes most curious, quality of all living organisms is that they use their senses to approximate information from their external environment and apply it to adjust themselves accordingly. If they fail to adapt to environmental changes sufficiently, they die, or even die out. Organizations follow similar patterns. A healthy organization appears to be in a continuous interaction with the environment. Only organizations that use the information they gather to adapt to the environment may survive over time. Circumstances change, abruptly or gradually, and organizations that are not sufficiently agile to adapt to the new environment begin to suffer from diseases.

Some years ago the Indian government set up a new organization to build advanced computers, in response to the restrictions on computer export from the United States to India. Out of the feeling of insult, a new organization was born. The mission was to develop a supercomputer, by many well-educated, skilled people. In a very short time, this not-for-profit governmental institution developed an advanced computer. However, difficulties in funding forced the government to change the organization's status to for-profit. All of a sudden, the organization had to earn profit by selling the hardware and software it was developing. The identity and brand continued; it was still the centre of development of advanced computing, but operations now had to include commercial activities. The mission changed abruptly, but the talented group of people carried on with the new mission.

A healthy organization not only adapts to its environment, but is also able to cope with environmental stresses and challenges, to withstand, and to rise above them. Let us consider an individual who falls and hurts her knee. If this individual is healthy, within a few days her knee recovers. If she is unhealthy—already suffering from a disease, such as diabetes—she may not recover, or at least not so quickly. Her body is not able to cope with this new problem. The minimal definition of organizational health is that a healthy organization, like a healthy body, is able to cope with attacks, stresses, and negative influences originating from the environment. If problems become chronic, it is a sign of ill-health.

To be able to survive in the long term, organizations have to continuously define how to treat environmental inputs. This implies having different sensors, receiving various and necessary information from the environment, interpreting it and divining its meaning, and having the ability to adjust to the changes demanded by this information. It sounds complex, and it is indeed a complex task.

I was working in a department of the government-started Postgraduate Management Education Institute. Our group joined the established institute to form one of its departments, although it was substantially different culturally from the rest of the institute. The institute's mainstream departments issued certifications required by regulations to the participants of their programs. The government financed these programs. We, on the other hand, sold our services of organizational development. The considerable differences in our cultures were reflected even in our names, "departments" versus "laboratory." Initially, we were under a lot of pressure to conform, to give up our very identity, an identity which made it difficult for us to exist as part of this bigger entity. Then, economic reality took a sharp turn at one point. The government commissioned a feasibility study, and was advised to abolish the monopolistic position of the institute and stop financing postgraduate education. "The Institute should sell its services if it wished to continue." You can imagine the effect this final recommendation had! Departments that offered services that customers were willing to pay for gained enormous esteem. The status of our group changed overnight, from being an annoyance to being the most respected. Very quickly, we became a role model for the rest of the departments.

Environmental input is not always a resource; sometimes the impact from the environment is dangerous and unhealthy. In certain cases, the organization has to insulate itself from those impacts. Bribery and corruption, if they are rampant in the environment, are good examples of a negative environmental impact. If an organization wants to avoid their negative ethical and material consequences, it has to make a special effort to select decision makers who could reliably insulate against this effect by developing procedures to minimize their impact. Knowing when to adjust and when not to are integral adaptation skills.

A healthy organization pays attention not only to the quality of the input it takes in, but also to the output it releases to the environment so that it can filter out the harmful ones in both cases. For this purpose, a healthy organization has "valves." Inlet valves ensure that only good things are received, and unnecessary, harmful things are prevented from entering the organization. In the same way, outlet valves ensure that internal information and bad outputs do not get into the environment. However, a living system is not necessarily a perfect system. In its interactions, an organization can work out how the harmful outputs will be managed in the environment itself. Reversible energy and reusable outputs are good examples.

Healthy organizations do not only just react to inputs from their environment, including other organizations, government, marketplace, and society at large; they are also proactive. They visualize possibilities and prepare themselves to deal with different scenarios. Flexibility in handling and responding to environmental events is a very important aspect of health.

But being proactive is not enough. There is an even more involved way an organization can relate to its environment, and that is by actively shaping it. The organizational vision reflects how the organization would like to see itself within the environment in the future. By developing scenarios for how it can get closer to the vision, an organization can actually create its future. Turning a vision into reality is more than being proactive.

RELEVANT ENVIRONMENT

When we talk about the environment of an organization, we need to qualify it by saying "the relevant parts" of the environment, because the environment, as such, is infinite. Relevance, from the perspective of an organization, means those elements that either have an impact on or have some relationship with the particular organization. If the organization inadequately identifies its relevant environment, on the one hand it will waste resources and, on the other hand, it will not pay appropriate attention to some stakeholders or events. In both cases, the organization ends up with higher entropy. A healthy organization consciously defines its relevant environment and its input/output mechanisms, while its sensors continuously monitor changes. It continuously redefines what is relevant.

In case of a radical change, for example, a paradigm shift in the market, or a scientific discovery, the organization can also choose to reselect its relevant environment. Considering its strengths and uniqueness, it can move to another market or identify its market niche differently. It can still build on existing strengths up to the point of finding customers. Though the organization may become weaker in its relation to the new environment, it can in actuality be healthier than it was before.

STAKEHOLDERS

Several important stakeholders provide the inputs an organization uses in its operation, and they receive outputs from the organization. A stakeholder is not an abstract concept, but a specific individual or group of individuals. For example, families employees belong to; the community within which the organization exists; the local government; the town, whose resources the organization is using or polluting; suppliers; the government, which collects taxes and enforces regulations, all constitute important stakeholders. These stakeholders retain an interest in the organization, which essentially means that they expect to derive some benefit from the existence of the organization, or, at the least, they expect that the organization will cause no harm to them. A good, healthy organization considers—or at the minimum, is aware of—all its stakeholders, their particular interests, and lives in harmony with them.

Vendors and suppliers are special stakeholders, since in a sense they are an extended part of the organization. The quality of their services and products impinge on the quality, delivery, and prices of the organization's services and products. At the same time, a supplier and a purchaser are perceived to have directly opposing interests. To successfully manage this relationship requires layered communication. On the one hand, there are ongoing negotiations of price, features of the product, and terms of delivery, yet on the other hand, cooperation of the highest degree possible is beneficial to both parties. Maintaining regular communication and giving feedback is essential for overcoming the perception of conflicting interests and succeeding in this cooperation.

When, for example, an organization in a monopolistic situation dictates payment terms to its supplier, it is shifting the burden. In this context, the organization tries to minimize entropy by decreasing costs and improving cash flow beyond the accepted industry standard, at the cost of other organizations. Reducing entropy at the expense of other organizations or the environment beyond what is socially accepted is unhealthy.

Vendors of financial services occupy a special position among suppliers. Some organizations are reluctant to share information with financial institutions, being afraid of negative reaction. Yet when organizations continuously inform financial institutions of operational issues and ways of addressing them, financial institutions are in a better position to assist in overcoming them.

Governments have a stake in organizations because they derive revenue from organizations in the form of taxes of various kinds and because they are concerned about economic growth and employment. This relationship, however, is not one-sided. An organization may engage in continuous dialogue with the government, so that it also conveys its requirements to the government. This is particularly important, because governments create the regulatory environment determining important aspects of the existence of the organizations. Regulating the economy is a political process by its nature, and enforcers do not always foresee specific consequences of a particular regulation; in this case, a good dialogue providing the necessary information to both government agencies and organizations is beneficial for both parties.

Local governments also regulate the environment of an organization. They represent the local community where employees live. They may provide land, utilities, transportation facilities, infrastructure, or access to these. For an organization, this is a closer relationship than with the federal government. Local governments have a strong interest in organizations that act socially and responsibly beyond the direct financial interests of the organization. Some organizations are good in supporting local constituencies, such as educational institutions, whose graduates form the workforce of the future, or cultural institutions, theaters, and festivals that contribute to a community's strong sense of identity. Sometimes it is difficult to differentiate the local government from the local community, because local governments operate a variety of institutions, including schools, theaters, and hospitals.

A healthy organization has the capacity to go beyond its business interest in developing a relationship with its environment, which is not purely transactional and exploitative. If an organization is able to do that, it will have a different relationship not only with the community in a broader sense, but with employees as well, because they are part of the community. Neighbors and family members are the most efficient agents of shaping a positive view of the organization in the community. Organizations that care for the local community and, within their limits, support it gain a respect that is hard to measure in financial terms, but is easy to sense among employees.

The location of the organization is an important issue. Lots of organizations have several plants scattered around a country, a continent, or around the world, which makes the situations more complex.

One of our multinational clients had headquarters in the capital and plants located in the countryside. Ninety percent of the employees worked in the plants. It has been known as a socially responsible organization that maintains a good relationship with the local government. During the vision-building seminars, top executives engaged in a heated discussion: Those managers who were from the countryside felt strongly that the organization should give donations to a local school while executives from headquarters or other countries wanted to see a direct financial return on this investment and questioned how the organization benefits from these donations. The discussion was about reaching a consensus on basic values, seemingly very different in the two groups.

Organizations everywhere in the world try to optimize their taxes. Benefiting from exploiting different tax systems is common, and companies operating across borders may develop techniques to best utilize differing tax systems. Occasionally, this puts employees in a difficult situation. They want to be loyal to the organization they are working for, but they also want to be loyal to their local community and their country. In a healthy organization, decision makers try to avoid putting employees in a position that challenges their loyalties.

Governments often grant a variety of concessions and subsidies to multinational organizations for moving into economically backward areas. These negotiations that follow are not only about accessing a cheap workforce and creating workplaces, but also about the organizations' contribution to the development of the community, or the potential harm operations may cause to the community and the environment.

A healthy organization welcomes competition. Competition helps an organization to remain healthy by meeting the performance standards of those who are better. Competitors are stakeholders in the sense that they have an interest in the performance of others. Competitors can be mutually beneficial for each other when an ethical code of conduct is in place. In order to be able to follow the ethical code, an organization needs a healthy self-esteem: We are ready to welcome competition, even share ideas, when we trust and have faith in ourselves. If we feel that the organization is too weak, capitalizing on little advantage that can be replicated easily, it is hard to be cooperative. A healthy organization approaches cooperation with competitors from the win-win perspective of regarding competition as an additional opportunity to improve performance and increase added value to customers.

Competitors clearly have a common interest in enlarging the market, educating customers, representing certain issues to the government, and sharing some information. Healthy organizations, on the one hand, compete with each other, doing their best to provide the most attractive product, and, on the other hand, negotiate issues of common interests with competitors.

We invited the main management training firms of the country to a National Training Round Table. During the first few meetings, representatives were suspicious, to say the least, but they came anyway. Within a short time, the ice melted, and our meetings became very productive. We developed practice guidelines, which benefited everybody, including clients. We adopted a code of ethics, which included self-imposed rules of ethical behavior with clients, ways of handling copyright issues, submitting professionally adequate proposals, following professional bidding processes without backdoor offers, and not commenting negatively on other training firms adhering to these rules. Nowadays, we perform market surveys and invite well-known foreign speakers together. All this does not mean that we don't compete for clients. We participate in the same tenders, and naturally do our best to win the engagements. By collaborating, we created a win-win situation where only a zero-sum game existed before.

Needless to say, a healthy organization has to keep up with technical advances, and nobody can be complacent with outdated technology. Healthy organizations manage contacts with professional and academic institutions to learn about the latest ideas and discoveries to use them as a source of innovative ideas for the organization. Members participate in conferences, meetings, and research projects. Universities and professional institutes therefore form an especially important part of any organization's stakeholders and keeping close contact with them is also vital for recruitment.

As much as the physical and mental health of employees can be considered the output of the organization, we regard individual employees and their families as external stakeholders to an organization. When organizations overwork, weaken, and exhaust employees, they shift the burden to families and the local community in the form of increased stress for the family and increased cost of health care and hospitalization for the larger community. While losing the balance between professional and private life is a topic that has been discussed earlier, it is important to point out again that families do pay the price when an organization ignores them as stakeholders.

Given the environmental complexities, the increasing circle of stakeholders due to globalization, and the possible delay in understanding the consequences of organizational impact on the environment, many organizations err to some degree in their approach to their surroundings.

Disease: Aggressive Approach to the Environment

It is a jungle out there; "all is fair in war."

Description

Relationships with different stakeholders may vary, but the typical attitude toward the environment is that it is a battlefield, full of danger, threat, and rivalry. This overall perception of the environment defines the approach to external stakeholders. If members of the organization perceive the environment as violent, their first reaction is aggressive and defensive. This of course provokes negative behavior, which reinforces the negative perception of the environment. This organization then has a wide range of conflicts with the different stakeholders in the environment.

Symptoms

- A substantial legal department exists, and/or the organization extensively uses external law firms.
- Regular visits to courts occur for a continuous flow of lawsuits.
- Conflicts exist with the local government and local people.
- Bad supplier relations exist: contracts are short and suppliers regularly change.
- Lobbies with competitors form against local interest, regulations, or other interest groups.
- There is a lack of strategic partners.
- Conflicts exist with tax agencies and other government agencies.
- The vision statement lacks specific statements associated with the social responsibility of the company or with external stakeholders (e.g., suppliers).
- When problems occur, the first reaction is to try to deny the responsibility.
- A lack of young people coming for internship to familiarize themselves with the company exists because the organization does not have a good reputation.
- The organization does not provide a chance for people to visit or take part in developmental activities.

Causes

- The basic assumption about the environment is that a continuous win-lose game is going on with everybody out there. Others want to take advantage of us, so it is better that we strike first.

Origins

- The genetic origin is if the founders or the executives themselves carry a strong competitive and aggressive attitude to the external world, this model will take root in the organizational culture.
- The birth-related origin is that in its early life cycle the organization has experienced some significant losses resulting from aggressive, unfair behavior by some of the external stakeholders, which has led to a defensive, overly suspicious and violent attitude toward the external parties of the organization.
- The environmental origin is that the general business culture is very aggressive, violent, and has low moral standards. In order to survive, the organization adopts the same standards.

This disease often occurs together with Customer Exploitation, Money Mania, and Organizational Paranoia.

Table 9.1
Aggressive Approach to the Environment

Structure of Reasons	Possible Causes	Possible Actions for Improvement
Personal, Leadership Related	1. Executives are concerned only about the short-term financial interest of the organization, not about the environmental and the societal impact. 2. Executives have not realized and understood the advantages and importance of the environmentally responsible operation. 3. A "why should I be concerned, since I am so small and cannot influence the total outcome anyway" attitude prevails.	***Executive Coaching, Training Workshop, and/or Other:*** • Provide executive coaching to introduce or reinforce disciplines of systems approach and assessments of long-term impacts. Change attitudes: What are market- and competition-related aspects of the organization's approach to the environment? Are environmentally friendly approaches discussed as an alternative or ignored all together? • Facilitate executive discussion; plan a forum on environmental impacts, possibly with outside experts.
Organizational, Operational	1. Planning and incentive systems include only a narrowly defined group of the directly impacted stakeholders (owners, employees, and customers); other stakeholders are ignored or exploited.	***Coaching, Training Workshop, and/or Other:*** • Introduce the main dimensions of environmentally friendly operations.

Structure of Reasons	Possible Causes	Possible Actions for Improvement
	2. There is a lack of competence expertise, skills, and interest on corporate social responsibility (CSR) issues. 3. Information to show the impact of organizational operations on the environment does not exist or is not accessible.	• Introduce leading example practices and trends. Benchmark by visiting other companies with positive examples. • Facilitate a forum with participation of different external stakeholders to develop a better understanding of the impact the organization is having on its environment. • Audit CSR practices: what is done and how can the organization improve.
External, Market Related	1. In economic, political, and civic circles the interest of the wider environment (natural, economic, and societal) are usually ignored, and there are no consequences for the individual organizations not to do so. 2. Industrial development has not reached the level where the environmental impact becomes an aspect of further development.	*Interventions:* The organization can initiate societal changes after it has changed internal practices. Opportunities include the following: • Supporting higher education such as specific educational programs, such as by donation, running charity programs, presentations, case studies, and internships, all related to environmentally conscious practices. • Participating in different societal or international forums.

A structured list of causes and possible actions for improvements for this disease can be seen in Table 9.1.

Disease: Insufficient Interaction with the Environment

The organization is out of touch.

Description

The organization recognizes too late the changes taking place in customer needs, habits, structure, technical discoveries, or important shifts in the competition's strategies. Sensors may be developed, but their voices are not heard in the organization or the means of adaptation including these sensors, valves, and insulation are not working properly, and the organization is not optimizing its interaction with the environment. Procedures that can ensure that the organization keeps a healthy, living, active, and adequate relationship with its environment do not function. The organization cannot adjust to the changes or challenges emanating from the environment, a clear sign of dysfunction.

Symptoms

- Board and other executive meetings spend little time on discussing what is going on in the environment and its impact on the organization; instead they are preoccupied with internal issues.
- Even if marketing has a lively relationship with the environment, its relative weight among the departments is insufficient to influence the organization. It is perceived to be too late and too costly to adjust.
- The relevant environment is not properly identified; therefore, lots of irrelevant information is received that preoccupies resources, increases cost, and is not itself helpful in managing the relationship with the environment.
- Intake systems are not working properly: an unorganized flood of information and impact comes from the environment because the valves do not filter out enough and do not specify and classify according to organizational needs, thus becoming overwhelming. Such a flood of information does not help to define the reactions or actions toward the environment for the rest of the organization.
- Intake valves are too selective: the information allowed in is biased, influenced by internal politics. Some information is missing while other input is exaggerated.
- Information is not interpreted accurately.
- The management engagement calendar rarely includes attendance at conferences, professional visits, and meetings with government officials.
- Outlet valves work improperly: used water, air, soil, and so forth are polluting the environment as socially indicated by protest, litigation, and a low respect for the company by the local community.
- An insulation problem exists: The organization allows certain products that are not needed, and it purchases services that do not add value to the whole organization. This may also apply to the hiring practices: people with a destructive attitude or

Table 9.2
Insufficient Interaction with the Environment

Structure of Causes	Possible Causes	Possible Actions for Improvements
Personal, Leadership Related	1. Executives have more professional but less leadership skills. 2. Introverted management executives do not feel comfortable in unfamiliar environments. 3. A fear of releasing confidential business information exists. 4. Executives' energies are completely absorbed in focusing on immediate business issues and are left with no energy to deal with other, broader aspects/relationships of their organizational environments.	*Executive Coaching, Training Workshop, and/or Other:* • Promote or introduce new executives who have active and wide-ranged relationships and are able to utilize those for the benefit of the organization. • Allocate more time on executive meetings for discussing issues and sharing information related to the environment (occasionally invite outside experts). • Increase the activity of key executives in professional forums, events, conferences, study tours, and so forth. • Provide a broader range of information for executives (professional, technical, business, market, environmental, social, economical, and so forth) by organized and systemic use of the Internet. • Provide personal coaching for an executive to be more open in the

Table 9.2 (continued)

Structure of Causes	Possible Causes	Possible Actions for Improvements
		extroverted type of roles he or she has to play while representing the organization on different forums and at events.
		• Introduce management to the concept and practice of CSR and help to make it part of the everyday business operation.
Organizational Operational	1. An introverted organizational culture exists, one that is too absorbed in its own operation and activities and has little energy left for active and interactive relationships with the relevant environment.	*Coaching, Training Workshop, and/or Other:*
	2. Those members who have an active relationship with the environment and possess a wealth of information cannot take advantage of the information because they do not have sufficient power or impact on other members and parts of the organization. Lack of systematic collection,	• Extend the leadership development and CSR from the individual to the organization.
		• Invite outside experts to corporate forums to provide important, relevant information about what is happening in the relevant environment.
		• Provide incentives and time for employees to encourage them to play more extensive roles in the work of relevant outside organizations

196

Structure of Causes	Possible Causes	Possible Actions for Improvements
	channels, and use of this information exists.	(professional, scientific, local, and community).
	3. The organizational culture is exhausted, uninterested, indifferent, passive, and lacks a positive mission.	• Organize an open day at the company, where relatives, representatives, and local authorities can visit.
	4. Building business and other related relationships is regarded as useless and valueless.	• Change the management competency requirement to include consciousness of the environment.
	5. The information system does not actually provide information from the outside.	
	6. There is a lack of expectation that management will keep an interactive relationship with its relevant environment.	
Environment, Market Related	1. The local community has prejudice and/or a negative attitude toward the organization (for example, in some countries against the multinational companies).	• Initiate dialogue and positive gestures; sponsor local initiatives, educational and cultural institutions, and so forth.
	2. The environment is characterized by organizations and communities that are introverted, cultural islands of isolated groups.	• Implement careful first steps of opening toward the local community by inviting representatives and showing what is happening inside the organization.

inadequate skills/competencies are hired, causing problems, conflicts, and high costs.

Causes

• Management and leaders whose functions are to keep in contact with the environment perceive this activity as not a priority, and hence they neglect it. Because of their negligence the organization does not have the proper structures, procedures, and culture to keep a lively, healthy, and balanced relationship with its environment.

Origins

• The genetic origin is that the founder/key executive is too involved with the product/service and has little interest in the organization's environment. This influences the way the organization is structured, its resources distributed, and the culture developed.

• The birth-related origin is that at the early stage the organization had a secure, stable environment, a good position in its market, and could get along easily without paying too much attention to its environment.

• The environmental origin is that external stakeholders (local governments, suppliers, and so forth) are comparatively weak in comparison with the organization's power, so the organization can dictate its terms to the environment.

This disease often occurs together with Shortsightedness and Insufficient Value for the Customer.

A structured list of causes and possible actions for improvements for this disease can be seen in Table 9.2.

PART III

Leading Healthy and Joyful Organizations

CHAPTER 10

Leaders Make or Break Healthy and Joyful Organizations

What is the role of the executive in creating a healthy and joyful organization? Does the executive's capacity for experiencing joy limit the organization's capacity to be joyful? Are charismatic leaders better able to build joyful organizations? How does the executive's need to matter impact on the organization? How do previous experiences influence decision making? Why do we keep reinforcing our beliefs until a serious problem develops? How do we learn from these serious problems?

* * * * * *

Interpreting health and joy in the organizational context provokes almost everyone into exploring the role individuals and their specific character traits can play in shaping an organization. We have already seen that the culture and structure of organizations is determined, among other things, by the personal beliefs of founders or key executives. Therefore, causes of organizational disease symptoms frequently have a "genetic" origin. Most of us have few encounters with joyful organizations, and we possess definite expectations of executives, which puts the following question foremost in our minds: "Does the executive's capacity for joy define and confine the organization's capacity for joy?" It is best to address this question in several steps.

First, we have to turn our attention to the role leaders and managers play in an organization (or its parts) from the aspect of health and the specific ways leaders and managers add value to an organization.

Second, we have to scrutinize how value adding advances or confronts the personal needs of leaders and managers. This will enable us to better identify the inherent incentives of their actions and to understand what set of circumstances may lead an executive to experience joy from work.

Third, we have to look into the underlying mechanisms of decision making, learning to understand what ultimately shapes the decisions executives make and how and to what extent these factors may be changed.

All this could provide insight into whether their personal conduct is likely to further the organization they lead, manage, or work in on its way to health. However interesting this conclusion may be, it does not yet provide an answer to the earlier question; by definition, the answer has to include components specific to each individual. Therefore, we created a guide to enable the reader to complete the answer. Our intention in doing so is to actually turn the question around and ask, "How will you get closer to finding joy in your work? How do you intend to expand, rather than limit, your organization's capacity for joy?" In the next chapter, we will further discuss practical steps that will contribute to building a joyful organization. Be forewarned, though, that there is no shortcut; there is no way to skip further questioning and jump directly to "joy in three easy steps."

LEADERSHIP AS A FUNCTION

The leadership function plays an important role in our concept of the healthy organization. It is the leader who initiates the vision of the organization and who facilitates members who identify the vision as their own rather than as the leader's. It is also the leader who enables the organization to cope with internal problems and external stresses by mobilizing various human, financial, and information resources. He or she is ultimately responsible for how efficiently these resources are used, how much value added the organization creates for the customer, and that revenues exceed the costs of production, whether it be product or a service. To understand the role of a leader in a healthy organization, leadership is necessarily to be understood as a function and not a position: the leader has to be seen as a provider of services to the organization and its employees. The leadership function has the following five main aspects:

1. To Build an Organization around a Vision and Ensure that the Vision Is Shared

   Leaders have to ensure that the organization has a vision, either by projecting their own or facilitating the birth of one, thereby giving meaning and identity to the organization. The leader must articulate the vision in such a way that people find it personally fulfilling. When people feel strongly about the vision, they align with it, using their talents and competencies in its service. Members' commitments do not come from commands; they come from involvement, feeling good about the vision and therefore identifying with it.

2. To Mobilize Resources

   A leader has to attract the necessary resources to serve the vision. For an organization, one of the most important resources is people. Leaders need to attract talent in order to realize the vision. Members join an organization not only to perform a job and earn an income, but also to contribute to it in order to grow and make this aspect of their life meaningful. Therefore, the leader of a healthy organization creates an environment in the organization which purposefully attempts to satisfy members' needs. A leader also has to attract the necessary funds to first establish the organization or, once the organization is established, the means to support operations on an ongoing basis.

3. To Manage External Relations

A leader must be a good "spokesperson" for the vision externally and manage relations with the external environment. Ultimately, it is his or her responsibility to continuously assess feedback from the environment to decide whether the vision, as well as the processes followed to fulfill the vision, is still relevant and valid given the circumstances.

4. To Reduce Entropy

A leader has to facilitate organizational operations with the minimum waste of resources, especially the energy of people, through minimizing friction in the organization. To this end, a leader facilitates the installation of structures, processes, systems, and the development of an organizational culture whereby work is carried out with minimal diversion and interference.

5. To Ensure Value Creation

A leader must be concerned about adding value to the resources mobilized in the pursuit of the vision, ensuring that the product or service offered becomes increasingly desirable to the customers.

A leader is a person who is able to influence and create the environment. If a person cannot have this influence, his or her position as a leader is questionable. If a person in an executive position feels that he or she is a victim of circumstances, he or she is not leading anything or anyone; rather the environment is leading him or her. In this case, by definition, he or she is not a leader.

MANAGERS AND DAMAGERS

Managers often perform a balancing act like a tightrope walker. A good manager really knows how to manage this balancing act and enjoys doing it. Rather than perceiving this situation as "being under pressure," it is like a sport. Many managers, however, especially at the higher levels, become managers without having acquired coping skills. They have the technical skills and experience of many years of working in the same organization and culture. They have produced results at a particular level, and they become more senior by virtue of the passing of time. They may have gone to management education institutes, but only to acquire the vocabulary of management, not the skills.

Managers who lack interpersonal skills tend to experience an unfocused anxiety and insecurity. This is not insecurity about the job, but rather anxiety about whether they will be successful. This anxiety originates in the lack of sense of control over people, over the environment, and over the organization. Unskilled managers are very often "damagers," not managers.

Unskilled managers have very few tools at their disposal: They know only to use a hammer and the only way they can matter is by seeing everybody as a nail. Unskilled managers use the tool of authority exclusively. Another very interesting aspect of their behavior patterns is broad categorization. They show a tendency to feel that all human beings are similar in character and need the same treatment.

We worked with a hospital which was well-known for having the best equipment even measured by international standards. The director of this institute proudly publicly talked about the excellent technology, indicating that good doctors are secondary to having the best technology. One day I found this director in front of the intensive care unit. In the waiting area full of visitors, he was shouting at a nurse. I had to go there and point out to him that his shouting affected those around who were suffering and sick. For this person, other humans were there to operate the equipment, whether they were doctors or nurses, and not to show personal caring.

A skilled manager thinks in a larger perspective and has multiple tools. A skilled manager makes a more refined categorization of persons and situations. A skilled manager adjusts behavior as required by the situation. He or she uses a hammer on a nail and a screwdriver on a screw. A skilled manager is a person who uses power not only to get things done, but also to nurture and develop others. Skilled managers, whose skills increase, become gentle managers, but it does not mean they do not exercise power. Being gentle means that whatever they handle is done with the minimum force required. A skilled manager is a graceful manager.

CHARISMATIC LEADERS AND HEALTHY ORGANIZATIONS

Leadership skills are often mistaken as charisma. Nowadays most people in executive positions aspire to become charismatic leaders and to be one is their main personal purpose. Charismatic leaders have a quality of attracting others to a degree that they follow automatically. People buy into their vision, would like to be associated with them, and are eager to execute this vision. However, from the perspective of a healthy organization, charismatic leadership has a downside, too, because it develops dependencies.

A relationship between a charismatic leader and the follower is more like a "parent-child-" than an "adult-adult"-type relationship. They become charismatic leaders because they are able to articulate the needs and the wishes of the people around them. They are able to project a way to get there and let people see them as the leader of fulfilling that vision. Followers tend to give up some parts of their own personal identity and identify more with the leader, in the process, losing part of their independence. Followers become dependent on the charismatic leader. They would like to read his or her mind, understand his or her way of thinking in order to copy it, rather than be creative and come up with ideas on their own. When—for whatever reason—the charismatic leader disappears, the group remains helpless. A vacuum is created until somebody else with a charismatic character enters. Sometimes they do not differentiate themselves from the vision; nevertheless, their persona is extremely important to themselves. Charismatic leaders are likely to be self-centered, and often executives wear a charismatic mask in order to pursue their own personal needs.

What is charisma? There is a general understanding that charisma is an aspect of personality. However, if we examine so-called charismatic leaders, Jesus Christ, Mahatma Gandhi, John F. Kennedy, Martin Luther King, Jr., or indeed anybody with a large number of followers, we find that charisma is also contextual. A person who is charismatic is seen as charismatic in a particular culture, in a particular situation. It is hard to be charismatic all by yourself. You need a group of people who decide eventually whether you are charismatic for them or not. You have to understand the needs of the people around you so they become followers and you become their charismatic leader.

MANAGING UNCERTAINTIES

In open, dynamic, living systems, there is very little predictability; instead, much uncertainty exists. The subparts of organizations are also living systems; therefore, the level of uncertainty can rise due to internal processes as well as external interactions. The leader has to manage these uncertainties by getting continuous feedback about whether the organization is on track or not. A leader monitors the progress, and gives feedback to the organization, so that corrective action can take place as quickly as possible. Leaders initiate internal changes based on the demands of the external environment and make the organization continuously flexible. Because of the uncertainties inherent in these interactions, the importance of different functions in the organization can change from time to time. Leadership identifies how to give importance to critical functions relevant at any time.

MANAGING COMPLEXITY

Earlier we identified the main underlying objectives of organizations—satisfying customers' needs, employees' needs, and economic needs of the organization—which have to be balanced in order for the organization to be healthy. Whose responsibility is it to ensure that these three needs are taken care of and are satisfied simultaneously? The organization's structure and culture can guarantee that these needs are looked after continuously and that the balance is kept. Executives are responsible for crafting and developing this supporting structure and culture. We use structure in a broad sense here, including everything that is formally regulated, not only personnel and department roles, but also the connections among the different parts of organizations and the procedures they follow. The organizational culture of a healthy organization supports the structure by carrying these three important messages:

1. "We understand and care for customer needs, satisfy them, and think of them proactively."
2. "We care for our people, understand their needs to grow and develop, provide them with a sense of belongingness, and help them achieve their goals."
3. "We equally consider the financial aspect of the organization, making sure that the organization is financially stable and that it uses its resources efficiently, operating with minimal entropy."

LEADERSHIP SKILLS

Several different skills are required to perform the complex set of leadership functions well. When those skills are lacking, the level of health and joy of the organization is affected. As we know from personal experience, not everybody succeeds in managing these skills simultaneously. Instead of playing the leadership role, some executives act more like managers. What is the difference between a leader and a manager? A leader empowers people by giving meaning to tasks, whereas a manager directs, controls, and disciplines, in other words, "supervises" the task till completion. This difference does not depend on the level they occupy in the hierarchy. The chief executive can be a manager, and the department head can be a leader. Managers perform a supervisory role thereby providing a maintenance function. They enforce rules and regulations and continue tradition through maintaining awareness of organizational history. The manager is concerned about the completion of short-term tasks and the efficiency of the operations in terms of measurable, quantifiable indicators. The leadership function is creative in the sense of devising a vision that did not exist before. After the vision is in place, managers ensure that mechanisms required for pursuing the vision properly are provided.

Most managers who rise to a higher executive position do not acquire the corresponding leadership skills and competencies. It is common to spend, say, three years in a position and move to the next by doing nothing more than imitating the boss. People always complain about their bosses, but most nevertheless imitate them.

PEOPLE HIGHER IN THE HIERARCHY ADD MORE VALUE?

Organizations are preoccupied with examining their processes, identifying which activities add how much value to the outcome, and which ones are obsolete. On the other hand, with reference to the contribution of individuals, a tacit assumption is made that those individuals who are higher in the hierarchy automatically add more value, and that is why their compensation is higher. This assumption needs to be challenged because executives do not always add value; sometimes they take value away, creating a less healthy organization, one plagued with a higher level of entropy, alienation, and stagnation.

An exercise we often use in management training programs consists of two parts. In the first part, a participant plays the role of a worker who has to build the highest possible tower of blocks in five minutes, blindfolded, using only his or her left hand. Another participant is playing the role of the manager, who can help by talking to the builder.

As they set out to build the tower, managers usually interpret the task of helping workers by giving instructions, "Lift the blocks, move forward, backward, right, left, up, down." The harder they try, the more detailed the instructions become. Usually the team builds a 12- to 13-story tower. When they finish, both of them have a sense of success. Managers feel that their instructions guided the worker, and, therefore, they contributed much to the success of this enterprise. The builders feel good also because they got help, were not alone in this task, and did not have to take all the responsibility or too much risk. They are also happy with the result and give most of the credit for the success to the manager for providing detailed and helpful instructions.

During the second part of the exercise, the worker has the same task, but this time help is not allowed. When introducing the new rules, the facilitator attempts to increase the self-esteem of the builder with a few words. "You will be able to build the tower by relying on your sense of touch replacing vision. You can build a much higher tower than you would have imagined." Without instructions, regularly, they build a substantially higher tower, typically 16, 18, 20 blocks, or even higher. The participants of the training can hardly believe their eyes.

There are several conclusions from the result of this exercise, but we would like to emphasize the following two in this case.

First, what was the value the manager added during the exercise? Did the manager add value at all? After the first part of the exercise is completed, it looks as if that is indeed the case. However, after experiencing the second part the answer changes: by being aware of the sense of touch and taking ownership of the task rather than responding to minute supervision, the individual can, in fact, build a higher tower. Instruction actually slows the process down substantially, creating entropy. Far from adding value, the managers created entropy, as well as wasted resources of their own time, which could have been invested somewhere else for more benefits. Preparing workers by building up their self-esteem, identifying skills that they could use to replace vision, and making them believe that they are able to build a higher tower than they would have thought possible could have added value. Incidentally, doing so also would have helped the workers to develop and grow. This activity can be perceived as value adding because of the additional value expressed in a higher tower and less resources used, produced through increased self-esteem and more sophisticated skills. This increased self-esteem would carry on to executing other tasks as well.

Second, more likely than not, executives focus on satisfying their own needs, which they themselves are not necessarily aware of or would not care to acknowledge. Their own need of mattering, the feeling that they are powerful and in charge, and the feeling that without their instructions tasks could not be accomplished all influence their behavior in the exercise as well. Believing that the workers were able to achieve those goals through their direction and intervention satisfies their need for mattering. Thereby executives get satisfaction for themselves and have the illusion of adding value. It happens often in real life, too; when executives are not present and thus prevented from providing intervention, people are equally productive and usually even more so. It seems worthwhile, therefore, to examine when and how an executive adds value in more detail.

Adding value by executives is deeply rooted in their belief systems, their self-images, and their concepts of managerial and leadership roles. Some executives believe that people are capable, trustworthy, and can do a lot themselves. They conclude that if the task is clear and if people have commitment, the necessary skills, and support, the executive can add value by developing them. This belief system leads an executive to understand that the necessary conditions exist in order that each individual maximizes his or her potential. When he or she succeeds, the executive experiences the feeling of importance that "without me, the result would not be quite the same." Other executives believe that people are not trustworthy and will attempt to exploit the organization or any situation if they have the opportunity. They think that others want to put the minimum effort into work and get the maximum benefit out of the organization. This belief system would lead an executive to exercise tight control, give strong directives, and be involved in the operation in a detailed manner. Naturally, the group will be dependent on the executive since it will not take any initiative. The executive thus experiences a constant feeling of importance, which he or she calls adding value. The perception of people around or above the executive would be similar. Only, as we saw, to add value this executive would have had to do the opposite of what he or she actually did.

THE SELDOM REVEALED ROLE OF SELF-CONFIDENCE

When we join an organization, we would like to satisfy our needs, some conscious, some of those less so, independent of the level of position we occupy in the hierarchy. When executives keep tight control, they are not necessarily aware of the fact that they do so. Controlling behavior provides them with the feeling of importance and power. Exercising tight control is their way of gaining the attention of other people. They obtain the feeling of mattering through experiencing day to day the "I am in charge" high. It could easily happen, though, that instead of adding value they create entropy and reduce motivation, autonomy, and the feeling of mattering for other people. Thus, their satisfaction may increase, but the satisfaction of other members will decrease and the potential of the group as a whole will not be realized. It is a win-lose situation: Some people get more, while others get less.

Work situations are often perceived as a power game, where everybody tries to find out who influences whom, and who needs whom. Individuals who need to feel powerful try to de-emphasize the importance of other employees. "If you do not do what I say, if you do not perform well, if you do not follow my instructions, I can replace you, I can get somebody else easily, people are waiting outside the door to get in." The message is that others have no power over the manager; hence they are not important and do not matter. By doing so, managers attempt to take away the feeling of mattering from other people.

Trust is the tool with the most leverage an executive can have from the point of view of adding value. If a manager does not have trust, he or she reverts to tight control. That is very costly, time-consuming, ineffective, and demotivating. Trust always starts from inside. Those who trust themselves are able to trust others. Those who are insecure have a hard time trusting others. People whose self-esteem is low have to prove themselves repeatedly.

Executives who facilitate the growth of their employees are also interested in satisfying their own needs, only they happen to do it while contributing to achieving organizational purposes by adding value. They get positive feedback, and their activities are more beneficial for the organization by being more beneficial for the other members. "I help them grow day to day."

Why do some executives feel that they matter only by suppressing others or by professing to be helpful when they are not? Previously we have distinguished the three areas of motivation, or the three sources of mattering, that is, achievement, power, and affiliation. Achievement-motivated people suppress others because they want to achieve, to do better, but have an internal fear that they may not be able to do so because they lack the necessary skills. This is called the fear of failure. In the case of power motivation, it is the fear of impotence, of not being influential, and of not being able to exercise power over others. For this fearful person, because of their continuous need for approval and self-reinforcement, every interaction with another person is a test of their potency. An affiliation-motivated person fears rejection, not being accepted, loved, or appreciated. Though this person has a need for love, fear prevents taking active steps to achieve it. People may find secondary ways to compensate for their fears.

Different people handle this fear differently. Some handle fear by rejecting the goal itself. Internally they crave the goal, but they will say things against it, such as, "this goal is unrealistic." Other than demeaning the goal, they will stay passive. Others do tremendous planning. They have an inner urge to act, and they feel that the only way to get over their fears is by breaking down the action required into familiar pieces of tasks, so they conquer fear by extensive planning. After failure, people use defensive language like "goals must be realistic; you should not take too many risks to handle the situation." However, using defensive language does not prevent them from becoming miserable. Power-motivated individuals either talk about power negatively, as if it was a dirty thing, "power is bad, powerful people are bad, and power corrupts," even though inside they want to be powerful, or they turn to aggression. Power-motivated managers with fear of failure treat their staff by controlling and threatening them and by making other people feel small. They increase the distance between themselves and the individuals they manage.

Anxious people who believe that they are not clever enough and want to feel smarter than others always choose people who are less intelligent than they are. In the same way, a person who is stricken by a fear of impotence prefers people who are incompetent. Such a manager manipulates conditions so that employees feel incompetent and are forced to ask for help.

Executives who are self-confident and possess the ability to influence are aware of their potency and are interested in nurturing people. Their sense of mattering comes from developing people and gaining their respect, not from generating fear. People who are confident of their power and ability to influence like others around who are equal to them. Only then is interaction fun and can their talents come into play. Therefore, they use their managerial positions to nurture people to bring them to their potential. Often they believe that people can become better than they are. It is only after developing people that they derive satisfaction from influencing. Confident people are good listeners because it is through listening that they are open to being influenced. They believe that people are capable in themselves and give them autonomy because a person who is confident is willing to fail. Some failures do not lower the self-esteem of a confident person, but instead encourage learning and growth.

CONFIDENCE, HEALTH, AND JOY

A substantial amount of value loss in organizations happens through executives at all levels who may have so-called managerial knowledge, but who do not possess leadership skills and internal confidence. Those people slowly lower values in organizations.

Our experiences suggest that when the founders or key executives are healthy psychologically and have a capacity to experience joy in life, there is a higher chance that their surroundings will be healthy and joyful as well. This is not to suggest that individuals who may not be called completely healthy—in the holistic sense of having one or more of the indicators fall out of a given range—cannot create a healthy organization. However, in this case they need a strong self-awareness and a good understanding of themselves, of their strengths and weaknesses, and the ability to compensate for their weaknesses by including others in the leadership with different personalities. If that person has a strong determination, they can create a healthy and joyful organization. It is also possible to create a healthy and joyful organizational subsystem around an individual, even if the whole organization itself is not healthy and joyful, similar to creating an oasis in a desert.

When I think about people, who, in spite of their personal hardships run a joyful organization, a particular executive comes to mind. He is a talented individual, happily married for decades, who was chief executive of a company which was part of a larger group. He was well known for his ability to create an organization where employees loved to work. The company he led was so successful that he was expected to be promoted to a higher position. Unfortunately, he lost his dearly loved wife in a car accident and was turned down for the promotion. For some months he only felt devastation, but he soon took charge. He never complained or made cynical comments about the holding company or its executives, and he did not allow other members of the organization to continue to show sympathy for his loss. He made a conscious effort to stop his depression impacting on others in the organization. He continued to encourage people and was able to change other people's feelings in a genuine way. If anything, they respected him and enjoyed working for the company even more than before. His obvious success in the face of such hardships made a lasting impression on me.

PEOPLE CAN (AND OFTEN DO) PERCEIVE THE SAME EVENT DIFFERENTLY

We organize in order to bring things under control so that there is a higher probability that we will achieve our purpose. Organizing requires predictability, but the future is not predictable. Every person is guided by his or her belief in dealing with the unpredictable. Belief is our ideology, a view about "what is" and "what should be." We perceive the reality around us by using our belief systems as a filter and organizer. Perceptions in turn are important factors shaping our understanding about what is happening to us as individuals and to organizations. Armed with appropriate perceptions we can organize better. Achieving our purpose starts with perceptions. But perceptions have the most perplexing quality because different individuals can perceive exactly the same thing differently.

While reading this book, there will be a reasonable amount of differences among readers in how they will react to, use, or talk about this book, although they read the same text. If managers attend a meeting and afterwards separately explain to their subordinates what went on in the meeting, they all will tell different stories. If subordinates from different departments compare their notes, they may conclude that the bosses did not attend the same meetings! Since people who have attended the same meeting are different, the very same experience means different things to them.

When we perceive something, we look at things through a filter. The filter could be defined as previous experiences that actually influence what we see.

Every one of us has a history. Our individual belief system is based on those previously accumulated experiences in different situations; this includes our motivations, interests, values, and personality. Beliefs are generic, perceptions are specific. Using our beliefs as a filter, we can reconstruct reality in our mind, and while at it, conclude different things from the very same object. We actually see the present situation as similar to past experiences and circumstances and have a hard time recognizing variance. Sometimes we even go as far as to perceive only what is "convenient" to us and filter out all the "inconvenient" data.

I had been working in a business school and was the representative of the faculty. We were to select a new dean. Having worked closely with the candidate and having shared an office with her, I thought I knew the person quite well. I was one of the promoters of her becoming the new dean. She got the position. Sometime after she took office, we noticed that the administrative manager of the school seemed to be in constant conflict with the new dean. When the administrative manager complained, we professors were not sure whether she was justified in her complaints. We certainly did not want to confront the new dean. Personally, I did not see what the problem with the new dean was at all. The administrative manager was blaming the dean, accusing her of being unfair. Rumors began about the administrative manager. It got to the point that the dean decided that the administrative manager had to leave the organization. I had mixed feelings about how the new dean handled the situation, but I got over it without analyzing the incident. A few months later, I found out by accident that during a conversation in my absence, the dean made disapproving comments about me. Her comments seemed to be emotional and offensive, and her choice of the occasion to deliver them gave the definite impression of impertinence. However, when I heard from several more colleagues clearly inaccurate references to events related to me did I start to question my opinion of the dean. Our relationship turned bitter upon our confrontation about these reports. Finally, my perception of the new dean changed radically. I did not see her anymore as a trustworthy individual who was well positioned to run the business school. When I recollected the previous administrative manager, I recognized that the perception I had of the dean now resembled closely the administrative manager's before she left the school. I had to ask myself: why was I unable to see the problem before? Were there no signs? With hindsight, I easily identified the signals I had overlooked, because there was now a strong filter in front of my eyes. Probably, because I had been one of the promoters of the new dean, I wanted to see that I was right. In my perception, I filtered out information contradicting my image of this person.

These misperceptions happen quite often. We constantly filter out information and use restricted information to construct an image in our heads about individuals, organizations, situations, and about reality as a whole, and this limited image forms the basis of our judgments. When we enter a situation, we are unable to look at it objectively because we are subjects of the situation. We perceive something through our filters. After we have filtered out the information based on our previous experiences, we decide about the action we intend to take.

Let us say you are a manager of a department, and you find that somebody from the staff is coming late to work. Considering this information in the light of your previous experiences, you may say, "Well, people tend to be late; they do not care about work. Therefore, I have to act tough. To teach them a lesson, I will cut the salary of the latecomer." You selected this action based on your belief system, which indicated that since people do not care about work, only about the benefits they derive from working, cutting that benefit would make an impact. You perceive the outcome to be that the latecomer will feel bad and will arrive on time in the future. If you see this result—which you probably will—you reinforce your belief system, concluding confidently that you were right. If we face the same situation as a manager with a different belief system upholding that people are reasonable, our train of thoughts will be different. We will think, "If they happen to come late, there must be a reason." We would never start with cutting salary; rather, we would sit down with the latecomer to discuss what was going on, explain why it is difficult for the department to work without their presence, and ask whether they need support to ensure that it will not happen again. While doing this, we forge a good relationship with this person, and more likely than not, next time they will be on time. Perception has a tendency of reinforcing the belief system. Either way, in the above example we do not have to change anything. We do not have to learn. Our action is based on our belief system, and by acting we reinforce it.

LEARNING AND THE BELIEF SYSTEM

The process of learning may begin only after you acted, perceived the outcomes, realized that your goal was not achieved, stopped, and reflected. This time you do not separate yourself from the system that creates reality; you look at yourself as part of the system, which missed the goal. You analyze yourself, the situation, your role in it, and conclude from it. You see differently and build this new view into your belief system.

Some beliefs still originate in very limited experience. Sometimes the filter is so thick that whatever you sense does not influence you, unless something drastic happens; if you are shocked, your perception may change.

In India, the government initiated several programs to improve the living conditions in a concentrated population of former criminals. An extensive number of social workers worked in the area leading various rehabilitation programs. Conditions for establishing and operating companies in this area were extremely favorable. Over time, the effort was very fruitful, and economic activity flourished. I used to work with one of the companies in this region, in particular with two executives of a company. One of them talked about employees as "useless criminals," and often expressed that unless he was after them, they did not work. "Our workers are gangsters; you have to deal with them with a stick." He was convinced that it was this attitude which made them work. The other executive professed the opposite view. He said to me: "Once you train people in this region, you can just as well leave them alone to do it, and they will do an excellent job, while I spend my time planning the future. People work very well, I do not have to supervise them." What mattered was not where these workers were from but where these managers came from.

Another way our belief system is built up is through authority: "My grandmother used to tell me..." Developing our belief systems this way is socially convenient. Past experiences of an accepted authority lead us to a higher level of predictability and stability and, thus, to a higher level of security. That is how a significant portion of our belief systems is built. A wide range of people and sources can deliver past experiences to us, as long as we accept them as authority. However, we want to make a distinction between learning and building our belief system. Education illustrates this difference well. In school, we are told to trust what the teacher and our books say. When teachers do not like to be questioned, they are building belief systems by conveying past experiences in the role of authority.

During my second year in college, in the physics laboratory, I conducted an experiment to determine the value of gravity "g." I was an honest student and I conducted the experiment faithfully, putting various weights on to decide the "g." Using the measurement results the value of "g" with a mathematical formula can be calculated. My value of "g" differed slightly from the standard value. When I showed it to the lecturer, he said: "Manohar, don't you know the value of 'g'?" "The task was to conduct an experiment. I conducted the experiment; I did not copy the value out of the book." I still remember what he said: "Do you think that you are cleverer than Newton?" I was very angry. The lecturer and I were in the middle of a shouting match when the professor of physics walked into the laboratory. "What is happening?" I explained what I had done. He said: "Interesting. Let's carry out the experiment once again." He stood there as I repeated the experiment. The value was the result I got. He said: "Very good. I will give you good grades for this." But he did not stop there. He found it interesting too that the value of "g" differed from the value in the book. The professor explored the surroundings, and he found that there was a magnet under the table where I was conducting my experiment. I appreciated this more than the rebuke from the lecturer.

THE BELIEF SYSTEM OF ORGANIZATIONS

Organizations are built on belief systems because belief systems ensure predictability. The conflict of belief systems and perceptions is connected to individual, social, or organizational cultures. Very often, a person who was brought up in a particular culture gets "culture-bound" and does not know how to learn, or how to think out of the box. Culture is interpreted as tradition and accepted unconditionally. This results in a rigid belief system.

However, we do not suggest that being part of a culture and obeying it is all bad. Obedience to some extent is necessary. If we accept that order is required to reduce entropy, it follows that organizations always have a culture and a system to provide predictability in the process. Systems are designed and developed in a particular economic situation and social context.

Problems occur when the context changes and organizations stick to past experiences, beliefs, and actions. What is the origin of the belief system of an organization? It is typically genetic in the sense that the founder of the organization plays an important role in developing the set of beliefs. Others will of course add and take away. Nevertheless, those who start the organization have a defining influence in determining the type of belief system that will be valid for the organization. Since they play a very important role, and are often role models for others, the belief system gets disseminated.

An organization will attract people who have similar views to the founders and/or find their way easy to live with. Those who disagree to either would not join such an organization or would not hesitate to leave it. By a self-fulfilling prophecy, through the belief system, the organization will create its own reality. It is going to be very difficult to change such a situation.

We had been asked to make an organizational diagnosis in one well-known multinational company because of the concerns of the leadership over difficulties the company was experiencing. Quoting a short passage from the extensive and detailed diagnostic material will illustrate the difficulties that may occur when the belief systems and the leadership philosophies are not only unaligned, but are contradictory in a management team:

"Employees at every hierarchy level of the organization perceive that management is divided, and the organization suffers from the negative consequences of this divisiveness.... The internal problems troubling the top management appear to be one of the areas that need the most urgent attention. Lack of unity is the greatest problem, something that seeps over to everyday work and to lower levels of the organization... What makes the situation especially difficult is that there are significant differences in the deeply rooted beliefs, such as ones referring to the basic nature of people, how they can and should be managed, and what management tools are acceptable or unacceptable to use. In everyday life these differences are manifested in various ideologies that serve to provide a rational basis for enforcing a certain leadership style, be it an authoritarian, paternalistic, or a participatory style based on empowerment. There are various ways to direct an organization, but hardly any success if top management follow two completely different styles at the same time...The Toyota Production System [which our client was in the process of introducing] also demands a certain type of leadership style, philosophy, organizational, and management culture, since it builds on the inclusion, motivation, and initiatives of people—something that cannot be attained via authoritative methods. 'Bio-robots,' people who are considered disposable and replaceable and are treated as such, will never keep coming up with innovative ideas, will never improve efficiency and productivity on their own initiative. Therefore the management has to get its own act together in the first place: align its fundamental set of beliefs about the operation and leadership/management philosophy of the organization, in the course of which process a sense of mutual trust, acceptance, and respect will form between them. However superfluous and useless this may appear, it is inevitable for the harmonized management of an efficient, goal-oriented, and profitable company. Without this, vast amounts of money, time, and energy will be wasted and the entire organization will continue to suffer from the lack of harmonized actions..." After the top management team had received and read the Diagnostic material, we held a Data Feedback Workshop. The CEO said, "Well, guys, we cannot avoid facing ourselves in the mirror anymore, we cannot pretend we do not know what is going on, what is our responsibility in creating our problems. We cannot avoid acting on this..." Within a month two key persons (with a more authoritarian belief system and leadership style) got different jobs at different branches of the organization, and a major culture change program had been launched.

PERCEPTION IS INTERPRETATION

We discern what may be called reality through our senses, colored by our past experiences. However, sensing itself is not perception. Perception is different from sensing, because it includes judgment: Good, bad, right, or wrong, perception is interpretation. Perception ends with behavior or action of some sort. By behavior we do not mean only the externally visible patterns of acting; it can be internal as well.

Change, doing things differently, will come only if the belief system changes. In order to change the belief system, people actually have to recognize and be aware of what their belief system is. Sometimes it is not conscious at all. Sometimes you think it is something other than what you actually believe in. You have to be able to see the real consequences of your actions in order to reflect on the actual belief system, reconsider it, and change it.

I was running a program for the executives of an organization. The managing director was strong, a bit of an authoritarian type of person but open to learning. His deputies, the other directors, started to open up during the training session and gave feedback to the managing director. They said that sometimes he used threats toward them, and that they really felt uncomfortable when that happened. "When you threaten to fire us if this or that does not get done, do you believe we would work less hard if not for the threat? Is this the amount of trust that you have in us?" The managing director was surprised: "I really trust you." "If that is the case, then why do you threaten us?" Somebody said, "Do you remember what happened the other week? We had this crisis. It was 8:30 in the evening, and I was still in my office working out the alternative ways to tackle the problem. You called me and said if I do not solve this problem I would get into trouble. I told you that I am working on it but you insisted that if I do not find a solution, I would be fired. 'Your job is in danger' were your words. Do you know what I did? I shut off the computer, went to the door, put on my coat and left the office. That was the effect your threat had on me. There was a problem, I tried to find a solution to it as hard as I could, but when you started to tell me that I would be fired if the problem is not fixed, something in me rebelled. I reacted as a child. Of course, next day I came back and solved the problem." Then somebody else raised his hand and told a similar story. The managing director tried to defend himself. He thought in case of a serious problem, people should get the important message and the way to send that message has to be through a threat. He never had the chance to reflect on the consequences of his act before. It took him some time, but he started to give up this habit gradually.

Another way to change the belief system is to put people into circumstances where they have to face a new situation and then let them analyze it.

Another example from the same organization is the executive meetings. The managing director was extremely overwhelmed. Executive meetings had the following format: the managing director was running the show, he asked for the briefs, explained the issue, asked whether there were any questions, summarized the points, and made the decision. Most of the responsibility was directly on one person. When they decided to apply the empowerment team concept, they had to change the structure of the meeting as well. They decided that every time a different member would play the role of the chairman of the meeting. The managing director could equally participate in the discussions, and the others would have the experience of running a meeting and keeping it on track. Initially the meetings started off in a stilted manner, as although somebody else was running the meeting and it was still the managing director who often overpowered the rest of the group. They began to question whether it was a good idea or not, but they carried on anyway. At some point, we video recorded the whole meeting and then analyzed it together. They found many issues they could improve on. Nowadays, this is the way they run all their meetings and they cannot imagine doing it any other way.

If you change the structure and the context of the event, that will bring about new behavior. The new behavior will impact the belief system, and the new belief system will generate new action.

STABILITY IS NECESSARY, BUT WHEN IS CHANGE NECESSARY?

Stability is necessary. You do not have to experiment and to focus on new learning all the time. Sometimes you may use what you learned previously rather than relearn everything. The belief system is absolutely necessary in order to be functional. If you forgot what you have learned, you would be paralyzed and unable to take action. Organizations prefer stability; change is difficult, uncomfortable for most. However, some people are in favor of change just because it generates excitement and increases the adrenaline level. Both groups would give a long list of logical arguments why stability or change is required. The arguments are based on their attitudes, belief systems, and personalities. The question is, how do you decide if your belief system is already antagonistic to the circumstance?

SOME BELIEFS LEAD TO HEALTH, OTHERS TO DISEASES

A leader's belief system can be categorized based on the likely nature of the organization he or she will tend to create. So which beliefs of leaders lead to organizational health, and which cause diseases in an organization? You will find the major leadership-related belief systems provided systematically below. These are not exhaustive in reflecting all possible details of belief systems, but are rather examples of the main wave of beliefs, the actions that follow naturally from them, and the consequences of that action for organizational health or diseases.

We would also like to reiterate that creating a healthy organization (or parts of it) starts at the top, as this individual/group influences the character of the organization and is instrumental in managing change and transition. In either case, the need for a change is rooted in the reexamination of the key people's belief systems in the organization, however small or big that organization may be. The burden is always on the executive to understand their specific beliefs and the likely impacts, since nobody can change someone else's belief system. Healthy organizations will be created where the key players find that organizational health characteristics are aligned with their belief systems of how to run an organization, remain in business, deal with human beings, and organize human communities. Those who find these ideas strange would never initiate approaches leading to organizational health in the way we have defined it.

Belief systems have various aspects, and, in the following, we have picked the most prominent ones to illustrate their effects:

- One of the most important subjects [objects?] of belief systems are people. Executives have certain beliefs of how people work and how to "make them more efficient."

  - Related aspects include not only how to get more work out of people, but also how to provide facilities for them or how to exercise control.

- Important beliefs relate to how organizations work.

  - Other aspects of this group of beliefs are how vision defines operations and how work is to be organized.

- Important aspects of belief systems consider life itself and the meaning of life.

  - Beliefs about life define beliefs about personal growth, the desirable balance between private and professional life, and the meaning of work, among other important issues.

We have deliberately chosen straightforward, clear-cut examples to illustrate the range of possible impacts. While describing the examples in simple ways, we intended to establish a pattern that every reader can extrapolate to identify the consequences of more peculiar beliefs on the health of the organization. However, we are aware that our intent necessarily resulted in oversimplification of the examples and that in real life the situations we face are more complex and have many more alternative outcomes. We believe that the listed beliefs, actions, and consequences are typical examples of the patterns. The two central columns explain the two extreme sides of a belief, and the actions and consequences of each can be found following the arrows toward each side in Tables 10.1 through 10.8.

Table 10.1
Vision-Related Beliefs

Leading to Diseases				Leading to Health	
Consequences	Actions	Beliefs	Beliefs	Actions	Consequences
Vision statements do not provide guidance and focus for the activities of the organization. Different groups within the organization consider different factors as key components for direction and are not aligned with each other.	The vision—if there is one—contains vague, unconnected statements, reflecting current management ideas and buzz words.	Vision statements are made up by consultants and have little relevance for the organization other than being a more or less effective component of PR (public relations).	A vision is needed because it gives direction and keeps the organization on track and focused on priorities.	Develop a vision strategic enough to address direction and detailed enough to identify the most important objectives to reach.	The organization is aligned and activities are coordinated by the common focus provided by the vision.
Not all members understand and internalize the vision; consequently, some do not develop commitment and thus feel alienated.	Vision is discussed only at executive forums behind closed doors.	The vision should be shared only among executives. Lower-level employees would not understand it and would not know how to apply it. It is none of their business.	The vision should be shared across the organization.	Different forums exist within the organization for sharing the vision. Members from all levels discuss it and contribute to its development.	All members of the organization understand and internalize the vision and develop commitment to it. Decision makers at every level consider the vision as the expression of the final objective for their actions.

Table 10.2
Customer-Related Beliefs

Consequences	Leading to Diseases Actions	Beliefs	Beliefs	Leading to Health Actions	Consequences
Alienated customers. Loss of market share due to lack of repeat purchases. Low image.	A substantial amount of promotion and advertising is done to attract customers even with unlikely promises. Customer complaints have no follow-up. Relationship with customers is not mutually beneficial or cooperative.	Getting the maximum out of the customer for the minimum investment. This way we can maximize our profit from all of our transactions.	Customers are vital stakeholders. Customers are partners and we have to understand their needs. We have to do our best to provide the best value to them, the best quality at the lowest possible price.	Keep close contact and frequent interactions with the customers using many different forums. Be open and listen to them. Actively utilize customers' knowledge and input in all activities of the organization from product design to distribution.	Loyal customers, repeat orders, long-term supplier relationships, word-of-mouth marketing, high reputation, and stability.

Table 10.3
Employee-Related Beliefs

Consequences	Leading to Diseases Actions	Beliefs	Beliefs	Leading to Health Actions	Consequences
Alienation. Employees try to get the maximum out of the organization for the minimum investment they can get away with. They are not fulfilled, they feel taken advantage of, and they retaliate.	Give the minimum compensation for work the organization can get away with. Spend the minimum on employee development. Hire-and-fire practices in the organization reflect short-term considerations. Employees are closely supervised.	Employees are cost factors, which should be kept minimal and out of which the maximum benefit should be gained. Employees are a means to an end. Employees are disposable resources, easily replaceable whenever necessary.	People are assets to the organization. Employees have their own objectives of personal growth, which should be encouraged and facilitated as much as possible.	Continuous concern for the personal growth, development, and well-being of employees. Decision making reflects that they are an important part of the organization. Employees are listened to; their contribution to problem solving is encouraged at every level.	Feeling of belongingness. Employees find working in the organization fulfilling. They provide creative solutions to problems. They are motivated, and they thrive mentally and physically.

Table 10.4
Organization-Related Beliefs

← Consequences	Leading to Diseases Actions	Beliefs	Beliefs	Leading to Health Actions	Consequences →
Problems recur; fire fighting is part of everyday operations. Unexpected additional costs to keep the operation going are common. Problems with quality and delivery are typical.	Work processes and practices are neglected rather than kept up-to-date.	Processes and operations run themselves; no intervention is necessary. There is no point in wasting time, money, and energy on fashionable and fancy improvement projects. These cost a lot and eventually fade without much to show for them.	The organization has to thrive continuously to operate in the most efficient way possible, with minimal loss of resources (with minimal entropy). One has to pay particular attention to processes and operational issues.	Processes are continuously monitored and reevaluated. People are trained and empowered to improve the efficiency of operations within their reach.	High-quality, low-cost operation with state-of-the-art solutions, which may often be considered as benchmarks by other organizations.

222

Table 10.5
Teamwork-Related Beliefs

← Consequences	Leading to Diseases Actions	Beliefs	Beliefs	Leading to Health Actions	Consequences →
People work by themselves. They do not have a lot of interaction with each other and usually do not assist each other. Rivalry is likely. Lack of synergy.	Individual work is encouraged. Executives delegate to individuals and monitor individual performance.	Teamwork results in great loss of time and energy. It leads to mediocrity.	People can achieve more together. Synergy comes from teamwork. Organizational learning can flourish where people are working in teams.	Work is organized in teams. Teams have time to do thorough work. Training programs are provided to ensure the efficiency of teamwork, delegation, and empowerment.	People are motivated working in teams. Teams perform successfully. People develop commitment and belongingness to the team and to the organization. They are eager to take on more responsibilities.

Table 10.6
Personal Growth-Related Beliefs

Consequences	Leading to Diseases / Actions	Beliefs	Beliefs	Leading to Health / Actions	Consequences
People are highly specialized, but narrow-minded. They have skills and understanding only in their own areas. Friction exists among different departments and functions. Management has to spend substantial time to sort out conflicts. Loyalty is for the department, not the organization. Suboptimization.	Hire people with a potential, but if they do not perform, do not worry about how to develop them; instead find somebody else. Strictly defined role and job descriptions. Minimal budget for training programs. No energy spent on career development planning. No cross-functional information sharing.	Hire people who already have the necessary competencies. People should focus on their area and tasks and focus their learning as much as possible. Specialization in its members is what makes an organization successful.	People join organizations not only for financial concerns, but also for enhancing their careers and for personal development. It is the organization's responsibility to provide opportunities for personal growth.	A good learning environment is created. People are encouraged to learn more about the work of the different functions in the organization. They are also given the opportunity to learn new skills across functions.	People not only develop themselves, but develop a stronger commitment to the organization, so they try to perform their best under these conditions.

224

Table 10.7
Private Life–Related Beliefs

Consequences	Leading to Diseases Actions	Beliefs	Beliefs	Leading to Health Actions	Consequences
Members are overwhelmed. They exhibit signs of being burned out and stressed. Psychosomatic diseases and private life problems occur frequently.	Staying longer than working hours is expected. People are expected to be reachable during vacations. People are called at home regularly.	Private life should be kept separate from professional life. Private matters should not be mixed with professional concerns. The organization needs the whole person; how an employee manages potential conflicts between professional and private life is his or her problem.	People have complex identities. Besides work, they have other roles. People are, first of all, human beings and only secondarily work for the organization and perform certain tasks. Private life cannot be fully separated from work. A balance is important between professional and private life.	People are encouraged to use their vacation times and to work only during working hours. Family members are invited to events to spend time together in organizational surroundings. The organization supports its employees in sorting out important private life–related concerns.	People are less likely to develop psychosomatic diseases, burn out, or be stressed. They feel that they have dignity as human beings. They grow more in this organizational context. They have a stronger commitment. They contribute more creatively to organizational purposes

225

Table 10.8
Work-Related Beliefs

← Consequences	Leading to Diseases Actions	Beliefs	Beliefs	Leading to Health Actions	Consequences →
People are not given the chance to feel connected to a greater purpose and do not see the meaning of their work. Work is a burden. Strong unions may come to life to minimize working hours, working efforts, and to maximize workers' benefits. Alienation.	Employees are identified by tasks. Work is designed to be a series of tasks, divided so it can be supervised easily. Close control is prevalent.	Work is a burden. We have to work in order to make a living: "I work to live." Life comes after the work is done. Work itself is not something to enjoy. No wonder people try to distance themselves from the difficulties of work.	Work is a natural part of life. Work should be enjoyable. Work should provide opportunities for self-realization, success, and feeling good about oneself.	Work is organized in a way that people can enjoy it. Working conditions are designed to minimize difficulties. More interesting and challenging work is continuously provided.	People are motivated to accomplish tasks and perform well. They experience continuous enrichment from work. They feel that they contribute to a greater purpose. Their competencies increase while working.

CHAPTER 11

Creating a Joyful Organization

Once we have a healthy organization and are aware of how our belief system influences it, can we do anything specific to encourage joy? What are the sources of experiencing joy? How do we lose the capacity to experience joy? How do we revitalize people and create an ambience for joy?

JOY IS THE FUNCTION OF ORGANIZATIONAL HEALTH AND LEADERSHIP

We began this book by observing the enormous gap between how people experience work and what kind of experiences would make an organization more likely to endure and fulfill its vision. We scrutinized specific characteristics of the joyful organization in the hope that a more analytical approach would not only lead us to understand why such organizations are so few, but would also offer insights into how to create them. The most important conclusion from this investigation is that getting closer to this desired state often requires action that is counterintuitive and not immediately obvious.

The first layer of complexity comes from the fact that the existence of organizational diseases prevents joy from being a frequent enough experience at work. We discussed what a healthy organization is and what comes in the way of becoming healthy. We have defined the most frequently occurring organizational diseases and their causes and suggested a variety of interventions to overcome them. We have differentiated between health criteria on the basis of how directly they impact joy, the feeling of belongingness having the most direct effect on joy in an organization.

The second layer of complexity is added by the nature of human belief systems, especially the fact that we often do not consciously recognize the important impact they have on the organization. We argued that leaders make or break a joyful organization by virtue of their beliefs. We also argued that awareness of our specific beliefs plays the most critical role in consciously shaping the organization or the part that we lead. This is due to multiple reasons related to human nature and cultural characteristics. Humans rarely demonstrate the tendency to follow a holistic approach. Instead, we have limited skills and live in a culture that makes us focus and prioritize, addressing one area or another of organizational health, instead of trying to harmonize them. Thus, if we are not aware of our beliefs and the impact we as leaders have on the organization, we can hardly counterbalance it to be more holistic.

One conclusion we draw is that creating a joyful organization is not a linear process, which we can describe in a finite number of steps. Rather, it is a process that takes place in multiple layers, with some steps having the capacity of generating a greater effect than others. Our experience shows that acting on the insights from applying this framework increases the likelihood of success.

HEALTH AND LEADERSHIP ARE NECESSARY BUT NOT SUFFICIENT

Using the framework in this book yields insights through applying its analytical approach to behavior patterns in the organization. Based on those insights an organization can follow specific recommendations to make the organization healthier. In addition to applying this framework and acting on the diagnosis, we have identified supplementary techniques, such as raising awareness, that can further facilitate joyful experiences in an organization. However, organizational health and leadership awareness both happen to be necessary but not fully sufficient conditions in facilitating joyful experiences. They remove the barriers from experiencing joyful work, but they do not guarantee it.

Disease: Joylessness

Work is compulsory struggle; try to avoid it as much as you can.

Description

The general attitude toward work, the job and the organization, is that it is compulsory, brings difficulties and boredom, and has to be done. People do not look forward to being at work, do not enjoy what they do, and do not have a feeling of accomplishment. They regard their work solely as an income source and would abandon it as soon as they could afford to do so.

Symptoms

- People perceive that routine, repetitive activities make up their day. They do not face new challenges, but instead they feel they only execute the same task over and over.

- They may feel stuck at this workplace, feeling their potential was much higher.

- People do not look forward to being at work. Occasionally they arrive late or stretch other activities that may keep them away from the workplace (meetings somewhere else, sick leave, and so forth).

- People feel as if they are floating alone in the organization without the support of their colleagues. It appears as if their colleagues are even less committed and work even less than they do.

- The general approach to quality is "it's good enough"; what nominally fulfills the quality requirements is done, but there is a lingering feeling that real good quality would be something else entirely.

- People do not feel committed to their work; they occasionally experience a feeling of struggling, or working against all odds. They do not focus on the task at hand; instead they focus on the barriers, excuses, and reasons why it is not possible to do what they would consider a really good job.

- The general mood is quite depressed and unhappy. There is not much joking, or leg pulling, and if there is any, it is unrelated to the work, or at the expense of others or the organization.

- People do not express pride at belonging to the organization; they do not tell family and friends about it, or if they do, they talk only critically. They do not like to wear the company logo T-shirts, and they have no enjoyment of corporate functions.

- Employees feel empty, they do not identify with the larger goals or mission of the organization, and they do not have the recurring feeling that they are actively contributing to the good of society by their everyday activity.

- Members do not consider their organization as a model for any of its activities and do not actively compare their organization or practices to others unless as a negative example.

- Even the managers are not exempt from all these symptoms.

Causes

- Executives do not enjoy their work and believe that nobody should.

- The organization is struggling for survival, has many diseases, and is not operating healthily or moving toward the fulfilling of its vision.

Origins

- The genetic origin is that the founder's approach to life is defined by struggling and is not letting anybody else enjoy their work either. In general terms they are not happy people or definitely do not think that joy and work have anything to do with each other. Another possible origin can be that the leader is an exploitative

Table 11.1
Joylessness

Structure of Causes	Possible Causes	Possible Actions for Improvement
Personal Leadership Related	1. Key executives believe that work is not joyful and enjoying it excludes hard work. 2. Key executives believe that it is not their responsibility to create a joyful environment at work. 3. Key executives do not feel that the organization's objectives contribute to the common good of the society. 4. Managers believe that their job is to squeeze the maximum out of people at any price.	*Executive Coaching, Training Workshop, and/or Other:* • Provide people individual assessment of their priorities, values, and objectives. • Help people discover their own joy at a certain type of work. • Develop an understanding of how executives influence the workplace and the work experience of others. • Discuss with other executives who have gone through a similar phase in life. • Experience joy in other than work circumstances, from art, gastronomy, science, or other activities together. • Implement creativity training.
Organizational, Operational	1. People have not internalized the vision and do not think the vision is positive or that they have anything to do with it. 2. In the case of multinationals, the objectives of the operations are controlled from	*Coaching, Training Workshop, and/or Other:* • Assess the organizational objectives and vision.

230

Structure of Causes	Possible Causes	Possible Actions for Improvement
		abroad; local operations disregard local circumstances and culture.
	3. People feel alone in the organization; they do not feel that colleagues are committed and hard working.	• Work together with the corporate headquarters to adapt and localize the objective of the organization or at least modify communications so the vision is understood locally.
		• Implement teamwork training emphasizing reliance on each other.
	4. People sense that the quality is not right, or just nominally right. They do not feel that they can/should do anything about it, leading to a generally skeptical, demoralized climate.	• Develop forums for quality proposals. Establish a feedback system from customers on improvements.
		• Bring in lighthearted, fun experiences for the teams.
	5. The constant struggle has eaten up all the energy of the people.	• Organize events for celebrating success; create opportunities for experiencing appreciation of good performance, and organize other events where people can feel good about themselves. Include outdoor training, combining teamwork with physical exercises and endurance training.
External, Market Related	1. Joy is not regarded as part of work by society.	*Interventions:*
	2. The broader society is depressed.	• Reveal the impact of executives on how members of the organization may feel at work and what the negative consequences are.
	3. Economic indicators are unfavorable, including high unemployment, and employers take advantage of this situation so exploitation of employees is common.	

character who wants to use people for personal gain or the organization's benefit, without seeing them as human beings.

- The birth-related origin is that the initial challenges of the organization put too much pressure on everyone, and the initial stress and struggle meant they just got used to the idea that work is more of a struggle than anything else.

- The environmental origin is that when the external circumstances in the society are depressing, things are not very much different within the organizations itself. For example, most organizations within a dictatorial system tend to be quite depressing places as well. On the other hand, in strongly individualistic societies joy from work may be considered a personal objective for the individual for which the organization and its leaders can contribute nothing. This puts all the burden on the individual and implies that if there is no joy at work it is really the individual who has failed.

This disease often occurs together with Organizational Paranoia, Self-Centered Leadership, and Alienation.

A structured list of causes and possible actions for improvements for this disease can be seen in Table 11.1.

In addition to removing the barriers from experiencing joyful work, joyful experiences can be actively encouraged. In this last chapter, we suggest specific alternatives that leaders can consider to advance the creation of a joyful environment.

EARLY SOCIALIZATION SUPPRESSES OUR NATURAL INSTINCT OF JOYFUL DISCOVERING

In the process of growing up and becoming adults, many of us actually lose the capacity to experience joy. Every newborn has an inherent capacity to experience joy. It is very instructive to observe how and from what sources small children get joy. Early childhood learning aims to obtain information about the world in a joyful way. Children discover their physical surroundings by touching, taking a close look, and tasting everything that can possibly fit into their mouths. They engage all their senses in gathering information. It is striking to an observer how deeply absorbed they are in the activity. As they grow a little older, they love being able to manipulate the object of their discovery, turn it every which way, and make sounds by pushing or shaking it. When they succeed, they react with a radiant smile and hearty laughter. Learning by defining is a natural and basic instinct in us. By discovering and understanding the world, we give ourselves a better chance to adapt to it. However, this is not simply a survival function. The very action of discovering and understanding new things becomes a rich source of experiencing joy. Experiencing joy is a fundamental inborn capacity we all have.

If in early childhood we universally possess and exert the capacity to experience joy, why not later? As children grow older, the expectations of what and how they learn changes radically. Before we enter school, the steps of discovery are voluntary. Children decide what they are interested in, which senses to employ in the particular discovery process, and for how long. Especially at the very early stage, outside influence, even parental intervention, is likely to be minimal. By the time we reach school, this transforms thoroughly into its opposite. Others decide for us where and when we learn, for how long we should be engaged in the particular learning, and what is and what is not acceptable behavior in the class. Others decide the content of our learning. As time goes on, others evaluate whether our learning was appropriate or not and give feedback accordingly, regardless of whether we need it or not. Others even decide when we can go to the toilet.

Experimenting requires autonomy, but granting autonomy makes things unpredictable for teachers. Learning therefore is likely to be equated with memorizing and recalling approved answers rather than with experimenting and enjoying the process. Some teachers teach students; most teach a subject. In most schools around the world, the voluntary element of our automatic learning instinct, which earlier on was so important in motivating us, ends up being repressed. The more we feel the obligation to learn things, the less we possess enthusiasm and joy. In the name of discipline children are taught obedience, and it is no wonder that a lot of children rebel against studying. Efficiency drops in correlation with the diminishing motivation for learning as the motivating force behind our learning is transformed into the feeling of obligation. It is what a responsible citizen or a responsible child is supposed to do. Thus the sharp drop in joyful experiences in time leads to the reduction of the capacity to experience joy. Joy, at best, remains associated with hobbies or family activities, not school, and certainly not work.

Most of us carry this pattern from the school to the workplace to some extent, where consequently people expect to be either a commander or an obedient executor. For the majority in the workplace, it is the latter. Somebody else determines when, where, and how long we work. It is others who set the performance criteria, others who judge our accomplishment, giving feedback according to their standards. No wonder we resent the situation and do not even consider work as a possible source of joy. The similar structure of the teacher-student relationship in schools to the manager-employee relationship at work provokes a similar type of unconscious, childish set of behavior patterns by employees.

In school, success is mostly defined by the grades we get, not by how we understand the subject. We memorize what we have to repeat: the correct, accepted, and preapproved answers. Education is designed to prepare for employment, to pass exams, to qualify for obtaining positions, not to successfully interact with the environment and even less to learn. The same pattern is observable in organizations. According to common understanding, a manager's role is to get things done. It implies that people who work for the manager do not have ownership of what they do. We are there to perform a task; our thinking has to be limited to what is relevant to that task. Naturally, people often lose the sense of the meaning of their task.

IDEAS AND EMOTIONS CAN ALSO BE A SOURCE OF JOY

In addition to our senses, employing our minds also has the potential to become a source of joy. When we think creatively, come up with new ideas, discoveries, and "play with information," we can experience joy. In many organizations, creativity is discouraged. We often find ourselves controlled to such a degree that we feel cornered to do the right, approved, thing, not to cause friction, and not ruffle any feathers. Unless we have a strong intrinsic motivation in addition to succeeding in the organization, sooner or later, we lose the capacity to experience joy.

Most social conditioning around the world holds that in professional life, a person is not supposed to be emotional and that emotions are considered to be inappropriately subjective. In spite of this convention, undeniably, emotions guide us in important ways and can also be a potential source of joy. Positive emotions about our experience in an organization, such as being part of a community, being surrounded by people who care about us and whose well-being we care about, and feeling that we contribute to achieving some common objective, all of these also have the potential to generate joy. On the other hand, when we experience negative emotions and do not trust our emotions enough to allow them to guide us, we float without attachment. Our behavior is likely to become "robot-like," and our capacity of experiencing joy is diminished.

THE IMPACT OF INJUSTICE ON OUR CAPACITY TO EXPERIENCE JOY

In addition to socialization, there is another important reason why people might lose the capacity to experience joy. When people feel that they are subjected to immense injustice, they become negative, and their capacity to experience joy can significantly diminish. Perceiving injustice leads to either being passive or being rebellious. Villains need different counseling than heroes. Villains, by their rebellion and passivity, will have a negative impact on the organization. Counseling is effective if it focuses on them as persons rather than on what they contribute to the organization. Heroes, on the other hand, do not need counseling as persons. They work from inner motivation, and, instead of missing personal attention, their issue is that groups often try to pull them down. Counseling, in this case, should focus on patience, and foremost on actively developing group acceptance. Once that is in place, heroes can be rewarded, and both they and the group will experience joy.

A group leader I used to know was once a tremendously joyful person, who later became bitter, because of the injustice he experienced. He was not what is commonly called a charismatic leader, but he was highly respected by all his colleagues. After 12 years, he did not get the promotion he felt he deserved, and he became so passive that he almost stopped working. The culture of the group he led started to change, too, reflecting his bitterness and change of attitude. A new manager came to his office and heard about how this individual had earlier made a significant impact on others, and how the group was known to be a joyful one. Everything the new manager saw now was passivity. Once when they ran into each other on the street, the manager initiated a discussion about their private lives. After that, they openly discussed various issues. One day, the new manager invited the group leader to lunch and asked what he was most curious about: "I heard legends about the joy you and your team experienced at work in the past, but the person I see now is completely different. Why? I would like to see the person you were before. It is painful to see how you hurt yourself, and your team." Suddenly he felt better—the new manager was interested in him as a person, and not only in his results. This was a new attitude he had not experienced before. It took him several months to recover, but with the help of coaching from the new office manager, he came out of the shell of passivity.

HOW CAN WE INCREASE OUR CAPACITY FOR JOY?

By now, it is obvious that we want to create organizations that become joyful places. Executives who succeed in creating such organizations for sustained periods usually have traveled a journey that shows two similar patterns.

First, either consciously or instinctively, they understand the deeper dynamics of organizations. They are not only able to provide a compelling and shared vision, but also to impartially observe how members of the organization behave; thus they are more likely to develop healthier organizations.

Second, joy has a distinguished rank among their personal values. It is important for them personally that the work experience of employees is not miserable, and that the quality of the part of their life influenced by work is high. For this reason, in some form or another it is their explicit objective to lead an organization that provides this environment, as well as profits from it. They themselves do not regard work as purely a burden or sacrifice and thus consciously or instinctively create an environment that is more conducive to joy for others.

I was developing a training program for branch managers at a bank, and so I decided to study what branch managers do and what it means to be a good branch manager. I studied one branch that was identified as a very good one and had about 25 people working there. Upon entering the place I was struck by the overall positive impression it gave. I started interviewing people and found that they talked highly of the branch manager, something I had not found before. They explained that when this manager arrived, he introduced interesting initiatives. First, he involved everybody in community contact. He persuaded them to talk to the traders and colonies of the community to attract more business. It had never been done in other branches. Initially employees opposed this. "Why should we do it? Our work is inside the bank." Slowly the bank manager persuaded a few people who did and came back with wonderful stories: "We went to this family, we spoke to that trader, and we were able to increase deposits threefold in two years." Employees also commented that the branch manager often came out from his office smiling, talking, and walking around. He encouraged people to get together after work, invited them to his own house to meet his family. Twice a year, they had picnics with their whole families. They also said that though the branch manager was very serious about work, he did not like to push work to the next day and encouraged everything to be finished promptly. They were proud of their work environment. They concluded that they were happy and the branch manager did not treat them as clerks, but as persons.

I also spoke to the union leader and told him about my negative experiences at other branches. I said to him, "I am happy that you are so proud of what happens in this branch, but what if tomorrow there is a national strike? What will you do?" He replied, "If there is a call for strike, we will go on strike." I asked, "What is the point then in having a good branch manager?" He said, "Oh, there is a difference. When there is a strike, we will not do anything against that branch manager. I will personally defend him. I will not even allow strike notices and strike posters to be placed on the branch walls, because this branch looks really nice. When the strike is over I will myself take responsibility to ensure that all backlog accumulated during the strike is cleared promptly." It was a remarkable statement coming from the union leader. Finally, I spoke to the branch manager. He talked about his good people. "They were developing this branch so well. I am just helping them." People were as proud of him as he was of them.

CAN ONLY JOYFUL PEOPLE CREATE JOYFUL ORGANIZATIONS?

At the end of our exploring the creation of a joyful organization, we would like to come back to whether or not only joyful people are able to create a joyful organization. Judging from the intensity of questions we have received, this is a crucial question for most people. Of course, it is very likely that somebody with a higher capacity for joy and desire to experience joy from life, including work, has a better chance to build up a joyful place and spread joy around. Since this person inherently understands the importance of joy and feels responsible for the organization, he or she will actively facilitate joy across the organization, operating in ways that spread health and joy. Yet, we do not think that only joyful people are capable of creating a joyful organization. People who are less capable of experiencing joy personally are still able to create a joyful organization. Individuals have their own purposes, just as organizations do. Managers who are convinced that it is important for the organization to become healthy and joyful can start to act to facilitate this experience. If they do not experience joy, it is better to start the process within themselves. Self-awareness and determination, not just the key people's capacity to experience joy, are the most important factors in creating the kind of organization we have suggested in this book.

After a few intense months of work with a significant new client, I decided to extend a national long weekend into a short ski vacation. I needed a break and wanted to ski with my sons, something we had not done for a long time. When I returned, I felt revitalized. The clean mountain air, the beauty of the snow on the slopes, playing on the slopes, the cozy dinners all had their effect. Little did I realize they also affected my colleagues, until one of them said jokingly, "We shall send you back at regular intervals. Since you returned, it is much more fun to be around you. You gave us much less trouble, came up with more solutions to problems and new ideas than during the half year before."

Key persons have the highest influence in nurturing the culture of the organization—spreading the right messages, modeling the expected behavior across the organization—and therefore they should be aware of the implications of their own behavior patterns. They also must have an honest concern for other people's well-being. Without this self-awareness, and concern, they are unable to push the organization to this higher level. Depending on what part of the organization we look at, a key person can be anyone who works with others in some capacity. The fact that the highest executive of an organization does not embrace this concept should not make it impossible—though admittedly it makes it more difficult—for sections of the organization to become joyful. To underline how much this is subject to the purpose and personality traits of the individual, here is an example of building an "island" in an organization against all odds.

One of our clients received a restructuring loan from the World Bank. This company also had a lead engineer, who designed the harvesting equipment the company produced. Motivated by personal desire to construct the best harvester of its kind, he and his team followed the life of every one of their "creations" over a span of 15 years. They knew the extent of the machines' utilization in the cooperatives (often much higher than they were designed for), under what conditions, when and how they broke down, and how they were maintained (often poorly). Based on this information, the engineer led his team in improving the construction over the years to withstand the most difficult conditions and lack of maintenance. They made a game out of keeping score on the machines and the improvements and around whose solution was simpler and more elegant. Members developed their own language and jokes, set their own visions, standards, and measured their own results. They had absolutely no outside requirement to do so; the harvesters were sold for the same centrally defined price and the employees had the same compensation, independent of the quality of the product or their contribution. This team was clearly an "island" within the organization with strictly internal motivation. Not until the company restructured, introduced using financial measurements, and started to sell the harvesters on foreign markets did any incentive come from the outside.

However, belief systems are not always conscious. Even beyond the belief systems, there are deeper motives that drive behavior. Here is an anxious manager with deep fears, who creates a diseased climate thanks to his diseased behavior, and excludes a chance for joy.

We knew an excellent, technically very competent senior manager. He was demanding to such a degree that most people were usually apprehensive when they had to interact with him. Though they respected him for his technical competencies, they became paralyzed when confronted by him. The common sentiment was that he was unbearable and that he should be told of the negative impact he had on others. However, nobody had the courage to tell him how he affected others, until finally a young employee blurted it out. "We like you because you help us, but there is one thing we are all concerned about. We live in terror anticipating your demands." For several days thereafter, the executive felt so offended that he had no reply to this outburst. Everybody waited for what he would do. He reflected on what happened, hoping that it did not represent common opinions and some people felt otherwise. To his dismay, he found that the feeling was universal. Sorting out his feelings he decided that instead of ignoring the incident or retaliating, he should listen and try to change. Later, this story was retold frequently and with great amusement.

We cannot stress enough that self-awareness is not just a useful or even fashionable thing for executives, but an obligation. Their characters, their personalities, their beliefs, and their inner feelings influence others as they accomplish the goals of the organizations. A leader who does not know himself or herself can cause significant damage in an organization, alienating people and even making them unhealthy. On the other hand, if the leader understands the mechanisms through which he or she is impacting the organization, the effect can be exactly the opposite, and other people may have valuable, pleasant experiences, in addition to the fact that the organization will flourish. They really have to understand this very well in order to use it well.

We have discussed the socialization process we go through and its profound effect on the learning behavior we carry in ourselves from early childhood. This insight can help us in considering our personal values and beliefs and, if necessary, in "reprogramming" ourselves, our belief systems about work, and life in general. We may then regain or increase our own capacity for feeling joyful and consider practical steps toward creating a joyful organization.

Once the organization is approaching a level of health, leaders can support the act of creating a joyful organization by increasing people's capacity to experience the feeling of joy, initiating the ambience for joy, and making work itself more joyful. It is important that these steps are taken simultaneously, not one after the other since they reinforce each other in making an organization healthier and helping to increase self-awareness.

REKINDLING THE SENSES AND CREATING AN AMBIENCE FOR JOY

We would like to share the following unique experience, which illustrates our point.

The managing director of one of our clients explained the dilemma he faced. The majority of the managers in the organization were in their mid-forties and fifties. The economy was going through rapid changes and this financial organization needed to keep up. His question was, who among the managers had the mind-set and the ability to handle more responsibilities and renew operations to match the changes.

During my initial visits, I found that people looked weary, they considered work as a burden; they even considered family as a burden. They clearly felt overwhelmed. They went through the routine of work everyday, but they had lost interest in it long ago. There were no smiles, no feelings, they just performed routine tasks. They did not interact with the external world; rather they confined themselves to the inner working of the organization. They did not appear to be equipped to meet the requirements of the new circumstances; indeed, they all gave the impression of having lost interest in life. There was an overall feeling of low self-esteem thanks to pressures from every corner.

It appeared that their senses had become dull. As far as the requirements for work and adapting to changes were concerned, they seemed unable to obtain the necessary information from the environment, become excited about it, and act creatively and innovatively. They appeared to have lost their capacity to be energized by new challenges. I shared my assessment with the managing director and suggested a very simple experiment: expose everyone to a variety of experiences, and their senses would be revitalized, and as their confidence grew, their skills would also grow as would their added value to the organization. He went along with the suggestion. We invited a conductor and went to a concert to enjoy music together. We visited museums together with an art historian and an artist, who helped us appreciate the different aspects of art. We took them out to a forest at night to look at the stars with an astronomer who related fascinating stories about them. We went out to dine with a gourmet cook to different kinds of restaurants. We smelt perfumes! We organized discussions of literary and economic topics. At first people thought the program was insane. They were skeptical of it and suspicious as to the purpose. They did not like being taken out of their routine and resisted being involved in the activities. Slowly, as word spread about the individual events, they became curious. After a few months, faces started to change. Participants started to show interest, ask questions, and contribute to the discussions. They felt younger. Lifeless routine meetings became livelier. Participants joked, creative ideas popped up, the atmosphere lightened, and the meetings became more productive. The place felt re-energized. One-third of the participants were promoted and started to handle higher responsibilities. The managers felt that the organization cared for them as persons. Their commitment to the organization increased substantially. To close our program we organized a party to which all the spouses were invited as well. One of the spouses came to us during the party, looked around to check that nobody could hear her, blushed, and thanked us for the program, alluding to the impact it had had on their relationships and home lives as well. Ten years later they still talked to me about the impact the program had on their lives.

JOYFUL WORK THROUGH CONTRIBUTING TO A LARGER PURPOSE OR EXERCISING CREATIVITY

We found that work itself can be joyful in two different ways. If it is perceived as connected with the larger purposes of the organization, then people see their work as a value addition to that purpose, and they experience that their contribution is meaningful. It is a necessary condition that the larger purpose of the organization is clear and shared among members across the organization. When this condition is fulfilled, members develop a commitment to work, because work becomes the means to a larger purpose, which then becomes the purpose of each individual. Through this, people experience an increased sense of self-worth and connection to the broader community. These feelings then contribute to avoiding alienation, loneliness, anxiety, and prepare the individual to experience joy from the work.

Work can also be joyful when it is not seen as a routine task, but as an exercise with various aspects and challenges. In a fertilizer factory, whenever the machines broke down, employees of the shop floor simply waited for maintenance to fix them. We enriched their work by training the workers themselves to do operational maintenance as well. Tools were kept at the workplace, and shop floor employees helped optimize machine performance by intervening when necessary. When a wider variety of functions are involved in a job, people's full capacity is better utilized, which leads to higher self-esteem and a potential experience of joy from work.

Learning new competencies is also a way of enriching work. Another way of doing this can be job rotation. Job rotation can be beneficial not only for the individual, but for the organization as well, if, as a result, the workforce becomes more flexible. By learning new competencies, both the work they perform and the employees themselves become more valuable. Working in teams also has the potential to enrich work. The relationship aspect of that environment may contribute to members feeling that their work has many interesting aspects.

In several cultures, people are less likely to develop skills of working smoothly and in an enjoyable way with others. If we grew up in a family where fights were typical and in school experienced the emphasis on individual performance and competition rather than on cooperation, we did not have a lot of opportunities to learn to cooperate with equals. If our colleagues also lack those skills, even with the best intentions, it will be very difficult to create a constructive, helpful, and relaxed creative work climate. However, we found that even in a place with a lethargic, depressing working climate, people can develop cooperation skills—such as listening, appreciating others, resolving conflicts, and striving together for common goals—over a period of time, if they have the motivation to make the effort. Using these skills, they get positive reinforcement, which establishes a positive climate, which is a good environment for a joyful place. Since entropy and joy are mutually exclusive, when entropy created by infighting starts to decrease, the situation, by definition, allows more opportunities for joy.

In performing every task, people possess a variety of goals. The first goal is usually to do work ending in a result. The second goal is, given the result, to get compensation for doing it. The third goal is, after reaching a certain result, to get a promotion. If we see each goal as a means to the next goal, then we are unlikely to experience joy; instead we will feel stressed. When joy comes from the work itself, we immerse ourselves in it and focus on realizing our vision, not achieving the above mentioned goals. Work is no more a means to an end. If it is considered legitimate to experience joy from work, the physical and social surroundings create an ambience for joy, and efforts are aimed to enrich work, that place is likely to become a joyful organization. In these organizations, members do not work only for a salary, the work itself becomes a goal for them.

* * * * * *

It is not by mistake that we decided not to title this book "Five Quick Steps to a Joyful Organization." Not only do we not know such steps that apply in the same way for every organization in all circumstances, we do not exactly believe that such steps exist. What we do believe, however, is that the ideas and viewpoints presented here will provide the reader with insights to discover his or her own journey toward a joyful organization.

We hope that reading this book will increase readers' desires to act in their own organization and environment toward this effect. The more people who do this, the less alienated organizations will exist, and the higher the expectations will be toward all organizations. The more people who experience joy, the more real the belief will be that we are all capable of creating joyful organizations.

Further Reading

BROADLY RELATED FURTHER READINGS

Adizes, I. *Corporate Lifecycles: How and Why Corporations Grow and Die and What to Do about It*. Englewood Cliffs, NJ: Prentice-Hall, 1989.

Adorno, T.W., E. Frenkel-Brunswik, D.J. Levinson, and R.N. Sanford. *The Authoritarian Personality*. New York: W.W. Norton & Company, 1993.

Argyris, C. *Understanding Organizational Behavior*. Homewood, IL: Dorsey, 1960.

———. *Integrating the Individual and the Organization*. Reprint ed. Somerset, NJ: Transaction Publishers, 1990.

———. *Reasons and Rationalizations: The Limits to Organizational Knowledge*. New Ed ed. Oxford, UK: Oxford University Press, 2006.

Aronson, E. *The Social Animal*. San Francisco: W.H. Freeman, 1976.

Beckhard, R. *Organization Development: Strategies and Models*. Reading, MA: Addison-Wesley, 1969.

Bennis, W. *On Becoming a Leader: The Leadership Classic—Updated and Expanded*. Rev. ed. Cambridge, MA: Perseus Publishing, 2002.

Berne, E. *Games People Play*. London: Andre Deutsch, 1964.

Block, P. *Flawless Consulting: A Guide to Getting Your Expertise Used*. San Francisco: Jossey-Bass/Pfeiffer, 1999.

Festinger, L. *A Theory of Cognitive Dissonance*. Stanford, CA: Stanford University Press, 1957.

Fiedler, F.E. *A Theory of Leadership Effectiveness*. New York: McGraw-Hill, 1967.

Flamholtz, E.G. *Growing Pains*. San Francisco: Jossey-Bass Inc., Publishers, 1990.

Fromm, E. *The Art of Loving*. Scranton, PA: HarperCollins, 2000.

———. *Escape from Freedom*. New York: Henry Holt and Company, 1995.

Fukuyama, F. *Trust: Human Nature and the Reconstitution of Social Order*. New York: Touchstone Books, 1990.

Goffman, E. *The Presentation of Self in Everyday Life*. Garden City, NY: Doubleday, 1959.

Goleman, D. *Emotional Intelligence*. New York: Bantam Books, 1997.

Handy, C. *The Age of Unreason*. New Ed ed. Cambridge, MA: Harvard Business School Press, 1998.

————. *Understanding Organizations*. London, Penguin Books Ltd., 1993.

Hasselbein, F., M. Goldsmith, and R. Beckhard, eds. *The Leader of the Future*. San Francisco: Jossey-Bass Inc., 1996.

Hofstede, G. "Motivation, Leadership and Organization: Do American Theories Apply Abroad?" *Organizational Dynamics* 9, no. 1 (Summer, 1980).

————. *Culture's Consequences*. Beverly Hills, CA: Sage Publications, 1984.

Katz, D., and R.L. Kahn. *The Social Psychology of Organizations*. New York: Wiley, 1966.

Kohn, A. *No Contest: The Case against Competition*. New York: Houghton Mifflin Company, 1986.

Kolb, D.A., I.M. Rubin, and J.M. McIntyre. *Organizational Psychology*. Englewood Cliffs, NJ: Prentice-Hall, 1971.

Kotter, J.P. *Leading Change*. Cambridge, MA: Harvard Business School Press, 1996.

McClelland, D.C. *The Achieving Society*. Princeton, NJ: Van Nostrand, 1961.

————. *Human Motivation*. Cambridge, MA: Cambridge University Press, 1998.

Mintzberg, H. *The Nature of Managerial Work*. New York: Harper & Row, 1973.

————. *Power In and Around Organizations*. Englewood Cliffs, NJ: Prentice-Hall, 1983.

Morgan, G. *Images of Organization*. Newbury Park, CA: Sage Publications, 1986.

Peters, T. *Thriving on Chaos*. London: Macmillan, 1988.

Peters, T.J., and R.H. Waterman. *In Search of Excellence*. New York: Harper & Row, 1982.

Schein, E.H. *Organizational Culture and Leadership*. San Francisco: Jossey-Bass Inc., 1986.

————. *Organizational Psychology*. Englewood Cliffs, NJ: Prentice-Hall, 1989.

————. *Process Consultation*. Reading, MA: Addison-Wesley, 1969.

Senge, P. *The Fifth Discipline*. New York: Currency Doubleday, 1990.

Simmons, A. *Territorial Games*. New York: Amacom, 1998.

Trist, E.L. *Socio-Technical Systems*. London: Tavistock Publications, 1960.

Watzlawick, P., J.H. Weakland, and R. Fisch. *Change, Principle of Problem Formation and Problem Resolution*. New York: W.W. Norton & Company, 1988.

Whyte, W.H. *The Organization Man*. London: Cape, 1957.

RECENT, RELATED LITERATURE

Albion, M. *Making a Life, Making a Living: Reclaiming Your Purpose and Passion in Business and in Life*. New York: Warner Books, Inc., 2000.

Avolio, J.B., and F. Luthans. *The High Impact Leader*. New York: McGraw-Hill, 2005.

Bakke, D.W. *Joy at Work: A Revolutionary Approach to Fun on the Job*. Seattle, WA: PVG, 2005.

Barrow, S., and R. Mosley. *The Employer Brand: Bringing the Best of Brand Management to People at Work*. 2nd ed. Red. and updated ed. New York: John Wiley & Sons, 2005.

Bellman, G.M. *The Beauty of the Beast: Breathing New Life into Organizations*. San Francisco, Berrett-Koehler Publishers, 2000.

Blair, M., and T. Kochan. *The New Relationship: Human Capital in the American Corporation*. Washington, DC: Brookings Institute Press, March 2000.

Brandon, M.A., P.A. Cole, and R.S. Hunsberger. *Finding Power, Passion and Joy Being at Work*. Traverse City, MI: Book Marketing Solutions, 2006.

Buckingham, M. *The One Thing You Need to Know:...About Great Managing, Great Leading, and Sustained Individual Success*. New York: Free Press, 2005.

Chowdhury, S. *Organization 21C: Someday All Organizations Will Lead This Way*. 1st ed. Upper Saddle River, NJ: Financial Times Prentice Hall, 2002.

Ciulla, J.B. *The Working Life: The Promise and Betrayal of Modern Work*. New York: Times Books, 2000.

Coffmann, C, and G. Gonzalez-Molina. *Follow This Path: How the World's Greatest Organizations Drive Growth by Unleashing Human Potential*. New York: Warner Business Books, 2002.

Daft, L.R., and H.R. Lengel. *Fusion Leadership: Unlocking the Subtle Forces That Change People and Organizations*. 1st Pbk. ed. San Francisco: Berrett-Koehler Publishers, 2000.

Deal, T.E., and M.K. Key. *Corporate Celebration: Play, Purpose, and Profit at Work*. San Francisco: Berrett-Koehler Publishers, 1998.

Dive, B. *The Healthy Organization: A Revolutionary Approach to People & Management*. 2nd ed. London: Kogan Page, 2004.

Drake, S.M., M.J. Gulman, and S.M. Roberts. *Light Their Fire: Using Internal Marketing to Ignite Employee Performance and WOW Your Customers*. Chicago: Dearborn Trade Publishing, 2005.

Hamel, G. *Leading the Revolution*. Cambridge, MA: Harvard Business School Press, 2000.

Hemsath, D., and L. Yerkes. *301 Ways to Have Fun at Work*. San Francisco: Berrett-Koehler Publishers 1997.

Katzenbach, J.R. *Peak Performance: Aligning the Hearts and Minds of Your Employees*. Cambridge, MA: Harvard Business School Press, 2000.

Komisar, R. *The Monk and the Riddle: The Art of Creating a Life while Making a Living*. With Kent Lineback. Cambridge, MA: Harvard Business School Press, 2000.

Kunde, J. *Corporate Religion: Building a Strong Company Through Personality and Corporate Soul*. Upper Saddle River, NJ: Financial Times Prentice Hall, 2000.

Lencioni P. *The Five Dysfunctions of a Team: A Leadership Fable*. 1st ed. New York: Jossey-Bass, 2002.

Maier, C. *Bonjour Laziness: Why Hard Work Doesn't Pay*. New York: Vintage Books Random House Inc., 2005.

McEwen J.W. *Married to the Brand: Why Consumers Bond with Some Brands for Life*. New York: Gallup Press, 2005.

Morgenstern, J. *Making Work Work: New Strategies for Surviving and Thriving at the Office*. New York: Fireside, 2004.

Pfeffer, J. *Human Equation: Building Profits by Putting People First by Peak Performance*. Cambridge, MA: Harvard Business School Press, 1998.

Richards, D. *Artful Work: Awakening Joy, Meaning, and Commitment in the Workplace*. 1st Ed ed. San Francisco: Berrett-Koehler, 1995.

Ridderstråle, J., and K. Nordström. *Funky Business: Talent Makes Capital Dance*. Upper Saddle River, NJ: Financial Times Prentice Hall, 2000.

Rosen, R.H., and P.B. Brown. *Leading People: Transforming Business from the Inside Out*. New York: Viking, 1996.

Rushkoff, D. *Get Back in the Box: Innovation from the Inside Out*. New York: Collins, 2005.

Sartain, L., and M. Schumann. *Brand From the Inside: Eight Essentials to Emotionally Connect Your Employees to Your Business*. San Francisco: Jossey-Bass, 2006.

Solomon, R.C. *A Better Way to Think About Business: How Personal Integrity Leads to Corporate Success*. New York: Oxford University Press, 1999.

Taylor, J., and W. Wacker. *The 500 Year Delta: What Happens after What Comes Next*. With Howard Means. New York: HarperCollins Publishers, 1998.

Taylor, W.C., and P. LaBarre. *Mavericks at Work: Why the Most Original Minds in Business Win*. New York: William Morrow, 2006.

Thomas, K.W. *Intrinsic Motivation at Work: Building Energy & Commitment*. San Francisco: Berrett-Koehler Publishers, 2000.

Thomson, K. *Emotional Capital: Maximising the Intangible Assets at the Heart of Brand and Business Success*. New Ed ed. Oxford, UK: Capstone, 2000.

Ulrich, D., and W. Brockbank. *The HR Value Proposition*. Cambridge, MA: Harvard Business School Press, 2005.

Ulrich, D., and N. Smallwood. *Why the Bottom Line ISN'T!: How to Build Value Through People and Organization*. 1st ed. New York: Wiley, 2003.

Weinstein, M. *Managing to Have Fun*. New York: Fireside, 1997.

Index

About the Authors

IMRE LÖVEY is Managing Partner and founder of CONCORDIA Inc., Budapest, one of the first organizational and experimental management training firms to be set up in Hungary. He has over 30 years of experience in consulting to multinationals, joint ventures, governments, international agencies, and socialist enterprises undergoing transformation to a market economy and publicly traded companies. He worked on different assignments in countries such as the United States, Thailand, India, the United Kingdom, Germany, Macedonia, Slovakia, Montenegro, and Ukraine. Imre Lövey was instrumental in introducing organizational development in Central and Eastern Europe and pioneered using and raising the awareness of organizational development methodologies. He founded the Hungarian Organizational Development Society in 1986 and was its first president and has also founded commercially successful consulting enterprises. Dr. Lövey was a regular visiting professor of management at the University of California, Los Angeles, between 1990 and 1997, and is a member of the National Training Laboratories of Applied Behavior (USA) and of the Executive Committee of the International Organization Development Association.

His e-mail address is **ilovey@concordia-od.hu**

MANOHAR S. NADKARNI was the founder Chairman, Behavioral Science Center (India) Pvt. Ltd., Mumbai. He had over 40 years of experience in organizational development practice in India and was a consultant to multinationals, government agencies, and local communities. He worked in rural development, small industry development, and in large industrial and nonindustrial organizations. Manohar Nadkarni undertook several international assignments and United Nations' missions in developing entrepreneurship, management, and organizational development and trained a number of OD consultants in several countries such as Russia, Hungary, Papua New Guinea, and Nigeria. Manohar Nadkarni is a former president of the Indian Society for Applied Behavioral Science. He spent four years at Harvard University as a senior member of Professor David McClelland's team, developing and running training programs for Achievement Motivation Development. He also worked as a consultant for several American corporations.

ESZTER ERDÉLYI has been a management consultant for over 12 years. She began her career in Hungary consulting to the government, international development agencies, and new enterprises. She has consulted to multinational companies and nonprofit organizations from London, Paris, and New York and is currently based in San Francisco. Ms. Erdélyi received her MBA degree from the Harvard School of Business Administration in 1992, her master's degree in International Economics from the Budapest University of Economics in 1985, and completed the European Union comprehensive program at the Foundation Nationale des Sciences Politique in Paris in 1992. She has worked with A.T. Kearney, Crédit Lyonnais, and Coopers & Lybrand Consulting.

DATE DUE

| 3 2008 | | |